ADAM SMITH'S THEORY OF VALUE AND DISTRIBUTION

Adam Smith's Theory of Value and Distribution

A Reappraisal

Rory O'Donnell
Economist
National Economic and Social Council, Dublin

St. Martin's Press   New York

First published in the United States of America in 1990

Printed in Great Britain

ISBN 0–312–04508–5

Library of Congress Cataloging–in–Publication Data
O'Donnell, Rory.
Adam Smith's theory of value and distribution/Rory O'Donnell.
p. cm.
Includes bibliographical references.
ISBN 0–312–04508–5
1. Smith, Adam, 1723–1790. 2. Value. 3. Distribution (Economic
theory) I. Title.
HB 103.S6035 1990
330.15′3—dc20   89–70271
                                                            CIP

Contents

Acknowledgements

It is a pleasure to acknowledge my great debt to John Eatwell for his valuable guidance and support during the research for this book. Without his keen theoretical comments and considerable patience this work would not have been possible. I am grateful also to Prue Kerr, Geoffrey Harcourt and Murray Milgate for helpful comments. At an earlier stage of my studies I received a valuable intellectual stimulus from Patrick Lynch and Cormac Ó'Grada, and encouragement from Paul Andrews. A special debt is owed to my parents who provided continuing support and encouragement. I am extremely grateful to Jacqueline O'Connor for her first-class secretarial work and immense patience. The research for this work was funded by the Economic and Social Research Institute, Dublin, the Robert Gardiner Memorial Foundation, and Trinity Hall, Cambridge.

RORY O'DONNELL

1 Introduction

It is now generally accepted that Adam Smith was primarily concerned with the causes of the increase of the annual produce of society, and that this explains his stress on the division of labour, linked with the accumulation of stock; that this explanation of the accumulation process required the concept of productive and unproductive labour, so often misunderstood, while his confused elaboration of the concept of labour as a measure of value was due to his desire to have a constant *numéraire* in which to express changes of wealth in time and place. (Black, 1971, p. 10)

The perception of Adam Smith's economics described by Black came into general acceptance largely as a result of Myint's celebrated article 'The Welfare Significance of Productive Labour' and book on *Theories of Welfare Economics* (Myint, 1943 and 1948; and see Black, 1976, p. 61). However, any idea that Smith was concerned with growth *to the exclusion of value and distribution* was, inevitably, destined to be challenged. Any attempt to spell out Smith's theory of growth in terms of dynamic laws of accumulation, productivity and population inevitably involves some mechanism determining value and distribution – however minor a role this was assigned in the overall model and however rudimentary its specification (see, for example, Lowe, 1954, p. 139 and 1975, p. 417 and 421). And, however great was Smith's interest in growth and capital accumulation it is clear that the *Wealth of Nations* contained an enormous amount of detailed analysis of issues which necessarily involve the question of value and distribution.

Given this, a number of developments have served to re-open controversy on Smith's treatment of value and distribution. First, Sraffa's re-interpretation of Ricardo, and his own theoretical work, have provided an new view of certain aspects of the value and distribution theory of the classical political economists, which must inevitably influence how Smith's work is understood (Sraffa, 1951 and 1960). Second, Hollander, while accepting Myint's view that Smith's primary concern was growth through capital accumulation, has disputed his corollary that Smith ignored the question of the allocation of resources (Hollander, 1973).

1

1.1 CONTEMPORARY INTERPRETATIONS OF SMITH

It is from these two developments that the dominant contemporary interpretations of Smith's treatment of value and distribution have emerged. In his *Economics of Adam Smith* (1973) Professor Samuel Hollander argues that Smith should be seen as an important forerunner of the neoclassical general equilibrium theory of value, distribution and output. This is a revival of a view that has been stated intermittently (see, for example, Robbins, 1935, p. 68 and Boulding, 1971, p. 229) and, to judge from the reception accorded Hollander's book, would seem now to be accepted widely (see, for example, Bowley, 1973b; Jaffe, 1977, p. 20; Recktenwald, 1978, p. 62; Moss, 1976).

The second recent interpretation of Smith's treatment of value and distribution is that of the late Maurice Dobb and the late Professor Ronald Meek. In his *Theories of Value and Distribution since Adam Smith* (1973) Dobb argued that Smith contributed to the development of *both* the classical or surplus theory found in the work of Ricardo and Marx, *and* the neoclassical or marginalist theory which later became the dominant theory of value and distribution (for support for this interpretation see Groenewegen, 1975, p. 193 and 1975, p. 142). This 'two streams' view of Smith involves the combination of a number of arguments drawn from different sources. It involves, first, adoption of much of Marx's interpretation of Smith – indeed, Bradley and Howard argue that the 'two streams' view of Smith itself originated with Marx (Bradley and Howard, 1982, p. 34). In addition, Dobb endorsed Sraffa's interpretation of Ricardo. Finally, the 'two streams' view of Smith involves a restatement of a traditional view that Smith had a 'cost of production theory of value', and that a theoretical continuity of cost theory can be identified from Smith, through Malthus and Mill to Marshall (see, for example, Marshall, 1890, pp. 671–6; Stigler, 1952 and 1958, pp. 69 and 197; Bladen, 1938; Blaug, 1978, p. 43 and Viner, 1930).

Clearly, these two interpretations of Smith's work have one important conclusion in common – namely, that Smith can be seen as having made a significant contribution to the development of the 'supply and demand' or marginalist theory of value, distribution and output. Consequently, whether they accept or reject Sraffa's interpretation of Ricardo, and the wider dual development hypothesis which has grown from it, historians of economic thought would seem, in large measure, to agree with this proposition concerning Smith. The purpose of this study is to examine the validity of the arguments put forward by Hollander and Dobb concerning Smith's role in the development of the classical and neoclassical theories, and thereby to establish a more accurate view of just what kind of value and ditribution theory was developed by Adam Smith.

1.2   THE APPROACH TO INTERPRETATION

Each of these interpretations of Smith involve propositions concerning the *content* of his writings and his *influence* on subsequent theorists. In order to keep the exercise of interpretation to manageable proportions, and in order to put first things first, this study involves, primarily, an evaluation of the arguments of Hollander and Dobb concerning the *content* of Smith's work.

However, there are a number of reasons why the *influence* of Smith's work cannot be kept rigorously separate. It is inevitably the case that in the view taken of Smith by major thinkers, insights will be found which would otherwise be missed. More specifically, the case presented by Dobb rested more heavily on arguments concerning Smith's *influences* than on arguments concerning the details of his work. In particular, he cited the way in which Smith's work was seen by Ricardo and Marx. But Dobb was not alone in this. Ricardo and Marx set the terms for discussion of Smith to such an extent that rejection of Marx's interpretation of labour embodied and labour commanded in Smith would seem to have been considered, by some, as sufficient grounds for rejection of the view that there may have been theoretical similarities between Marx and Smith (see, for example, Blaug, 1978, p. 66; and Bowley, 1973a, pp. 117-21). Consequently, this study includes a detailed examination of both Ricardo's and Marx's criticisms of Adam Smith.

Given that the major focus of this study is on Smith's major *text*, the *Wealth of Nations*, and the propositions being evaluated concern the explanation of *value* and *distribution*, the approach adopted is to examine his work and interpretations of it against a yardstick provided by the classical and neoclassical theories of value and distribution. For this purpose, rigorous definitions of the classical and neoclassical theories are set out in Chapter 2. Although these definitions are objective (being based on sufficient analytical conditions for explaining value and distribution in two different ways) their use as points of comparison with Smith's work on value and distribution inevitably involves a considerable measure of judgement. Therefore, the approach adopted in this study, while indispensible for an evaluation of the sort of propositions put forward by Hollander and Dobb, ultimately needs to be supplemented by a detailed historical examination which will relate Smith's work to a given theory of value and distribution *as it stood in his day*. However, the approach is strongly defended because, as will emerge from the following pages, a lot can be learned from a detailed examination of Smith's great work, the *Wealth of Nations*, as a piece of economic theory.

1.3   OUTLINE OF THE ARGUMENT

The argument proceeds in two stages. Part I consists of a detailed examination of Smith's work on value and distribution in the *Wealth of Nations*. Part II presents an examination of selected interpretations of Smith.

Part I surveys most of the statements by Smith which deal with value and distribution, and which are pertinent to an evaluation of the central propositions of Hollander and Dobb. In conducting this survey the approach adopted is to ask to what extent Smith intended to develop a theory of value and distribution based on the concept of economic surplus, and to what extent he succeeded in doing so. There are two reasons for adopting this approach. The structure of a logically coherent surplus theory of value and distribution has been clarified only relatively recently; consequently, many arguments linking Smith's ideas with a surplus theory (or denying his use of a surplus theory) have been based on unsatisfactory definitions of that theory – definitions derived from the work of Ricardo and Marx. Second, Dobb did not undertake a detailed examination of Smith's work with a view to identifying what elements of a surplus theory may be found there. This is probably explained, in part, by the fact that his 1973 book was a *general* history of economic thought. But it would also seem to result from his view of *how* Smith contributed to the surplus tradition of theory: this contribution did not lie in Smith's use of the core concepts of a surplus theory (the analysis of outputs and necessary inputs), but in the fact that certain of his doctrines were 'inverted' by Ricardo and Marx (Dobb, 1973, p. 115).

Consequently, Part I opens with an examination of the concept of surplus in Smith's work. It is shown in Chapter 3 that his definition of surplus has been obscured by his definitions of net and gross revenue and by his resolution of prices into wages, profits and rents. But it is revealed that when dealing with accumulation Smith defined profits and rents as the surplus of the economic system. As for a surplus *theory* or *explanation*, it is indicated that he adopted a surplus type explanation of the magnitude of *aggregate* profits plus rents. Chapter 4 examines Smith's development of the concept of competition and its creation of a tendency towards a uniform rate of profit; interpretations of this analysis as an 'equilibrium theory' of value are examined. The next step is to consider Smith's famous and much debated labour command *measure* of value. A new interpretation of this labour command measure is presented, and it is shown that this measure played an important, and to date unrecognised, role in Smith's analysis of the effects of taxes and bounties. It is shown in Chapter 5 that his choice of a labour command measure, and his use of a corn measure, were predicated on his assumption of a constant production cost of corn, and not merely on an assumption of a constant corn wage. His measure of value is shown to have been used to measure *changes* in the *value* of commodities due to changes in methods of production. This demonstration affords an opportunity to examine certain historically important propositions concerning labour embodied and labour commanded in Smith's work. It is then possible to turn, in Chapter 6, to Smith's *explanation* of value and distribution. Smith is shown to have made considerable progress in analysing the relations of price to production costs but to have failed to provide an adequate theory of distribution, and, consequently, to have had an indeterminate theory of value. In particular, the central conclusion of Part I is that Smith did not use his surplus explanation of the *aggregate* profits plus rents to derive a *theory* of the *rate* of profit.

Part II opens with an examination of Ricardo's development of Smith's economics and asks whether the differences between their work were such as to warrant the conclusion that they belonged in two different traditions of value and distribution *theory*. Drawing on the account of Part I it is shown that Ricardo's substantial *theoretical* addition to Smith's analysis was his new theory of the rate of profit. Several important misunderstandings of the relation between Ricardo's work and Smith's ideas are revealed when their different assumptions concerning the production conditions of corn are carefully noted. Chapter 8 provides a detailed examination of Marx's extensive commentary on Smith and, besides illustrating a number of inaccuracies in his account, shows that it is incorrect to equate his division of Smith's work into two parts with Dobb's 'two streams' view of Smith.

In Chapter 9 the structure of Hollander's case in the *Economics of Adam Smith* is identified, and the textual evidence cited in support of each element of the argument is considered, both textually and analytically. The conclusion is that Hollander has not provided sufficient evidence to sustain his strong proposition concerning Smith's use of analytical concepts akin to those found in subsequent neoclassical theory. Finally, the structure of Dobb's 'two streams' proposition is identified. In evaluating the first part of the argument I draw heavily on my earlier chapter on Ricardo to dispute the view that Ricardo saw Smith's work as an example of the 'supply and demand' explanation that he was combating. Using the findings of earlier chapters, and the definition of surplus theory, it is argued that it can scarcely be correct to see Smith's contribution to surplus theory to have consisted in his treatment of the *labour theory of value*. The second part of Dobb's argument concerns Smith's contribution to the, so-called, 'cost of production' stream of value theory. The analytical validity of this concept is challenged and this undermines this part of Dobb's argument.

The detailed examination of Smith's text and the analysis of the commentaries of Ricardo, Marx, Sraffa, Dobb and Meek allow a new and, I submit, a more accurate view to be formed of where Smith's work stood in the development of the classical approach to value and distribution. This shows that the problems in Smith's analysis of value and distribution were not always accurately identified in existing commentaries. When the true nature of Smith's approach is clarified it is seen that Smith's work was further from the fully developed classical theory of value and distribution than has hitherto been thought. Indeed, most previous interpretations do not sufficiently differentiate between the analytical problems faced by Smith, on the one hand, and Ricardo and Marx, on the other. But it is also shown that the element of surplus in Smith's work was far more *certain* than one would gather from existing accounts which, focussing excessively on the labour theory of value, see Smith as having vacillated between conflicting approaches to value and distribution.

2 Theories of Value and Distribution

Therefore the foundation of modern political economy, whose business is the analysis of capitalist production, is the conception of the value of labour-power as something fixed, as a given magnitude. (Marx, 1861–63, I, p. 45)

As forerunners of the theory, we may name generally all those who have derived value from utility; specially those who were persistent in basing even exchange value altogether on utility, particularly when they did not shrink from their principle in spite of the obvious influence of costs of production. (Wieser, 1888, p. xxxii)

This chapter provides definitions of classical and neoclassical theory and establishes criteria by which the propositions outlined in Chapter 1 will be evaluated. The distinction between classical and neoclassical theory, which forms a point of reference of this study, is based on the identification of the essential analytical elements of each theory. In the view of many writers the logical structure of these theories are significantly different to warrant their treatment as two distinct schools of thought (see Schumpeter, 1954, pp. 567–8; Dobb, 1973). In many studies which make use of this distinction the precise logical structure of these theories of value and distribution are presented in mathematical form. Here I outline them verbally, preferring to illustrate them by drawing on the words of the great economists who developed them.

2.1 THE CLASSICAL OR SURPLUS THEORY

The classical or surplus theory explains value and distribution by reference to the size and composition of the social product, the technique of production in use, and the real wage. This concise definition of the logically coherent surplus theory of value and distribution will be considered further below, but it is important,

7

especially when considering any possible role for Smith, to identify the larger set of propositions of which that theory of value and distribution forms a part. The existence of wider and prior concerns than the theory of value and distribution is indicated most simply by the title of Smith's major work.

2.1.1 The elements of the theory

The classical economists considered that they had significantly advanced understanding of the nature of wealth (see, for example, Malthus, 1820).[1] Adopting a definition of wealth as useful material objects implied a shift in emphasis away from the analysis of *trade* towards that of *production* (Roll, 1973, p. 98). Examination of production and, more significantly, of *reproduction* naturally involved identification of that part of output which must be put back into production. What remained of the product constituted a *surplus* which could be disposed of in various ways, without encroaching on what was required for future production.

To these basic concepts were added three elements which shaped the development of classical political economy and greatly influenced the final form that the theory would take.

First, if the subsistence of workers involved in production could be included in the *necessary inputs* then the remainder, or surplus, became synonymous with the non-wage share of total product. For example, Sir William Petty identified the surplus product of land as the sources of rent (1662, I, p. 43; see also Walsh and Gram, 1980, p. 17). The implication of viewing the subsistence of workers as necessary for reproduction was that the analysis of *reproduction* became an analysis of *distribution* of the product among the classes into which society is divided (Garegnani, 1984, p. 293).

This link between reproduction and distribution became a feature of classical political economy. It meant that if the primary task of the theory was to determine the size of the social surplus then it had, perforce, to determine the size of the non-wage share of the product.

Within this common framework the definition of surplus differed from one theorist to another. Petty's original notion of surplus as consisting of land rent was adopted by Cantillon and Quesnay, and developed into the doctrine that only in agriculture is a surplus produced (Cantillon, 1755, p. 15; Quesnay, 1757). The British economists eventually broke free of this doctrine that surplus originated in agriculture alone, and they included profits, with rent, in the non-wage share of produce. It was surplus defined in this way which became the object of analysis of developed classical distribution theory (see Ricardo, *Works*, I; Marx, 1867).

The basis on which wages could, like the material inputs to production, be taken as given, for the purpose of determining the size of the surplus or non-wage share, also differed somewhat from one classical writer to another. Indeed, it is important to note that much classical writing was preoccupied with *this* particular part of the theory of distribution and value. But Wermel, in surveying the evolution of wage theories from the late seventeenth to the early nineteenth century, claimed to have identified a distinctly 'classical' school of thought. The later examples of this were characterised by belief in a conventionally determined norm of *subsistence* and a regulating mechanism of population and migration (Wermel, 1939). This judgement is confirmed by Eltis who says 'All the classical economists saw wages as necessary costs of production which were almost wholly consumed' (1984, p. 335; see also Garegnani, op cit. pp. 294–5).

The second element that was added to the basic notions of reproduction and surplus was the adoption of the view that the key determinant of the level and rate of progress of wealth was capital accumulation. When combined with the view that profits and rent were a residual, this stress on capital accumulation clearly placed this non-wage share of produce at the very centre of the whole classical view of the economic system. Analysis of the magnitude of the non-wage share was analysis of what was considered to be the engine of the economy.

Again, the *formulation* and *documentation* of this theory of economic progress absorbed much of the effort of classical writers, *especially early in the classical period*. And, of course, the theory of exactly how capital accumulation was related to the magnitude of profits and rents, and how the progress of wealth was related to accumulation, differed from one writer to another, depending on the circumstances prevailing at the time and on the complexity of the social and institutional analysis undertaken.

The third element which conditioned the development of the theory based on reproduction and surplus was its application, from the very start, to a *capitalist exchange economy*. The theory explained the size of the social product, the material inputs to production (technology), and the real wage in such a way that these three appeared as independent variables in the determination of the surplus (profits and rents). But since each of the three aggregates consists of a heterogeneous bundle of commodities they could not be related to one another when measured in physical units. Garegnani has argued that it 'is in connection with this problem of measurement that the surplus theories of distribution meet the question of value and with it, their chief analytical difficulty' – a difficulty which was not to be overcome for many years (Garegnani, 1984, p. 229). It will be of interest to see whether this statement applies to Adam Smith's work.

2.1.2 The problem of value

However, if the problem of value was ultimately to pose the chief analytical difficulty, the stress on production and reproduction provided the early classical economists with a first approach to the theory of price. As Groenewegen says in an account of this early work, 'Both exchange and distribution play a crucial role in ensuring that at the end of the production period (say, a year) the output is distributed in such a way that the required inputs are available to producers in the right proportions to start the production process afresh' (Groenewegen, 1982b, p. 123). Such a role for prices is evident in Cantillon's 'Intrinsic Value' and Quesnay's 'Prix Fondamental' and remained central to the classical approach to price (see, for example, Ricardo, *Works* IV, p. 19; and Vaggi, 1983).

This conception, of prices covering costs and containing an element of surplus, was developed into a much sharper idea once it was seen that, in a *competitive* capitalist system, such necessary prices must not only ensure reproduction, but must also yield a *rate* of profit which is uniform across all producers. This insight was the outcome of remarkable progress in the understanding of the economy as a *system*, and this will form the subject matter of Chapter 4 of this study. It meant that the non-wage share of the product now appeared as a *rate* of profit and a rate (or rates) of rent. Consequently, the 'natural prices' of commodities could be calculated once their method of production and the rates of wages, profits and rents were known.

It was in this form that Ricardo faced the problem of explaining the determination of the non-wage share. Two related developments in political economy, with both of which he was closely involved, greatly facilitated his provision of an explanation of profits and rent. These were: the adoption of the idea of diminishing returns in agriculture, and the development of the differential theory of rent. The latter separated the question of rent from that of the rate of profit, and the former, once he posed the question of profits clearly, provided a definite prediction of the path which that rate would follow.

Having formulated the theory that the rate of profit was determined by the rate of wages, which in turn depended on the state of cultivation in corn production, the difficulty which Ricardo faced was precisely that problem of measurement mentioned above. The aggregates upon which he drew to determine the rate of profit (the size and composition of the social product, the material inputs to production, and the real wage) were not commensurate when measured in physical units, and really required to be measured in *value* terms. Yet, if any of these value magnitudes were to depend on the rate of profit, then the determination of the rate of profit by reference to these 'given' quantities would fall into circular reasoning (Garegnani, 1984, p. 301).

Ricardo's successive attempts to solve this problem have been documented by Sraffa, and I will have reason to refer to them in more detail in Chapter 7 (see Sraffa, 1951). The general tenor of his attempts to solve the problem is well expressed in his statement to McCulloch 'after all, the great questions of Rent, Wages and Profits must be explained by the proportions in which the whole produce is divided between landlords, capitalists and labourers, and which are not essentially connected with the doctrine of value' (Ricardo, *Works*, VIII, p. 194).

Marx also tried to solve the same problem and, in doing so, adhered to the same view that the rate of profit could be determined independently, and prior to the determination of relative prices (Marx, 1894, Ch ix; see also Garegnani, 1984, pp. 305-9; Eatwell, 1974, 1975). In addition, Marx wrote an extensive history of the surplus theories. That history is an important source in an examination of a possible role for Smith in development of the theory, and consequently is examined in detail in Chapter 8 of this study.

2.1.3 The logically coherent classical theory of value and distribution

Sraffa has shown that the general problem of the classical economists, and the specific one addressed by Ricardo and Marx, does, indeed, have a solution. Taking as given:

1. the size and composition of the social product,
2. the technique in use, and
3. the real wage,

these data are sufficient to determine the uniform rate of profit. However, he demonstrated that this determination of the rate of profit necessarily involved the simultaneous determination of the relative prices of commodities. So the theory does not, in fact, entail the circularity which seemed to threaten it; but neither can the rate of profit be determined *first* (purely by reference to the product, technology and wages, each *measured in physical units*), and *then* used to calculate relative prices, as both Ricardo and Marx would seem to have believed, or at least hoped, it could (see Sraffa, 1960).[2]

In describing the logical structure of the surplus theory, Garegnani has identified a 'core' which is isolated from the rest of the analysis, because the wage, the social product, and the technical conditions of production, appear there as already determined (1984, p. 296). Within this core the rate of profit is determined and, as demonstrated by Sraffa, this entails determination of relative prices. Furthermore, it is possible to derive quantitative relations between the independent variables (the real wage, the social product, and the technical conditions of production) and the dependent variables (the non-wage shares and prices). As Garegnani points out, it follows that the 'surplus' aspect of the theory (the determination of the non-wage share as a *residual*) has its logical basis in the view that the real wage and the social product can be determined *prior* to those non-wage shares. And, of course, the validity of the theory rests on the validity of that view. But, as Garegnani notes, the adoption of this logical structure did not entail denying altogether the existence of influences of one of these independent variables on the others nor, indeed, of the dependent variables on the independent. An example of the latter was the view that the level of profits could eventually influence the real wage, via the speed of accumulation.

This distinction between the 'core' (within which were calculated necessary quantitative relations between the independent and dependent variables) and the rest of the theory would seem also to have a useful historical dimension. For, prior to Ricardo, classical writers were pre-occupied with developing a clear conception of reproduction and surplus, a theory of wages, a theory of the 'stages' of economic development, a theory of the role of capital in growth and its relation to technical change, a theory of competition, and *definitions* of the distributive shares and the components of price – all elements which were analysed *outside* the 'core'. *Since* Ricardo, theorists were very largely concerned with the possible solutions to the analytical problem of determining profits and prices and, in particular, with the labour theory of value – which arose precisely in that context. This historical pattern clearly has a bearing on the central questions of this study. One of these questions is to ask: can Adam Smith be assigned any role in the development of the classical or surplus theory as outlined above?

2.2 THE NEOCLASSICAL THEORY

The neoclassical (or marginalist) theory was developed to give foundation to the view that relative prices are determined by the mutual interaction of the forces of 'supply and demand'. It does this by showing the conditions under which, in a market system, agent's maximisation yields a set of consumption and production choices that can be represented as supply and demand. These choices, being functions of price, will be made consistent by variation of price in a process of 'substitution' By consistent is meant that at some set of prices the demand for each good and service is equal to its supply. Since demands and supplies are derived from maximising choices then, at that set of prices, all consumers are maximising utility and all producers are maximising their profit.

The theory takes as data the preferences of consumers, the endowments of the system (their size and distribution), and the technology of production. These data, says Debreu, provide a 'complete description of a private ownership economy' (Debreu, 1959, p. 79). Given certain assumptions on the form of preferences and technology, discussed below, these data are sufficient to determine the consumption and production choices and all relative prices. It will be seen that these data embody the three features which are essential for the contruction of the neoclassical theory: *utility* functions, which are maximised subject to the constraints of *fixed initial endowments*, in a context in which these initial endowments have *alternate uses*. Without these three elements, it would be impossible to develop the 'supply and demand' view of the market system into a *theory* of value and distribution. To see *why* these three elements proved necessary it is instructive to consider briefly the process by which the theory was developed.

2.2.1 Supply and pure exchange

The neoclassical view developed out of a rejection of the classical idea that although *market* prices were determined by the relation of the quantity brought to market to the effectual demand, *natural* prices were determined by other forces. The new doctrine asserted that *both* natural and market prices were determined by 'supply and demand' (Malthus, 1820, p. 46). This assertion had no clear meaning in the absence of a theoretical explanation of 'supply' and 'demand'. In defence of the assertion that price was determined by supply and demand Say and, to a lesser extent, Malthus went some way towards deriving demand from utility.[3] Yet while asserting that natural price was determined by supply and demand they simultaneously acknowledged that price was equal to the sum of wages, profits and rents.

As long as wages, profits and rents were each considered to have independent determinants, arising from the requirements of reproduction or necessary 'abstinence', there remained a contradiction in the 'supply and demand' position, the very essence of which was that price (the sum of wages, profits and rents) was determined in the market (see Cannan, 1929, pp. 187–9). John Stuart Mill stated the problem as follows:

> It seems to me necessary, when we mean to speak of the *ratio* between the demand for a commodity and the supply of it, that the two quantities should be, in the mathematical sense, homogeneous - that both of them should be estimated in numbers of the same unit. (Mill, 1945, p. 143)

The problem was to reconcile supply and demand with cost of production: could there be a theory of cost congruent with a theory of demand based on utility?

Paradoxically, the solution to this problem lay in concentrating on *pure exchange* and extending utility theory to all economic choices, not just demands (Jevons, 1871, pp. 93–4). By beginning with the theory of pure exchange (no production) Jevons, Walras and Menger were able to take the existing quantity of goods as *given*, and derive individual offer from utility and disutility at the margin. Consequently, all costs, regardless of what form they may take, could be thought of as consisting ultimately of disutility; as Jevons stressed 'the Theory of Exchange, as explained above, rests entirely on the consideration of quantities of utility, and no reference to labour or cost of production has been made' (Jevons, 1971, p. 137). In contrast with the confusion of earlier formulations Walras could state that 'In the last analysis, the utility curves and the quantities possessed constitute the necessary and sufficient data for the establishment of current or equilibrium prices' (Walras, 1874, pp. 143 and 399).

The *way* in which these data are necessary and sufficient is the derivation from them of demand functions and supply functions. These relate utility maximising choices of demand and offer to price. Assumptions on the forms of the utility functions guarantee that constrained maximised choices will *vary continuously* with prices. The key assumptions are convexity and continuity of preferences (Debreu, 1959, pp. 55–6 and pp. 59–60). Because individual utility is defined as being a function only of the *same* individual's consumption, individual choices are *independent*, and so the demand and offer of all individuals for a given commodity can be summed to form market demand and offer functions (or correspondences) (Walras, 1874, p. 94). These functions determine the equilibrium price as that at which total demand equals total offer.

This method, developed by Jevons, Walras and Menger in the 1870s, forms the core of neoclassical theory and illustrates *why* the three elements cited above are essential to that theory.

The specification of utility functions, which is today presented in axiomatic form, is essential because it established a *single* principle underlying all economic behaviour, and guarantees that that behaviour assumes a certain form. Thus, the application of the principle of utility by Jevons, Walras and Menger, solved the problem identified by John Stuart Mill.

It was commencing with the case of pure exchange that allowed these writers take the *endowments* of each good as *given*. This provided the ground for the application of utility maximisation to derive offers on the *same basis* of demands. For, it is the existence of given endowments which provides the constraints on maximising choices and thereby guarantees that these choices will be determinate. In this analysis it is necessary that there be a single price in each market and, more importantly, that each agent take this as *given* when deciding their demand and offer. The idea of perfect competition was developed to provide the assumptions on which this can be guaranteed (see Eatwell, 1982).

The necessity of the third element cited above (that the given endowments have *alternate uses*) arises from the need to guarantee that elasticities are not zero. This was recognised by Jevons. In reply to criticism by Thornton, who 'suggests that there are no regular laws of supply and demand, because he adduces certain cases in which no regular variation can take place', Jevons was quite clear, saying: 'Of course, laws which assume a continuity of variation are inapplicable where continuous variation is impossible' (Jevons, 1871, pp. 108–9).

This theory, consisting of utility functions which are maximised subject to the constraints of given endowments which have alternate uses, implies what Marshall called the 'fundamental symmetry of the general relations in which demand and supply stand to value' (1890, p. 675). At last there was a definite answer to the question – what does it mean to say that price is determined by 'demand and supply'? If all costs are ultimately disutilities, then clearly supply is merely another aspect of demand (see Jevons, 1871, p. 137). This 'fundamental symmetry' was stressed by Wicksteed who said:

> But what about the 'supply curve' that usually figures as a determinant of price, co-ordinate with the demand curve? I say it boldly and baldly: there is no such thing . . . what is usually called the supply curve is in reality the demand curve of those who possess the commodity. (Wicksteed, 1914, p. 785)

As he pointed out, this accurate description of the theory, in contrast to vague references to the two forces of 'demand and supply', serves to make explicit the 'definite assumption as to the amount of the total supply possessed by the supposed buyers and the supposed sellers taken together' (Wicksteed, 1914, pp. 785–6). In doing so, it serves to make explicit an element - given endowments - without which the neoclassical (or 'supply and demand') vision of the market system cannot be formulated as a logically coherent theory of value.

2.2.2 Production and exchange

The analysis of pure exchange established for the pioneers of neoclassical theory the method by which they would take account of production. Their treatment of production, rather than modifying the account of the theory given above, confirms that view of what are its essential elements. In Lesson 10 of his *Elements* Walras outlined the major proposition derived from the analysis of pure exchange: that exchange of goods in perfect competition is an operation whereby individuals maximise their utility. He then set out, with absolute clarity, the programme of work required for construction of the full neoclassical theory:

> The main object of the theory of social wealth is to generalise this proposition by showing . . . that under perfect competition, it applies to production as well as to exchange. The main object of the theory

of production of social wealth is to show how the principle of organisation of agriculture, industry and commerce can be deduced as a logical consequence of the above proposition. We may say, therefore, that this proposition embraces the whole of pure and applied economics. (Walras, 1874, p. 143)

Once the supply of goods can be augmented by production these quantities can no longer be taken as *given*, but must be determined within the theory. This implied that the *data* of the problem must be redefined to include the endowment of *factors of production* (rather than of consumers goods) and the *technology* of production. It is then shown that by a process of *substitution* agents allocate these resources to different uses, in such a way as to yield an equilibrium of production and exchange. Walras said that equilibrium in production, 'which implies equilibrium in exchange', has three features. First, there must be zero excess demand for productive services. Second, there must be zero excess demand for products. Third, 'it is a state in which the selling prices of products equal the cost of productive services that enter into them' (Walras, 1874, p. 224).[4]

These three conditions imply that, in equilibrium, it cannot be more expensive to obtain a final commodity by exchange than by using factor services to produce it. In other words, the price of one commodity in terms of another cannot exceed the opportunity cost - where opportunity cost is derived directly from the resource constraints and technology. Modern formulations make it clear that it is not of any significance (to the coherence of the theory) whether the margin of constraint defines a single opportunity cost of one good in terms of another, or a range of such values (Bliss, 1975; Dixit, 1977).

The factor service endowments and available technology define the constraints within which producers maximise the value of production, given prices (Debreu, 1959, p. 43). As Debreu says, this constitutes a 'complete analogy' with the consumer's maximisation of utility subject to a wealth endowment and given prices (ibid., p. 67). So the theory of utility functions which are maximised subject to the constraint of fixed endowments that have alternate uses, allowed *production* to be treated as an *extension* of *pure exchange*. Walras drew attention to this aspect of the theory:

It is evident, now, that the theory of production, like that of exchange, starts with the problem of the attainment of the maximum satisfaction of wants by each trading party, and ends with the problem of the establishment of equality between supply and demand in the market. The only difference is that *services* take the place of commodities. In fact, in the mechanism of production, services are exchanged for services. But, whereas one part of the services we buy is composed of services as such, another part is composed of services in the form of products. (Walras, 1874, p. 478)

The necessary assumption, that all inputs exist in fixed amounts, implies that in a neoclassical theory a distinction be made between goods used in production (factors of production) and goods which are produced (Menger, 1871, p. 58). The result, which is an indispensible starting point in a 'supply and demand' theory of value, was well expressed by Walras who, precisely in criticism of the 'English theory of the price of products', said that 'All things which form part of social wealth – land, personal faculties, capital goods proper and income goods of every kind – exist only in limited quantities' (Walras, 1874, p. 399).

2.2.3 Distribution

If the neoclassical analysis of production is merely an extension of its analysis of pure exchange, then the theory of distribution is a *part of* the theory of value in exchange. Maximisation of profit implies that, in equilibrium, the price of a commodity cannot exceed the cost of the factor services used in its production (see the third part of Walras' definition of equilibrium). This equilibrium condition adds to the resource constraints a set of price constraints in the form of a relationship between factor prices and commodity prices.

Perhaps the most important aspect of neoclassical theory, for the purposes of this study of value and distribution debates on Adam Smith, is that 'distribution and exchange are fundamentally the same problem, looked at from different points of view' (Marshall, 1898, p. 66; see also Menger, 1871, p. 164; Schumpeter, 1954, p. 568; Knight, 1956, p. 11). The concept of distribution as found in classical theory is not appropriate in this structure. Debreu stresses that 'by focussing attention on changes of dates one obtains, *as a particular case of the general theory of commodities* . . . a theory of saving, investment, capital, and interest' (1959, p. 32, emphasis added). Distribution and exchange are parts of a process in which each price is determined simultaneously with each quantity from all the equilibrium conditions, in what Marshall called a 'manifold mutual action' (1885, p. 161)

Although both Walras and Marshall were clearly aware of this 'fundamental symmetry' between demand and supply, and between valuation and distribution, both would seem to have, occasionally, lost sight of this necessary implication of their theory (see Eatwell, 1975). In one place Marshall said that in long run equilibrium 'both machines and human beings would earn generally an amount that corresponds fairly with their cost of rearing and training, conventional necessaries as well as those things which are strictly necessary being reckoned for' (Marshall, 1890, pp. 479–80; and see Walras, 1874, p. 271).[5] This, if it was intended as an *explanation* of wages, would introduce a second principle for the determination of value and distribution and is, therefore, incompatible with the neoclassical theory (see Wieser, 1888, p. 186).

The neoclassical theory of distribution can be seen to have the exact same essential elements as the theory of value and the theory of production. Its familiar proposition concerning distribution – that each factor receives a reward equal to its marginal product – can be seen to reflect, and depend on, these elements. It is the fundamental requirement of given endowments which confers importance on *margins* (see Wicksell, 1901, p. 133). The fact that it is *utility* functions that are maximised makes *value* and not physical productivity, at the margin, significant (see Hicks, 1968, p. 111). It is the possibility of using endowments in alternative ways that guarantees the responsiveness of agents to price (the non-zero value of elasticities), and hence the consistency of unco-ordinated maximising choices.

This brief account of the development of neoclassical theory reveals a striking continuity in the elements which underlie 'supply and demand' explanations of value and distribution. Whether it is the work of Walras or Debreu, whether it is analysis of exchange or of distribution, the essential elements of a 'supply and demand' theory are utility functions, which are maximised subject to the constraint of given endowments, which have alternate uses. We are, therefore, justified in adopting these as a definition of neoclassical theory in asking our second question: What validity is there in the claim that Smith had an essentially neoclassical theory of value and distribution, or contributed substantially to the development of that theory?

2.3 ANALYTICAL THEMES IN THE STUDY OF SMITH

In statements of the proposition that Smith was the forerunner of neoclassical and/or classical theory, reference is seldom made to definitions of these theories akin to those adopted here. It will be seen that, instead, particular ideas – such as the labour theory of value or cost of production – commonly thought to be synonymous with classical or neoclassical theory, are said to be present in or absent from Smith's work. To simplify the argument of later chapters the relation of those ideas to classical and neoclassical theory, as defined above, are briefly identified here.

2.3.1 The labour theory of value

Sraffa's examination of Ricardo's writings, and his own theoretical work, allow an identification of the role of the labour theory of value in the classical theory of value and distribution. In the work of Ricardo and Marx the labour theory of value played the analytical role of facilitating a statement of the surplus theory of the rate of profit (see Sraffa, 1951; Eatwell, 1974, 1975; Garegnani, 1984). However, the labour theory is not necessary to this theory of profit; indeed, the general solution to the analytical problem posed by the surplus theory involves a rejection of the labour theory of value (Steedman, 1977). Consequently, it is not necessary that Smith held or approximated a labour theory of value in order that he can be said to have contributed to the classical theory.

Of course the identification of value with a quantity of labour did not begin with Ricardo. In some seventeenth- and eighteenth-century writing the quantity of labour was cited as the source of wealth, the origin of use-value, the basis of property rights, a measure of value and, on occasion, the determinant of exchange value (see Petty, 1662, I, pp. 68, 43; Locke, 1690; Vaugan, 1980, pp. 87–8; Cantillon, 1755, p. 29; Roll, 1973, pp. 98–127; Meek, 1973a, pp. 11–44). While this pre-history of labour theory is beyond the scope of this study it can be said that, just as acceptance of the labour theory of value is not a condition for Smith having been a surplus theorist, nor would *rejection* of these early labour theories be evidence of *departure* from the classical viewpoint.

2.3.2 Cost of production

The equality of money cost of production to price is merely the outcome of competition. Consequently, money costs of production *per se* cannot determine value, and from the equality of money costs and price *nothing* can be inferred concerning the theory of value (see Wicksell, 1893, p. 94, 1901, p. 21 and Wieser, 1888, p. 192).

Considering the role of costs in neoclassical theory, Wieser identified what later came to be called 'opportunity cost' (Wieser, 1888, p. 175). Once this concept is adopted it follows that 'between costs and utility there is no fundamental opposition' (ibid., p. 183). Given the simultaneous determination of factor and product prices, via the process of substitution, then 'factor prices will automatically reflect the relative subjective valuation of the various goods which could be produced with these factors' (ibid., p. 174). Therefore, it is possible in most situations, and necessary in many, to value goods according to cost - that is, by calculating the value of factors of production used in providing them (ibid., p. 184).

In this account the exact relation between cost and utility in neoclassical theory is made clear. It is not, as Marshall said it was, the same as the distinction between supply and demand, but rather:

> The opposition between costs and utility is only that between the utility of the individual case, and the utility of the whole . . . Thus where law of costs obtains, utility remains the source of value . . . The only thing is that utility and marginal utility are no longer determined in a one-sided way within the limits of each particular group of products, but over the entire field of cognate products. (Wieser, 1888, p. 183)

It follows that, despite the impression which is sometimes conveyed by Marshall's discussion of these issues, there can be no room in neoclassical theory for a separate *cost-based* explanation of supply (see Wieser, 1888, p. 196; Whitaker, 1904, p. 194; Wicksteed, 1914, p. 788; Robbins, 1934; Schumpeter, 1954, p. 924; Knight, 1956, p. 21). Therefore, where the question of cost and neoclassical theory is concerned we can adopt Wieser's criterion – as quoted at the start of the chapter.

The relation of cost of production to the classical or surplus theory of value can be briefly stated. First, the principle of competition of capitals means the price *will equal* money costs of production. In the logically coherent surplus approach to value and distribution relative prices are determined by methods of production and the manner in which the surplus is distributed (Sraffa, 1960, p. 11). Sraffa pointed out that although values determined in this way will equal the money cost of production, they should be called 'necessary price' or 'natural price' but *not* 'cost of production'. The correct solution of the analytical problem of determining the rate of profit revealed that money costs of production cannot be 'measured independently of, and prior to, the determination of the prices of the products' (ibid., p. 9). Consequently, the classical or surplus theory of relative price determination should not be called a cost of production theory of value.

These notes provide the basis for a consideration of the widespread use of the notion of a cost of production *theory of value* in the literature on the history of economics. The major instance of this is in work on Smith and Ricardo and, because of their importance, on classical economics in general. In many works the labour theory of value is contrasted with the 'cost of production theory'.[6] And, significantly, the idea that Smith and Ricardo had a cost of production theory (and not a labour theory) was seen as providing support for Marshall's view that neoclassical theory was not 'a new doctrine of value which is in sharp contrast to the old' (Marshall, 1890, p. 676; see also Viner, 1954, p. 358).

This line of interpretation can now be seen to have involved considerable historiographical inaccuracies[7] and, more significantly, to have been analytically misconceived. Neither classical nor neoclassical theory can properly be called a cost of production *theory*. If one adheres to analytically clear definitions then a priori there is no basis for the view (which, as will be seen, is the heart of this line of interpretation) that Smith's and Ricardo's rejection of the labour theory of value was necessarily a *move towards* a neoclassical or 'supply and demand' theory. Once Marshall's untenable perspective on cost is abandoned (as the leading theorists of his and our day insist it must) then it is clear that neoclassical theory is not a cost theory. In general, cost of production cannot be defined independently of demand, for it is the derived demand for factors which determines factor prices and hence cost of production (see Arrow and Starret, 1973, p. 128 and Garegnani, 1983).

2.2.3 Equilibrium and self-adjustment

A number of writers have identified Smith as a forerunner of neoclassical theory on the grounds that he introduced a *conception of equilibrium* which is still central to modern theory (Schumpeter, 1954, p. 189; Blaug, 1978, p. 43; Kaushil, 1973, p. 67 and Hollander, 1973, p. 114). The fact that in Walrasian theory the operation of supply and demand 'embraces the whole of pure and applied economics' tends to encourage the belief that to invoke *any* self-adjusting mechanism in an economic theory is to adopt the neoclassical theory. But, logically, there are no grounds for the belief that the existence of *some* self-regulating mechanisms in the capitalist economy implies the existence of the *specific* mechanisms upon which neoclassical theory is based (Garegnani, 1976; Milgate, 1982). Consequently, the task facing those who would adopt the above interpretation is not simply to cite Smith's belief that an uncoordinated economy tends towards a coherent outcome (as Arrow and Hahn, 1971, do), nor to cite his definition of natural price as a 'centre of gravitation' (as Blaug, Schumpeter, and Kaushil do), but to demonstrate Smith's use, in however primitive a form, of those particular mechanisms of adjustment which constitute neoclassical theory (Arrow and Hahn, 1971, p. vii and see also pp. 1–2)

2.3.4 Interdependence

A similar criterion must be adopted for evaluating the proposition that Smith's recognition of the 'interdependence' of the economic system indicates that he was a forerunner of neoclassical theory (see, for example, Schumpeter, 1954, p. 308; Kaushil, 1973, pp. 67–8; and Hollander, 1973, p. 281 and 292–3). Since both classical and neoclassical theories involve some element of interdependence between value and distribution this proposition would have to be defined much more precisely if it were to be used to support the case that Smith contributed to the development of neoclassical theory.

2.3.5 Summary

In summary, we can specify the two theories of value and distribution in terms of the *analytical data* which each adopts. The classical or surplus theory takes as data:

1. the size and composition of the social product,
2. the technique in use, and
3. the real wage.

These data are sufficient to determine the uniform rate of profit and the associated natural prices of each commodity. In contrast to this the neoclassical or supply and demand theory takes as data:

1. the preference of consumers,
2. the size and distribution of the endowments, and
3. the technology of production.

These data are sufficient to determine the price and quantity traded of each good and factor service.

In making sense of the long-running debates on Adam Smith's theory of value and distribution, and of the use of Smith's name in debates on the correct approach to the study of value and distribution, it will prove necessary to make reference to the concise definitions and histories of classical and neoclassical theory set out in this chapter.

Part I
Smith's Contribution

3 Surplus

> Smith did not, . . . despite the example of the physiocrats, . . . define
> net revenue, as Ricardo later did, to make it essentially identical with
> the supposedly main source of savings and tax revenue, namely,
> profits-plus-rent. (Spengler, 1959a, p. 410)

> Smithian 'net revenue' is a different concept from physiocratic
> *produit net* and from Marxian 'surplus value'. (Dobb, 1973, p. 63)

As Black has noted 'it is now generally accepted that Adam Smith was
primarily concerned with the causes of the increase of the annual
produce of society' (Black, 1971, p. 10).[1] Furthermore, it is also
generally agreed that Smith's theory of economic growth focused on
capital accumulation (see Lowe, 1954; Thweatt, 1957; Spengler, 1959a
and 1959b; Barkai, 1969; Hollander, 1973; Eltis, 1975 and 1984; and
Anspach, 1976). Yet Smith's account of capital accumulation is *not*
seen as a *surplus theory*, for – as indicated in the statements by Spengler
and Dobb – his concept of surplus is not seen as analogous to that of
the physiocrats, Ricardo, or Marx. In his celebrated article on Smith's
theory of economic growth Spengler said that 'Smith defined "*neat
revenue*" as the whole annual produce minus the maintenance of fixed
and circulating capital, *but he did not relate savings to this residuum*',
and he contrasted his own view with that of Marx whom, he said
'*asserted* that Smith's "surplus value" consisted of rent and profits'
(Spengler, 1959a, p. 410, emphasis added).
   Spengler's view has come to be accepted – especially among those
who examine Smith's work in relation to surplus theory. For example,
Lichtenstein, following Dobb, says that Smith 'regarded wages to be
part of the surplus along with profits and rent' (Lichtenstein, 1983,
pp. 68–9; Dobb, 1973, pp. 62–4 and 1975, pp. 333–4). Even Walsh and
Gram (1980), who stress the role of profit and rent as a surplus in
Smith's work, do not address the question of how he *defined* surplus
and how this definition related to his concepts 'annual produce', 'gross
revenue' and 'neat revenue'.
   If the prevailing view were correct it would indicate an important
difference between Smith, on the one hand, and the physiocrats,
Ricardo and Marx, on the other, and would consequently cast doubt

on the contention that he contributed, like them, to a surplus tradition of theory. The central task of this chapter will be to identify Smith's use of the concept of surplus in the *Wealth of Nations*. The stress will be on the concept of surplus *per se*, and its use in his theory of *accumulation*, rather than on surplus in a theory of *value and distribution*. (The latter aspect will be considered in Chapter 6.) It will be shown that in Book II, Chapter iii, 'Of the Accumulation of Capital', Smith defined surplus in a manner analogous to that of the physiocrats, Ricardo and Marx. This fact has long been obscured by his definitions of gross and net revenue in the preceding chapter (II.ii), and it was precisely concentration on this chapter which led Spengler, Dobb and others to the view outlined above. Smith's definition of economic surplus has also been obscured by some apparent ambiguities in his use of the concept of annual produce. Consequently, I devote considerable space in this chapter to close examination of what precisely Smith meant by annual produce. Then, having identified Smith's *definitions* of annual produce and surplus, it can be seen that he used these concepts to develop a surplus theory of accumulation.

3.1 SURPLUS AND ACCUMULATION

It was in Book II, Chapter iii of the *Wealth of Nations*, entitled 'Of the Accumulation of Capital, or of productive and unproductive labour', that Smith spelled out the definition of surplus which is relevant to accumulation. He defined 'productive labour' as that which 'adds to the value of the subject upon which it is bestowed (*Wealth of Nations*, Book II, Chapter iii, paragraph 1, hereafter abbreviated to *WN*, II.iii.1).[2] Though the whole annual produce is produced by productive labourers, both productive and unproductive labourers must be maintained by it (*WN*, II.iii.3). Consequently the growth or decline of the produce depends on the division of any given annual produce between productive and unproductive labour:

> This produce, how great soever, can never be infinite, but must have certain limits. According, therefore, as a smaller or greater proportion of it is in any one year employed in maintaining unproductive hands, the more in the one case and the less in the other will remain for the productive, and the next year's produce will be greater or smaller accordingly. (ibid.)

But he made clear that this division between productive and unproductive labourers is not arbitrary:

> When it first comes either from the ground or, from the hands of productive labourers, it naturally divides itself into two parts. One of them, and frequently the largest, is, in the first place, destined for replacing a capital, or for renewing the provisions, materials, and finished work, which had been withdrawn from a capital; the other for constituting a revenue either to the owner of this capital, as the profit of his stock, or to some other person, as the rent of his land. (*WN*, II.iii.4)

It seems clear that Smith subtracted from total output all that is necessary to production, *including workers, wages*, and the remainder was *profits and rents*. Here, therefore, we have a *definition* of the concept of surplus analogous to that of the Physiocrats, and identical to that which was to be adopted by Ricardo and Marx. (The question of measurement of these aggregates is examined in Chapter 5.) Smith's approach, at least in this chapter, seems unambiguous; and yet modern commentators are virtually unanimous in taking a different view of Smith's definition of economic surplus. To appreciate why this is so it is necessary to consider some possible objections to the very idea that Smith did divide *produce* into *capital* and *revenue* in the manner outlined above.

3.2 'ANNUAL PRODUCE' IN THE *WEALTH OF NATIONS*

3.2.1 Annual produce in the 'physiocratic sense'

This interpretation of Smith is dependent in part on the idea that by 'whole annual produce' Smith meant the total of goods produced during a year, and not 'national income', as understood in modern national accounts. It seems clear that in the passages cited above Smith's 'annual produce' consists not only of final goods but also of many intermediate goods. It therefore corresponds to what Leontief called 'total gross output', (1951, p. 19), or 'total output' (1965, p. 136), what Pasinetti (1977, p. 39) calls 'total gross product', and what Sraffa called 'gross national product' (1960, p. 11). This differs from 'national product', as defined in modern national income accounting, which includes only value *added* during the year (Beckerman, 1968, p. 12).

A similar view as to what Smith meant by 'annual produce', in Book II, Chapter iii, was taken by Cannan (1898, p. 53). However, modern scholars have tended to adopt a different interpretation: for example, Schumpeter (1954, p. 628), Hollander (1973, p. 204) and Blaug (1978, p. 55) all consider that Smith's 'annual produce' was roughly equivalent to the modern definition of national income. If this view is correct then either I am wrong to say that 'annual produce' consisted of final and intermediate goods, *or* Smith had (at least) two meanings of the term 'annual produce'. In this Section we explore this issue and argue that, despite what can look like evidence to the contrary, Smith had a single concept of annual produce, and that encompassed the total of goods produced during a year.

Cannan's argument on this aspect of Smith's work is interesting, because it arose in the course of his severe *criticism* of Smith – from the stand point of the new Marshallian outlook. He pointed out the extent to which Smith's definition of annual produce ('a mass of material objects'), conflicts with the modern view of income (a flow), and asked how a particular part of the year's produce (capital replacements), can be the same thing as a particular part of the accumulated stock. In his view:

> the answer is that Adam Smith had evidently imbued himself with the physiocratic idea of 'reproduction', and the difference between the daily or annual produce and the stock of articles which are supposed to be daily or annually reproduced is, if the time when the stock is largest be selected, nil. (Cannan, 1898, p. 61)

Cannan dismissed this physiocratic and Smithian idea of produce as 'a mere chimaera', but there seems to me to be little doubt of the accuracy of his view of what Smith meant by 'annual produce'.[3]

3.2.2 'Annual produce' and 'revenue'

However, there is a difficulty with this view of Smith's 'annual produce' (and with the associated view of his definitions and use of the concept of surplus). On a number of occasions Smith equated 'annual produce' to 'revenue' – where revenue referred to wages, profits and rents, (*WN*, I.iv.11 and 17; *WN*, I.xi. p. 7; *WN*, II.ii.1). Now Smith considered that these revenues consisted of the *value added* to the produce; if their sum is equal to 'annual produce', then annual produce would seem, in this context, to equal national income. It is perhaps on this ground that

Blaug and Hollander take Smith's annual produce to refer unequivocally to national income or value added. However, Cannan – who has
undertaken by far the most thorough study of this aspect of Smith's
work – has demonstrated that this view is impossible to reconcile with
Smith's statements in Chapters ii and iii of Book II, which
unambiguously refer to produce in the physiocratic sense (Cannan,
1898, p. 62).

Highlighting this problem in Smith's text Cannan drew attention to
the fact that, in Book I, that part of produce which is neither rent nor
profit is *wages*; whereas, in the chapter just considered (II.iii), that part
of produce which is neither rent nor profit is *capital* – or 'goes to
replace a capital'. But, as Cannan said, it seems clear that Smith did not
consider that part of produce which replaces a capital to consist *only of
wages* – for, he explicitly referred to the renewal of 'provisions,
materials, and finished work', which had been withdrawn from the
capital (*WN*, II.iii.4).[4] There would, therefore, seem to be a real
inconsistency in Smith's use of the term annual produce.

3.2.3 Two meanings of annual produce?

Cannan's own view was that Smith did indeed use the word 'produce'
in two quite different senses. This formed an important part of his
interpretation of the nature, extent and timing of the physiocratic
influence on Smith.[5] He said:

> The explanation of the discrepancy must lie in an ambiguity of the
> word 'produce'. When following his earlier or British train of
> thought, Adam Smith makes 'produce' exactly the same as 'revenue',
> or what we call 'income'; it is the necessaries, conveniences, and
> amusements which men actually enjoy *plus* any objects which they
> may add to their accumulated stock or capital. But when following
> his later or physiocratic train of thought, as in Book II, Chapter iii,
> he looks on the produce of a country as a mass of material objects.
> (Cannan, 1898, p. 59)

Cannan supported this interpretation by arguing that Smith was
'probably groping' to reconcile these two concepts of 'produce' when,
in Book II, Chapter ii, he distinguished between gross and net revenue
(1898, p. 60). This could offer a way out of the problem, and with no
evidence, and little conviction, Cannan noted this possibility: Very
possibly when Adam Smith divided the total produce into wages,

profits and rent, he was thinking of his 'net product', and when he divided produce into profits, rent and the part of produce destined for replacing a capital, he was thinking of his 'gross produce' (ibid.).

However, this is unconvincing, for Cannan himself agreed that Book II.ii (in which Smith distinguished gross and net revenue) must be considered an example of Smith's 'physiocratic train of thought'. (The meaning of Smith's distinction between gross and net revenue is explored below.) Furthermore, Smith's identification of 'annual produce' with revenue ('his earlier or British train of thought') was not confined to Book I; nor was his identification of produce with profits, rent, and *capital* ('his physiocratic train of thought') confined to Book II.

3.2.4 The 'resolution' of price into wages, profit, and rent

In fact it is possible to show that Smith's identification of 'annual produce' with revenue (wages, profits and rent) was consistent with his fundamental view of produce as total gross output (in the physiocratic or input–output sense) and his use of that magnitude in defining surplus. The key to understanding this consistency lies in the source of his idea that annual produce equals revenue – that is, in Book I, Chapter vi, on the 'component parts of price'.

There Smith said that the price of each commodity 'finally resolves itself' into wages, profits and rents (*WN*, I.vi.10); although any given price covers wages, profits, rent, *plus* the cost of raw materials and instruments used up, 'the whole price still resolves itself *either immediately or ultimately* into the same three parts of rent, labour and profit' (*WN*, I.vi.11, emphasis added). This was based on his argument that the prices of tools and raw materials used in production can themselves be resolved into wages, tool and material costs, profit and rent; and that these tool and material costs can in turn be resolved into wages, profits and rents, and so on (*WN*, I.vi.10–16). This proposition would seem to be the source of the idea that annual produce equals revenue or value added. For Smith's next step was to extend this idea that price *ultimately* resolves into wages, profits and rents, from the price of *individual* commodities to the price of any given *aggregate* of commodities, and then to the price of a *particular* aggregate – the 'annual produce'. He stated clearly that the whole value of the annual produce 'is in this manner originally distributed among some of its different members' (*WN*, I.vi.17 and 24). Since wages, profits and rent are revenues, therefore, the value of annual produce equals total revenue. This identity was restated at several places in the *Wealth of Nations* (see *WN*, I.xi.7 and *WN*, II.ii.1).[6] It would seem that it was this identity which led Cannan to the view that Smith had a second meaning for 'annual produce'.

We can conclude that there was no necessary inconsistency in Smith's use of the term 'annual produce'. He consistently used this to refer to total output – in the manner of the physiocrats. Any confusion that arises from his usage results from the resolution of price into wages, profits and rent. That resolution, while it may or may not have facilitated an advance in the theory of price determination (see Chapter 6 below), was clearly an obstacle when thinking about surplus and accumulation. Once the annual produce was resolved into wages, profits and rents, then the whole product was counted as *value added*, and one could not identify the amount of inputs which were used up in creating the total output. This rendered virtually impossible a clear analysis of gross and net product.

Although I have confirmed that Smith had a single meaning for the term annual produce, and that meaning was the input-output one of total gross output, I might seem now to have undermined my original argument (which the discussion of the meaning of the term annual produce was intended to bolster) that Smith had a clear definition of economic surplus comprising profits plus rents. However, it will be demonstrated now that the resolution of annual produce into wages, profits and rent, which dissolves the distinction between 'revenue' and 'capital', and consequently the distinction between necessary consumption and surplus, was, in fact, temporarily dropped by Smith.

3.2.5 Surplus and accumulation: suspension of the 'resolution'

It remains, in addition, to consider the congruity of Smith's division of produce into profits, rents *and wages*, in Book I and in Chapters i and ii of Book II (and at several other places), and his division of produce into profits, rents, *and that part of produce which replaces a capital*, in Chapter iii of Book II – on accumulation. If Smith did not consider all capital as consisting of wage-goods advanced, then there is clearly a certain inconsistency.

In examining Book II, Chapter iii, on accumulation, Cannan would seem to have overlooked a most significant sentence. Smith in fact abandoned, or suspended, the idea that the whole *annual* produce resolves itself into wages, profits and rents. This greatly enhanced the possibility of considering the division of the produce between necessary consumption and surplus:

> *Though* the whole annual produce of the land and labour of every country, is, no doubt, *ultimately* destined for supplying the consumption of its inhabitants, and for procuring a revenue to them; *yet when it first comes either from the ground*, or from the hands of the productive labourers, it naturally divides itself into *two* parts. One of them, and frequently the largest, is in the first place, destined for replacing a capital, or for renewing the provisions, materials and finished work, which has been withdrawn from a capital; the other for constituting a revenue either to the owner of this capital, as a profit of his stock; or to some other person, as the rent of his land. (*WN*, II.iii.4, emphasis added)

This suspension of the resolution of price into wages, profits and rent, is of the greatest significance. First, there is, therefore, *no need for consistency* between the division of produce into profits, rent and *wages*, and its division into profits, rent and *capital*. The former is true and relevant only 'ultimately'; the latter is 'immediately' relevant.

Any apparent paradox is dispelled once it grasped that profits plus rents in the *ultimate* resolution of annual produce into wages, profits and rents (equation 1) *will not be the same magnitude* of value as profits plus rents in the *immediate* division of produce into profits plus rent, and capital (equation 2).

1. Book I, Chapter vi: produce = wages + profits + rents.
2. Book II, Chapter iii: produce = profits + rent + capital.

Put another way, were this capital to be 'resolved' it would not all be resolved into wages.

Second, it is important that in *considering accumulation* Smith subtracted from total output the replacement of all means of production and identified the remainder, profits and rents, as the source of capital accumulation. Indeed, in this chapter he used the term 'revenue' to refer to profits and rents, and counterposed this to 'capital' (*WN*, II.iii.11).

3.3 GROSS AND NET REVENUE

It is my view that Smith's clear definition and use of the concept of surplus when considering accumulation (Book II, Chapter iii) has been obscured in two ways; first by his resolution of prices into wages, profits and rents (Book I, Chapter vi) and second, by his definitions of 'gross' and 'neat' revenue in the preceding Chapter (II,ii). The 'resolution' would seem to have led many authors to the view that by annual produce Smith meant value added. And then the distinction between gross and 'neat' or net revenue led Schumpeter (1954, p. 628) and Blaug (1978) to the view that Smith's 'gross revenue' was (roughly) equivalent to modern *gross* national product and his 'neat revenue' to *net* national product or national income – while it led Spengler (1959a) and Dobb (1973) to the view that Smith did not identify a net product or surplus analogous to that of the physiocrats, Ricardo and Marx. Given that these interpretations have been shown to be of doubtful accuracy the question naturally arises: what was the nature and purpose of Smith's definition of gross and net revenue in Book II, Chapter ii?

It was an attempt to define the wealth or welfare of the society – and on this point I am in complete agreement with Hollander (1973).

To see this it is helpful to start with the *first* Chapter of Book II, 'Of the division of stock', and to trace Smith's various definitions from there. Smith divided the total inventory of goods in existence into three parts: stock reserved for immediate consumption, fixed capital, and circulating capital (*WN*, II.i.11–22). The items in this circulating capital (provisions, materials and finished work) 'are either annually, or in a longer or shorter period, regularly withdrawn from it, and placed either in the fixed capital or in the stock reserved for immediate consumption' (*WN*, II.i.23). This definition is found in line 1 of Figure 3.1.

In defining gross and net revenue in Book II, Chapter ii, Smith began from his inventory of goods. From this inventory he subtracted the *stock* of 'machines and instruments of trade, etc., which compose the fixed capital' and the stock of money (*WN*, II.ii.14, see line 2 of Figure 3.1). The remainder was the *gross revenue*: the list of commodities, both intermediate and final, produced during a given year. But, of course, this is equivalent to the *annual produce* as understood by Smith. Indeed, he here restated that the whole value of this annual produce constitutes a revenue to its different inhabitants – basing this explicitly on the resolution of *prices* into wages, profits and rent (*WN*, II.ii.2–3).

36

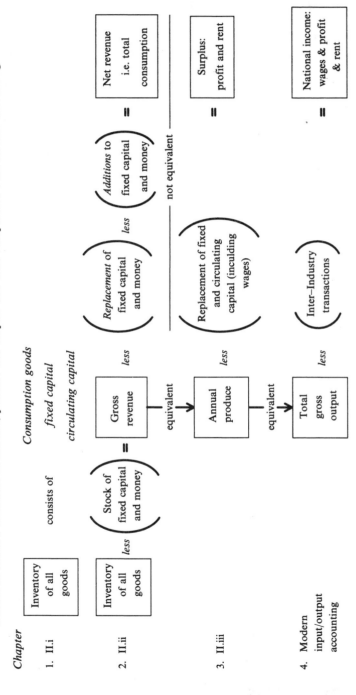

Figure 3.1

Outline of Smith's definition of revenue, produce and surplus and their comparison with modern accounting

Once again Smith confronted the limitations of the resolution of the annual produce into wages, profits and rents. It was clear that annual produce (gross revenue) was not an informative measure of the level of social *consumption*. But the idea that the whole annual produce resolves into revenues tempts one to equate these revenues (and hence annual produce) to what is available for consumption. For a second time Smith qualified the resolution of annual produce into wages, profits and rents. In the very next paragraph he proceeded towards a definition of the difference between the gross and net revenue of society (*WN*, II.ii.5). It is this paragraph which is most commonly cited as embodying the essence of his distinction between gross and net revenue (Spengler, 1959a, p. 410; Dobb, 1973, p. 62). However, the paragraph is quite misleading – especially if read in isolation from the remainder of Smith's account – and it has caused great confusion. It is misleading because of a difference between the way in which individual and aggregate circulating capital must be treated when measuring consumption – a difference which Smith went on to clarify two pages later (*WN*, II.ii.10). In order to set out clearly my interpretation of Smith I propose to place and discuss this misleading paragraph in a series of notes and follow Smith's actual accounting procedure in the main text.[7]

He pointed out that in the case of a private estate we can distinguish 'gross rent' (the amount paid by the farmer and received by the landlord) and 'neat rent' (what remains after deducting the expense of management, repairs, etc.), the latter being a measure of what can be placed in the 'stock reserved for immediate consumption' (*WN*, II.ii.4). He explicitly used this as an analogy in introducing the idea of the gross and net revenue of a whole country.

To get 'neat revenue', a measure of what the population 'without encroaching upon their capital, can place in their stock reserved for immediate consumption', (*WN*, II.ii.5) he deducted the following three items from annual produce (gross revenue):

1. 'the whole expense of maintaining the fixed capital' *less* the wages of workers employed in that maintenance – since those wages are part of social consumption[8] (*WN*, II.ii.6);
2. the expense of maintaining *one* part of the circulating capital, *the stock of money*: – the remainder of the circulating capital (provisions, materials and finished work) being consumed, and therefore making part of the net revenue of society[9] (*WN*, II.ii.9–11); and

3. the expense of *additions* to the fixed capital and money stock (*WN*, II.ii.13).

In effect, to get net revenue from gross revenue, Smith deducted only that part of produce which is used for replacement and enhancement of *fixed* capital. It follows that net revenue contains many materials and provisions which are needed for reproduction – workers wages being the most obvious. It is a measure of social consumption – *including productive consumption*.

We are accustomed to think of the price of each commodity which emerges as income as equal to the cost of intermediate commodities used up plus the value added (wages, profits and rent). Normally these intermediate commodities are considered to have been *produced in a preceding stage of production*. As Pasinetti says 'as one traces the productive process backwards through time, all of the intermediate commodities come to be eliminated from the calculation' (Pasinetti, 1977, p. 43). (Smith was the first to identify this result.) In Book II, Chapter ii, Smith in effect traced the production process backwards *in a single year*. The collection of goods produced (once maintenance of and additions to fixed capital have been subtracted) will be completely consumed and reproduced each year (for a similar view see Eltis, 1975, p. 435).[10]

This measure of what Smith called 'the value of what has been consumed and produced' (*WN*, IV.ix.32) or 'the consumable goods annually circulated within the society' (*WN*, II.iii.24) was, therefore, an attempt to measure the 'real wealth' or welfare of the society (see *WN*, II.ii.5 and 20). Hollander takes a similar view, stressing that 'the first two Chapters [of Book II] do not have the specific treatment of growth or "accumulation" in mind' (1973, pp. 199–204 and see pp. 144–6). It was precisely by concentrating on Book II, Chapter ii, and in particular on Smith's definition of 'neat revenue' (which includes wages), that Spengler (1959a) and Dobb (1973) were led to the conclusion that Smith's treatment of *produce* and *surplus* was altogether different from that of the Physiocrats, Ricardo and Marx. What has been shown here is that Spengler and Dobb were mistaken in seeking Smith's definition of economic surplus in Chapter ii of Book II. That definition is to be found in his chapter on the accumulation of capital (Book II, Chapter iii).

3.4 A SURPLUS *THEORY* OF THE NON-WAGE SHARE?

It has been shown above that in explaining accumulation Smith did isolate the non-wage share of output as an important magnitude. We have now to ask whether in the *Wealth of Nations* this surplus was *determined* by the level and composition of output and capital inputs, or whether all three were *ex post* magnitudes determined by some other set of forces. This question of the nature and extent of a surplus *theory* of the non-wage share in the *Wealth of Nations* is one of the central issues of this study and, consequently, it will be considered again in later chapters. Here I survey the evidence avoiding, as far as is possible, complications which arise from the problem of measuring and determining value. The evidence we must consider is how the annual produce and capital were determined in the *Wealth of Nations*, and whether any relationships between these two magnitudes and profits plus rents (revenue) were specified. It will emerge that there is considerable evidence that not only did Smith define the magnitude profits and rents, but also that he saw it as a *residual* determined by the independent magnitudes *produce* and *capital*. For he had separate theories of output, technology and wages.

3.4.1 The determination of 'annual produce' and 'capital'

It is hardly surprising that a theory of what determines the annual produce is central to the *Wealth of Nations*. Smith considered that output was determined by the accumulated capital stock, the methods of production, and the pattern of social consumption (*WN*, II.ii.37; *WN*, II.iii.13–20; *WN*, IV.i.18; *WN*, IV.ii.13; and *WN*, IV.iii.c.7). For example, the following statement is typical:

> The annual produce of the land and labour of any nation can be increased in its value by no other means, but by increasing either the number of its productive labourers, or the productive powers of those labourers who had before been employed. The number of its productive labourers, it is evident, can never be much increased, but in consequence of an increase of capital, or of the funds destined for maintaining them. The productive powers of the same number of labourers cannot be increased, but in consequence either of some addition and improvement to those machines and instruments which facilitate and abridge labour; or of a more proper division and

distribution of employment. In either case an additional capital is almost always required. (*WN*, II.iii.32).

Evidently Smith envisaged a fairly strict relationship between capital and output, saying 'the general industry of the country being always in proportion to the capital which employs it' (*WN*, IV.ii.12); and he saw fit to make explicit allowance for exceptions to this arising from differences in fertility and fluctuations in output caused by natural conditions (*WN*, II.i.29; *WN*, I.vii.17; and *WN*, I.x.b.46; and see Cannan, 1898, pp. 67–70 and Bowley, 1975, p. 372). As to the determination of capital accumulation itself, Smith considered that this depended on the quantity of produce that 'can be gradually saved from its revenue' (*WN*, IV.ii.13; and see Eltis, 1975). This in turn depended on whether revenue was used to hire productive or unproductive workers, and Smith had definite views as to which social class was 'naturally the most disposed to accumulate' and which social, political and economic conditions were conducive to this process (*WN*, IV.vii.c.61 and *WN*, III.ii.20).

The second determinant of output in Smith's theory was what would today be called the technology of production, but which he called 'the state of the skill, dexterity and judgement with which labour is applied in any nation' (*WN*, I.6). He would seem to have considered that at any given time these methods of production were given; he said, for example, 'the capital of the country being the same, or very nearly the same, the demand for labour will likewise be the same, or very nearly the same' (*WN*, IV.ii.42, and see *WN*, I.x.c.44 and *WN*, II.i.6). But he is, of course, renowned for this theory of how the division of labour develops (see *WN*, I.i–iii).

The composition of output was determined, in Smith's theory, by the pattern of social consumption as reflected in the 'effectual demand' (*WN*, I.vii.12). This determined what he called the 'natural state' of each employment (*WN*, I.x.b.44–6).

With output and the material and labour requirements of reproduction determined by the above forces, it remains to ask how the *remuneration* of those labourers was seen to be determined.

Smith's theory of wages was a prototype for all subsequent classical theory and, in many ways, a synthesis of earlier subsistence theories (Wermel, 1939, pp. 129–39, and, for a similar view, see O'Brien, 1976a, p. 135). In his view, the level of wages was determined by the 'state' or 'condition' of the society. He identified three such states: the 'progressive', the 'stationary' and the 'declining'. In the progressive state, capital was accumulating and the productive system required an increasing population; the stationary and declining states required stationary and declining populations respectively (*WN*, V.ii.i.1). This determined the subsistence of the worker; in a progressive state 'the reward of labour must necessarily encourage in such a manner the marriage and multiplication of labourers, as may enable them to supply that continually increasing demand by a continually increasing population' (*WN*, I.viii.40). Thus the level of wages will rise if the rate of capital accumulation exceeds the rate of population growth (which Smith considered to be the case in North America) but will not continue to rise once the required rate of population growth has been reached (*WN*, I.viii.23; see Tucker, 1960, p. 61n; Eltis, 1975, p. 430; but see Bowley, 1973a, pp. 183–206, for a somewhat different interpretation). Note that Smith considered each of these wages levels to be 'the subsistence of the labourer', regardless of whether it was a 'liberal, moderate or scanty subsistence' (*WN*, V.ii.i.1). However, each of these subsistence levels had a customary as well as biological element: 'by necessaries I understand not only the commodities indispensably necessary for the support of life, but whatever the custom of the country renders it indecent for creditable people, even of the lowest order, to be without' (*WN*, V.ii.k.3). It will be seen below that Smith adhered to his subsistence theory of wages with complete consistency. This completes our survey of how Smith considered output and capital (the requirements of production) to be determined.

3.4.2 Surplus relationships in the *Wealth of Nations*

Consequently, when in his crucial chapter on accumulation (II.ii) Smith considered the division of the produce into two parts (one of which replaces capital and one of which becomes the revenues – profits and rents) it can be seen that *produce* and *capital* were *given* magnitudes determined by previous capital accumulation, the state of technology, the wage rate, and the pattern of demand.

This is reflected in Smith's language: one part is '*destined* for replacing a capital' while the remainder, profits and rents, 'may maintain indifferently either productive or unproductive hands' (*WN*, II.iii.5 and *WN*, II.iii.20 and *WN*, II.iv.7). In addition, attention has frequently been drawn to his description of profits and rents as '*deductions* from the produce of the labour' (*WN*, I.viii.7).[11] However, if he had not made some attempt to *explain* the size and composition of the produce, the requirements of reproduction, and the level of the wage, these suggestive phrases could not validly be cited as evidence of a surplus theory in Smith.[12]

If these magnitudes are given it follows that revenue (profits plus rent) is a residual determined by them. Furthermore, this necessarily established a relationship between any *change* in *produce* or *capital* and the resultant change in revenue. If this really was Smith's theory of the non-wage share we should find in his work consideration of some such changes. In fact many examples of this can be identified. But, for reasons that will only emerge fully in Chapters 5 and 6, these do not always conform to what is found in the work of subsequent surplus theorists. The following are some of the *changes* or *differences* in the magnitude of produce or necessary inputs (capital) considered by Smith.

Falling share of profits and rents

First, in the chapter in which he divided *produce* into *capital* and *revenue* Smith compared the relation between these magnitudes in a rich and in a poor country. He related the fall in the share of profits and rents to the changing relative magnitude of produce and capital:

> That part of the annual produce, therefore, which, as it comes either from the ground, or from the hands of the productive labourers, is destined for replacing a capital, is not only much greater in rich than in poor countries, but bears a much greater proportion to that which is immediately destined for constituting a revenue either as rent or as profit. (*WN*, II.iii.11)

This path of development is consistent with increasing output per worker which is outweighted by increasing raw material and instrument requirements per worker (as a result of capital accumulation and/or increased wage costs per head – see *WN*, II.3 and Eltis, 1975, p. 445). Here the magnitude of the non-wage share would seem to be *determined by* the magnitudes of the annual produce and the 'capital'. But when we look to these passages for a more precise theory of distribution we are disappointed. Besides relating profits to this ratio of output to the inputs required for those outputs (or ratio of output to capital) Smith also related the rate of profit to 'competition', and thereby introduced a considerable ambiguity as to what was the *ultimate source* of falling profits. In Chapter 6 this ambiguity will be shown to have been an important feature of his treatment of value and distribution.

Removal of restrictions on trade

A second example of how *change* in capital or produce determined change in revenue can be cited. On several occasions Smith considered the effects of an extension of the market by removal of restrictions on trade. As a result 'the cultivators get a better price for their surplus produce' (*WN*, III.iii.20, and see *WN*, III.i.4 and *WN*, IV.vii.6–8). In analysing this change, produce seems to be implicitly taken as given – determined by the forces in Smith's theory of output. Of course, the improved *value* of a given *physical* surplus facilitates further accumulation: 'They are both encouraged and enabled to increase this surplus produce by a further improvement and better cultivation of the land' (*WN*, III.iii.20). Consideration of an extension of the market of this sort was common among the physiocrats, in whose opinion restrictions on trade were one of the two great inhibitions to capital accumulation in agriculture (Vaggi, 1983, pp. 13–14; 1987).

Surplus in different agricultural systems

Third, it was a feature of Smith's work that the concept of surplus as a residual magnitude was stated most clearly in his account of agriculture, and the significance of this is evaluated below. There he could make an unambiguous comparison between output and the requirements of production:

> Land, in almost any situation, produces a greater quantity of food than what is sufficient to maintain all the labour necessary for bringing it to market, in the most liberal way in which that labour is ever maintained. The surplus too is always more than sufficient to replace the stock which employed that labour, together with its profits. Something, therefore, always remains for a rent to the landlord. (*WN*, I,xi.b.2)

The central proposition of Chapter xi of Book I was that the rent of corn land, 'or whatever else is the common vegetable food of the people', regulates the rent of other cultivated land (*WN*, I.xi.b.14). In explaining this Smith made an interesting comparison which highlights the fact that in dividing *produce* into *capital* and *revenue*, *produce* and *capital* were considered given magnitudes. He compared the ratios of physical input to output in corn, rice, and potatoes, respectively (*WN*, I.xi.35–9; for a similar view see Walsh and Gram, 1980). Considering rice, for example, he said 'Though its cultivation, therefore, requires more labour, a much greater surplus remains after maintaining all the labour' (*WN*, I.xi.b.37). The clarity of this will be seen to contrast with the ambiguity of his account of why, in the economy at large, the share of profits and rents falls as capital accumulates.

It will be seen later in this study that Smith did not consistently focus on this relation between *produce*, *capital* (which includes wages), and *revenue* (profits and rent) in order to develop from it a theory of *distribution*. Although produce and capital were given and revenue was a residual, most of the *changes* he considered involved a change in *output* or, focussing as he did on capital *accumulation* rather than *distribution*, changes in all three magnitudes.

Taxes

However, in considering the effect of *taxes* levied on wages, profits, rents or interest, an examination of the relation *between* these three magnitudes (produce, capital, and revenue) was unavoidable. An analysis of the effects of these taxes clearly required a theory of price, and this aspect of Smith's account is examined in detail in Chapter 6. However, it may be useful to note his results here, for they provide further evidence that Smith had an independent theory of output, technology and wages – theories which were in many ways unconnected with the problem of value.

In analysing these taxes Smith made explicit use of the theory of output outlined above. He considered that a tax on rent would fall on rent, and a tax on profits would fall on interest. The explanation of this lay in their being *residual* quantities:

> The interest of money seems at first sight a subject equally capable of being taxed directly as the rent of land. Like the rent of land it is a neat produce which remains after completely compensating the whole risk and trouble of employing the stock. As a tax upon the rent of land cannot raise rents; because the neat produce which remains after replacing the stock of the farmer, together with his reasonable profit, cannot be greater after the tax than before it; so, for the same reason, a tax upon the interest of money could not raise the rate of interest; the quantity of stock or money in the country,

like the quantity of land, being supposed to remain the same after the tax as before it. (*WN*, V.ii.f.3)[13]

In contrast to this, a tax on wages or on 'necessaries' must raise the money wages of labour, thereby 'throwing the final payment of the tax upon the superior ranks of people' (*WN*, V.ii.k.44 and see *WN*, V.ii.i.2). These conclusions, and the basis on which they were reached, are strong evidence of a surplus *theory* of the non-wage share (Walsh and Gram, 1980, pp. 69–70).

Monopoly of the colonial trade

Finally, Smith's analysis of the consequences of a British monopoly of its colonial trade provides an opportunity to consider a most significant surplus relationship in the *Wealth of Nations*. He wished to highlight the effects of the monopoly on the quantity of surplus created and, consequently, on capital accumulation. The monopoly, by drawing British capital from agriculture and manufacturing:

> hinders the capital of that country, whatever may at any particular time be the extent of that capital, from maintaining so great a quantity of productive labour as it would otherwise maintain, and from affording so great a revenue to the industrious inhabitants as it would otherwise afford. (*WN*, V.vii.c.57)

Here Smith was making use of his theory that the value added in a given industry depends on how the capital is divided between productive labour and material inputs. It may be useful to sketch this theory.

Based on his fundamental distinction between productive and unproductive labour he had argued, in Book II, Chapter v, that the greater the proportion of labour to means of production the greater would be the value added to the produce, and he ranked industries in the order: agriculture, manufacturing, trade (*WN*, II.v.9–12 and 19).

> It is thus that the same capital will in any country put into motion a greater or smaller quantity of productive labour, and add a greater or smaller value to the annual produce of its lands and labour, according to the different proportions in which it is employed in agriculture, manufacturing and wholesale trade. (*WN*, II.v.23)

The case of the colonial trade is a good example of his use of this approach. Smith was, in effect, holding total inputs constant and comparing the effects on the *quantity* of *surplus* of two *different patterns of output* – one associated with a British monopoly of colonial trade, the other that would prevail if no monopoly was imposed. (See *WN*, IV.vii.c.15–63 *passim*; and Walsh and Gram, 1980.)

This line of argument was extremely important in the *Wealth of Nations* – underlying, as it did, Smith's criticism of the mercantilists and all his own most important policy prescriptions, including the famous 'invisible hand' argument (*WN*, IV.ii.3–10, and for a similar view see Campbell and Skinner, 1976, pp. 32 and 56). Its consistency with his theory of self-interest and advocacy of economic liberalism has been the subject of considerable discussion among scholars.[14] Its significance here is that it is undoubtedly the most often stated surplus relationship in the *Wealth of Nations*.[15]

The state of surplus theory in the WEALTH OF NATIONS

These examples provide an opportunity to evaluate the state of surplus theory in Smith's work. For these particular surplus relationships (and the distinction between productive and unproductive labour) most certainly cannot be cited as evidence of a surplus theory of *value and distribution* in Smith.

In evaluating policies according to the criterion of how they influenced the allocation of capital to different industries Smith's interest was in the consequences for accumulation, and he related that to the *amount* of surplus produced and not to the *rates* of profit or rent (*WN*, IV.ii.13; *WN*, IV.iii.c.15; *WN*, IV.vii.c.49 and 59 and *WN*, IV.ix.36; and for a similar view, see Bowley, 1975, p. 336). Furthermore, it will be seen that he did not draw on his analysis of these changes in the *amount* of revenue in order to calculate the change in the *rate* of profit. In general, his prediction about the direction of the rate of profit was derived by reference to the 'intensity of competition' (an idea which is examined in Chapter 6).

For example, in the case of the monopoly of colonial trade he considered that this drew capital from British agriculture and manufacturing into shipping, consequently reducing the *amount* of value added and surplus, 'and thereby diminishes their power of accumulation' (*WN*, IV.vii.c.49). At the same time he argued that the monopoly had *raised* the *rate* of profit on British capital as a whole (this is explained at *WN*, IV.vii.c.19 and 25, and 59). When drawing out the consequences for accumulation he consistently followed the *amount* of profit *rather than the rate* (*WN*, IV.vii.c.59). It is, perhaps, significant that it was exactly at this point of his somewhat unconvincing argument that Smith introduced what he admitted was an additional proposition: namely, that 'the high rate of profit seems everywhere to destroy that parsimony which in other circumstances is natural to the character of the merchant' (*WN*, IV.vii.c.61). Without this additional proposition it is not certain that the monopoly, which reduced the '*sum* of profit' but raised the *rate* of profit, would actually reduce the rate of capital accumulation (for a similar view see Campbell and Skinner, 1976, pp. 58–9 and see Campbell 1982, pp. 20–1).

This case, which is typical of many more in Smith, allows an interesting qualification of Spengler's view that Smith underestimated 'the capital-supplying power of surpluses' (Spengler, 1959b, p. 10). Paradoxically, the truth may be almost the opposite of this: Smith concentrated only on the capital supplying power of the *amounts* of profits and rents, and quite ignored the significance for accumulation of the *rate* of profit.

This is totally consonant with the state of the surplus theory in Smith. The distinction between productive and unproductive labour, and the ranking of economic sectors according to their surplus producing potential, was a useful enough way to approach accumulation; but of all possible ways of stating a basic surplus relation it is, perhaps, the one which least takes one towards a surplus theory of the *rate of profit*, and hence to a surplus theory of *value and distribution*.

In summary, there seems to be clear evidence of Smith having used his theory of output, technology, and wages to derive surplus relationships concerning the non-wage share. But in what we have surveyed so far, there is little evidence that he used these surplus relationships to derive a theory of *rate of profit* or rental rates.

3.4.3 Some qualifications

Smith's account of the physiocratic system underlines this argument that he had a surplus theory of the non-wage share and yet, as will be seen, qualifies it somewhat. These qualifications or ambiguities must be registered here.

In his commentary on the physiocratic system he focused on the central difference between their system and his own. In their system manufacturers are 'altogether barren and unproductive'. Consequently, the 'profits of manufacturing stock ... are not, like the rent of land, a neat produce which remains after completely repaying the whole expense which must be laid out in order to obtain them' (*WN*, IV.ix.10). In outlining the associated physiocratic view of accumulation Smith drew a most interesting distinction between 'parsimony' and surplus, as sources of funds for investment:

> Artificers, manufacturers and merchants, can augment the revenue and wealth of their society, by parsimony only; or, as it is expressed in this system, by privation, that is, by depriving themselves of a part of the funds destined for their own subsistence. (*WN*, IV.ix.13)

He contrasted this with the position of farmers (and country labourers, to some extent) who in the physiocratic theory:

> on the contrary, may enjoy completely the whole funds destined for their own subsistence, and yet augment at the same time the revenue and wealth of their society. Over and above what is destined for their own subsistence, their industry annually affords a neat produce, of which the augmentation necessarily augments the revenue and wealth of their society. (*WN*, IV.xi.13)

In the latter case it is clear that surplus can be defined prior to and independently of any decision to use it for accumulation or consumption and, consequently, this distinction would seem to be a potentially useful one when considering surplus creation and accumulation.

Smith's most famous comment on the physiocrats was, of course, that the 'capital error of this system, however, seems to lie in its representing the class of artificers, manufacturers and merchants, as altogether barren and unproductive' (*WN*, IV.ix.29). Yet there is no doubt that here, when defending his crucial extension to physiocratic theory, his account of surplus creation was by no means clear – a point which was to be noted by Marx (1861–63, I Chapter iv, and II, p. 360).

In contrast to his emphatic statements elsewhere that the value which the workman *adds* to the materials covers wages *and profits* (*WN*, I.vi.5 and 21; *WN*, I.viii.8–9; *WN*, II.iii.1; *WN*, II.iv.1; *WN*, II.v.11) he seemed, in the five points he raised against the physiocrats, to *accept* their premise that workers in manufacture 'do no more than continue' their own value, and to dispute only the physiocratic *conclusion* that this was justification for classing them as 'unproductive'. Now this

approach may have been adopted simply for the sake of argument –
and some of the points were valid in themselves[16] – but it would raise a
doubt as to what exactly was Smith's view of non-agricultural profits
and interest.

For example, instead of restating, what on all the evidence would
seem to have been his *general* view, namely, that manufacturing profits
are a 'neat produce', he argued here that farmers 'can no more
augment, without parsimony, the real revenue, the annual produce of
the land and labour of their society, than artificers, manufacturers and
merchants' (*WN*, IV.ix.34). This raises difficult problems of
interpretation. As we have seen, Spengler was of the opinion that
'his great and almost exclusive emphasis upon "parsimony" may have
led him to underestimate . . . the capital-supplying power of surpluses'
(1959b, p. 10). In part this results from Spengler's view that Smith did
not relate savings to his residuum 'neat revenue' (a view which, it has
been shown above, arises from mistaken interpretation of the 'neat
revenue' of Book II, Chapter ii, as Smith's definition of surplus), and in
part it may result from Smith not relating accumulation to the *rate of
profit*; but in part it may result from the line of argument which Smith
adopted in his criticism of the physiocrats – and, to that extent, may
have a certain validity.

It should be noted, however, that Smith's general use of the term
'parsimony' would not seem to have the connotation of privation and
encroachment on necessary consumption that it does in the passage
quoted above (see *WN*, II.iii.13–36; and also *WN*, IV.i.30; *WN*,
IV.vii.c.61; *WN*, V.ii.k.80; *WN*, V.iii.1–7). It is, perhaps, the contrast
between 'parsimony' and savings out of 'neat produce' which should
not be accorded too much significance.[17]

A further question about the clarity of Smith's extension of the
concept of surplus to all industries is raised by his frequent recourse to
an essentially physiocratic idea of surplus in agriculture. In arguing
that land used in the production of human food 'produces a greater
quantity of food than what is sufficient to maintain all the labour
necessary for bringing it to market' (*WN*, I.xi.b.2; and see also *WN*,
I.xi.b.34–42; *WN*, I.xi.c.35; *WN*, II.v.12) he invoked the idea that 'food
is always, more or less, in demand' (*WN*, I.xi.b.1), and traced both
profit and rent to this physical/value surplus: 'the surplus too is always
more than sufficient to replace the stock which employed that labour,
together with its profits' (*WN*, I.xi.b.2).

Finally, in his analysis of the effects of a tax on profits, the results of
which was reported in Section 3.4.2 above, Smith introduced a further

ambiguity about the surplus nature of profits. In his Chapter 'Of the profits of stock' he had explained that the rate of profit consisted of a 'compensation for occasional losses' and a 'surplus .. which is neat or clear profit' (*WN*, I.ix.18). 'The interest which the borrower can afford to pay is in proportion to the clear profit only' (ibid.). But in analysing a tax on profits he said that the part of profit 'which is over and above what is necessary for paying the interest . . . is evidently a subject *not directly taxable*'. It is to the rationale for this that I wish to draw attention:

> It is the compensation, and in most cases it is no more than a very moderate compensation for the risk and trouble of employing the stock. The employer must have this compensation, otherwise he cannot, consistently with his own interest, continue the employment. (*WN*, V.ii.f.2)

On this basis he argued that the employer must pass on the tax by paying less interest. This runs counter to his initial and fundamental definition of profits as 'altogether different' from wages, and his emphatic statement that profits 'bear no proportion to the quantity, the hardship of the ingenuity of this supposed labour of inspection and direction' (*WN*, I.vi.6, and see *WN*, I.x.b.36 where he confirmed that the effort involved does not increase in proportion to the capital). It also undermines somewhat his criticism of what he saw to be the physiocratic view, namely, that the profits of a manufacturer are a fund, 'for his own maintenance, and this maintenance he generally proportions to the profit which he expects to make by the price of their work' (*WN*, IV.ix.10).[18]

It should be noted that these ambiguities concerning the surplus *nature* of the undertaker's profits are, on the face of it, quite independent of any ambiguities which may be found in this theory of the *rate* of profit.

3.5 CONCLUSION

As Dobb and Meek have argued, there are good reasons to believe that we could find in Smith's *Wealth of Nations* an important foundation on which the theories of value and distribution of Ricardo and Marx were built. However, study of influential commentaries on Smith, such as that of Spengler, and including those by Dobb and Meek, reveals one major reservation to the view that Smith's work contributed to the development of a theory of value and distribution based on surplus. Smith is considered to have included wages in his definition of the surplus of the economic system – and, in general, his concept of net product, net revenue, or surplus, is said to have differed substantially from that of the physiocrats, Ricardo and Marx. As a result Smith's contribution to the development of the theory of value and distribution based on surplus is said to consist in all sorts of incidental similarities between his work and that of Ricardo and Marx – such as his occasional relation of value to labour embodied and hints at an 'exploitation' view of distribution (see Dobb, 1975).

In my view these commentators have not examined Smith's definition of economic surplus in sufficient detail. The central proposition of this chapter is that, when considering accumulation, Smith considered the surplus of the economic system to consist of profits plus rents. This fact was obscured by a number of other features of the *Wealth of Nations*. First, his resolution of prices into wages, profits and rents, in Book I, Chapter vi, has led to the impression that by 'annual produce' Smith meant value added or national income and not the total of goods, both final and intermediate, produced in a given year. This view of the meaning of annual produce strongly favours the idea that Smith defined the economic surplus to include wages. Second, in defining gross and neat revenue in Book II, Chapter ii, Smith definitely included wages in net revenue. Many commentators have looked upon this chapter as the location of Smith's definition of surplus or net product. Having stated and demonstrated my central proposition, that Smith defined the economic surplus to consist of profits plus rents, most of this chapter is devoted to showing that the objections to this view derive from these obscuring other features of the *Wealth of Nations*. Indeed, when the text is studied in detail it can be shown that these features do not even constitute conflicting evidence concerning Smith's definition of surplus. For, the resolution of price into wages, profit and rent was suspended by Smith when discussing accumulation and, consequently, is not at variance with his definition of surplus as the difference between annual produce and the requirements of reproduction, including workers' wages (i.e. surplus as the magnitude of profits and rents). Likewise, the distinction between gross and net revenue in Book II, Chapter ii, would seem to have been intended as a measure of *social consumption*, and not as Smith's definition of the surplus available for accumulation. Second, it has been shown that in dividing produce into capital and revenue, produce and capital were given magnitudes explained by Smith's theories of output, technology, and the real wage. Consequently, Smith can be considered to have had a *surplus* theory of the non-wage share. This is confirmed by his analysis of a number of relationships involving surplus. However, what is striking about these surplus relationships is that they were not used by Smith to develop a theory of the *rate of profit*, his concern being, almost exclusively, the *amount* of surplus and its implications for accumulation. Finally, this proposition, that Smith had a surplus theory of the non-wage share of produce, is subject to a number of qualifications arising from ambiguous statements concerning the surplus nature of non-agricultural *profits*.

4 Competition

> The plans and projects of the employers of stock regulate and direct
> all the most important operations of labour, and profit is the end
> proposed by all those plans and projects. (*WN*, I.xi.p.10)

We begin examination of Smith's treatment of value and distribution
by considering his use of the concept of competition. Skinner has
demonstrated that 'Smith had . . . attained a sophisticated grasp of the
interdependence of economic phenomena prior to his departure for
France in 1764' (Skinner, 1976, p. 114). Yet it was only in the *Wealth of
Nations* that he presented a complete statement of the *implications* of
the interdependence of a system of markets. Chapter vii of Book I, 'Of
the Natural and Market Price of Commodities', outlines the
implications that competition has for prices and the rate of profit. In
this chapter I identify the major features of this aspect of Smith's
contribution to the development of economic science.

4.1 NATURAL PRICE AND THE UNIFORM RATE OF PROFIT

The analysis of Chapter vii was, in fact, remarkably simple and is, for a
reason that will become apparent presently, very familiar. Smith stated
that there is in every society a natural rate of wages, profits, and rent
(*WN*, I.vii.1–3). Explicitly putting aside any consideration of how these
natural rates are regulated, he said:

> When the price of any commodity is neither more nor less than what
> is sufficient to pay the rent of the land, the wages of the labour, and
> the profits of the stock employed in raising, preparing and bringing it
> to market, according to their natural rates, the commodity is then
> sold for what may be called its natural price. (*WN*, I.vii.4)

The kernel of the chapter was the proposition that this natural price is
'the central price, to which the prices of all commodities are continually
gravitating' (*WN*, I.vii.15). The basis of this proposition was that when
the 'market price' ('the actual price at which any commodity is

53

commonly sold') is less than the natural price then either profits, wages or rent are below their natural rate and this will prompt the removal of capital (labour or land) from the industry in question – 'since by employing his stock in some other way he might have made that [natural rate of] profit' (*WN*, I.vii.5 and 13). A difference between natural price and market price will arise whenever the quantity brought to market differs from the 'effectual demand'. But the effect (of the consequent deviation of profits, wages and rents from the uniform natural rates) on capitalists, workers and landlords is such that the 'whole quantity of industry annually employed in order to bring any commodity to market, naturally suits itself in this manner to the effectual demand' (*WN*, I.vii.16). A condition for this tendency to 'supply, and no more than supply that demand', and hence for the 'gravitation' of price towards its natural level, was the existence of 'perfect liberty' – a situation in which a man 'may change his trade as often as he pleases' (*WN*, I.vii.6, see also *WN*, I.vii.30, *WN*, I.x.c.10). Consequently, Smith called natural price 'the price of free competition' (*WN*, I.vii.27).

4.2   FEATURES OF SMITHIAN COMPETITION

There are several features of this analysis which are widely agreed and which can, therefore, be stated briefly.

First, there is widespread agreement that this constituted an advance on previous attempts to provide an abstract characterisation of markets. One aspect of this is noted by Larsen who says 'Smith's inclusion of normal profit in natural prices is now generally accepted as a quantum leap over earlier efforts' (Larsen, 1977, p. 228; and see also Rosenberg, 1975, p. 377). This development of a clear conception of profit out of the disparate notions found in the works of Petty, Cantillon, Quesnay, Hutcheson and others has been studied in depth by Meek who considered that 'It was Smith's great emphasis on the economic role of profit on capital and capital accumulation which more than anything else gave unity and strength to the structure of the *Wealth of Nations*' (Meek, 1954, p. 139). Even Schumpeter, who was consistently critical of the idea that the *Wealth of Nations* contained significant theoretical advances, considered the 'rudimentary equilibrium theory of Chapter 7, by far the best piece of economic theory turned out by A. Smith' (1954, p. 189 and see also p. 308).

Second, it is widely agreed that this approach to competition became an important part of political economy for at least the next one hundred and fifty years. For, what Smith's analysis of competition did was specify natural prices and the associated natural rates of wages, profit and rent as the appropriate *object of analysis* of economic theory. Competition ensured that this long-period position of the economy was, to use Smith's own phrase, a 'centre of repose and continuance' (*WN*, I.vii.15). Although 'different accidents may sometimes keep them suspended a good deal above it they are constantly tending towards it' (ibid.). Consequently, it was the natural levels of these variables which must be explained by any theory which purported to have *general* validity.

Thus, theorists such as Ricardo, Marx, Mill, Walras, Wicksell, Marshall and Knight, who differed in their *explanation* of value and distribution, all addressed themselves to explaining those prices which were associated with a uniform rate of profit (see Knight, 1956, p. 25 and Milgate, 1982, pp. 19–23). They all accepted Smith's idea that it is competition which was the organising principle of the economy and which allowed the persistent forces in the system to make themselves felt. For example, Cassel, tracing the analysis directly to Adam Smith, said 'Free competition is thus the means whereby the exchange economy is automatically regulated' (Cassel, 1932, I, p. 118).

It should be noted that in Smith, and in subsequent economics, this object of analysis was an *abstract* or theoretical conception. The use of the notion of natural prices, associated with a uniform rate of profit, was not dependent on such prices being observable for any length of time, if at all. But its use did have an objective basis and was completely dependent on the existence of that basis. The existence of what Smith called 'competition between different capitals' is the basis for the idea that profit rates *tend towards* equalisation, and hence that actual prices tend towards their natural levels. It is the existence of these tendencies that justifies making natural prices the object of analysis when attempting to construct a general theory of the economy.

Third, those who have examined the question would seem to agree that Smith's concept of competition was not equivalent to the later notion of 'perfect competition'. Hayek pointed out that the idea of perfect competition excluded the actual competitive *activity* denoted by the 'truer view of the older theory' (Hayek, 1948, pp. 92 and 96; see also Clark, 1961, and Eatwell, 1982). McNulty applied this argument in order to show that 'the Smithian concept of competition was of a fundamentally different character than that which was later perfected by economic theorists' (McNulty, 1967, p. 395 and *passim*; and see also Stigler, 1957). In O'Brien's view the fundamental point about competition in Smith is that, in contrast with the role which competition plays in neoclassical theory, it was not applied to a situation of *fixed* and known *resources and technology* (O'Brien, 1975, p. 31). Focussing on a different aspect, Hollander considers that 'the Smithian conception of competition must be carefully distinguished from the modern conception which envisages sellers (and consumers) as "price takers" rather than "price makers"' (Hollander, 1973, p. 26). Finally, Richardson argues that Smith's theory of economic evolution presumes the general prevalence of *increasing returns*, and contrasts this with the neoclassical theory of perfect competition 'which postulates universally *diminishing* returns to scale' (Richardson, 1975, p. 354 and for a similar view see Hutchison, 1978, p. 20 and West, 1978, pp. 356–8; but see Blaug, 1978, pp. 44–5, for an argument that Smith's concept approximated perfect competition).

4.3   COMPETITION AND EQUILIBRIUM OF SUPPLY AND DEMAND

Some scholars have seen Smith's analysis in Chapter vii of Book I of the *Wealth of Nations* as evidence that he was a forerunner of later neoclassical theory. Schumpeter said:

> The rudimentary equilibrium theory of Chapter 7, by far the best piece of economic theory turned out by A. Smith, in fact points towards Say and, through the latter's work, to Walras . . . Market price, defined in terms of short run demand and supply, is treated as fluctuating around a 'natural' price – J.S. Mill's 'necessary' price, A. Marshall's 'normal' price. (Schumpeter, 1954, p. 189)

This statement is potentially misleading, because a detailed examination of Schumpeter's text reveals that by 'rudimentary equilibrium theory' he meant the concepts which underlie Smith's distinction between natural and market price and not the *explanation* of value.[1] Thus the adoption by Say and Walras of this concept of equilibrium does not, of itself, indicate any continuity in the *theory* of value from Smith to Walras – where by theory of value we mean *explanation* of how value is determined.

However, several modern writers borrow Schumpeter's argument, that Smith had an 'equilibrium theory', without making Schumpeter's distinction between this and an *explanation* of value. Kaushil, in an influential recent survey, cites Smith's analysis of natural price as 'the central price to which the prices of all commodities are continually gravitating', and concludes that:

> This is the long-run stable equilibrium, *à la* Marshall. There is also a clear understanding, if only at a rudimentary level, of the interdependence of the commodity and factor markets. Indeed, the process of adjustment is shown to be brought about via the necessary effects of any deviation of market price from natural price on factor rewards and consequent adjustment of factor supply and product supply to demand. (Kaushil, 1973, pp. 67–8, and see also Blaug, 1978, pp. 41–2)

Here it is implied first, that Smith's Chapter vii was his account of the *determination* of value and, second, that in that account value was determined by supply and demand as in Marshall's theory. The first of these points ignores the fact that the central statements in Chapter vii have nothing to do with the *determination* of value. The second point involves a confusion between price *adjustment* and price *determination*. Reference to the analytical notes on classical and neoclassical theories of value set out in Chapter 2 shows that this identification of a theoretical continuity from Smith to Marshall must be questioned. It was argued in Section 2.3.3 that a writer's use of the self-adjustment provided by competition does not imply his adoption of the specific self-adjustment mechanisms implicit in the supply and demand explanation of value. In particular, it should not be used to infer that Smith conceived of regular or 'natural' price-quantity relationships for both commodities and factors of production (for a somewhat similar view, see Groenewegen, 1980, p. 197 and 1982, p. 7). Indeed, the tendency for prices to gravitate to their natural level, and for the quantities of goods supplied to match effectual demand, are features of *both* classical and neoclassical theories of value and, consequently, should not be identified as a distinguishing characteristic of either.

In saying that this process of *gravitation* is distinct from the *determination* of value and, therefore, that it should not be used to identify Smith's *theory* of value, it is not intended to imply that it is theoretically unimportant nor, indeed, that it might not throw up problems which impinge on one or other *explanation* of value and distribution. Indeed, in both classical and neoclassical traditions the analysis of the details of this gravitation has proved a difficult theoretical problem (see Ricardo, *Works* I, p. 89; Jevons, 1871, p. 94; and Arrow, 1958), and one which is receiving increased consideration of late (see, for example, Fisher, 1983; Semmler, 1984; and Levine, 1980).

4.4   THE CONCEPT OF A CAPITALIST ECONOMIC SYSTEM

In examining Smith's analysis of competition Meek has stressed that the introduction of the concept of an average rate of profit required 'that the field covered by capitalist methods of organisation should be considereably enlarged, that competition in both internal and external trade should be reasonably free and that capital should be relatively mobile between different places and occupations' (Meek, 1954, p. 142, see also 1959). This observation, that Smith's treatment of competition involved remarkable progress in the conception of the capitalist economy as a system, can be further developed. Book I, Chapter vii was a concise statement of the *implications that competition has for the price system* – it demonstrated how prices are related to the organisation of the economy. But outside of that chapter, and particularly in Book II, that organisation of the economy by capitalist competition is developed in greater detail.

There is space here merely to note some of the features of this account. The concept of competition is to be found in Smith's analysis of 'the nature of stock, the effect of its accumulation into capitals of different kinds, and the effects of the different employments of these capitals' (*WN*, II. 6.). There were two elements in the development of this view of competition between different capitals: the nature of capital, and the interaction of many different capitals.

4.4.1 The nature of capital: production and profit

From his examination of the 'nature of stock' Smith deduced that capital exists in order to earn profits, and that it does this by hiring productive labour, setting it to work, and selling its produce (*WN*, I.vi.5 and *WN*, II.iii.6). The following steps in the argument can be identified. Smith began with the innate human quality of self-interest and deduced from it a propensity to exchange (*WN*, I.ii.1 and 2). However, this self-interest is not a simple thing; it consists of both a 'passion for present enjoyment' and a 'desire for bettering our condition' (*WN*, II.iii.28). 'An augmentation of fortune is the means by which the greater part of men propose and wish to better their condition' (ibid.). Social productiveness, or the existence of a social surplus, combined with the existence of private property, suggests one way of augmenting one's fortune: ownership of land or capital can confer a right to a share of the social product (*WN*, I.vi.8). The productiveness of *labour*, specifically, dictates that this method of augmenting one's fortune is viable – since labourers 'reproduce with a profit, the value of their annual consumption' they can share the product with the owner of capital and still survive (*WN*, II.ii.35 and *WN*, II.iii.1–2). The existence of a group of property-less labourers, who 'stand in need of a master to advance them the materials of their work', guarantees that this method of augmenting a fortune, production for profit, will be widely and continually used (*WN*, I.viii.8). Smith, therefore, linked the subjective desire to better one's condition, via augmentation of one's fortune, to the objective nature of capital, and concluded that 'the most likely way of augmenting their fortune, is to save and accumulate some part of what they acquire' (*WN*, II.iii.28). It is apparent that this set of conditions effectively transformed the nature of self-interest. The moving force was no longer the innate human propensity or desire. Instead, the desire, or will, was re-defined to coincide with the nature of capital. That nature was revealed by examination of the process whereby a surplus is produced in production for profit.

4.4.2 The interaction of different capitals

However, for the purpose of looking at competition, this pursuit of profit in production is less instructive than the conditions in which this search must operate, and the economy-wide phenomena it produces when it does. This *interaction of different capitals* was the second step in Smith's construction of the concept of competition.

In order to examine this he made two assumptions: 'perfect liberty' (*WN*, I.vii.6) and 'security' (*WN*, II.i.30). Perfect liberty was initially defined as a situation in which 'every man was perfectly free both to choose what occuption he thought proper, and to change it as often as he thought proper' (*WN*, I.x.a.1). This was clearly both an institutional and an economic condition. While its institutional dimension can be defined as the absence of factors such as corporations (*WN*, I.x.c.17), statutes of apprenticeship (*WN*, I.x.c.5–16) and poor laws (*WN*,

I.x.c.41–55), it was not possible to define the *economic* freedom to change trades without having first examined the circulation of capital within and between different industries. Smith's detailed examination of these questions in Book II of the *Wealth of Nations* was central to his theory of 'competition between different capitals'.

He examined the movement of capital within and between industries by considering three conditions that confront production for profit: (1) the technical constraints of the various methods of production (see the first chapter of Book II); (2) the economic constraint of having to sell in the market all commodities produced, and the tremendous outlets for production created by a system of markets (see the second chapter of Book II; and, in addition, Book I, Chapters iii and iv, and Book II, Chapters iii and iv; and Book IV, Chapter vii); and (3) the possibilities created by the existence of a credit system (see the fourth chapter of Book II).

Having set out these limitations on, and opportunities for, the use of capital in production for profit, Smith finished Book II with an examination of the most general form of interaction between capitals – the competition between different capitals. In Chapter v, 'Of the different employments of capitals', he studied the implications of the original postulate that 'Every individual is continually exerting himself to find out the most advantageous employment for whatever capital he can command' (*WN*, IV.ii.4). The result which Smith derived was that the pursuit of maximum profits will cause changes in the structure of production until there is a uniform rate of profit:

> The consideration of his own private profit is the sole motive which determines the owner of any capital to employ it either in agriculture, in manufacturing, or in some particular branch of the wholesale or retail trade. (*WN*, II.v.37)

It is here, in Book II, that we find the major statement of his theory of competition proper – *only* the *price implications* of which, were stated in the brief Chapter vii of Book I. It is this migration or mobility of capital that was at the heart of Smith's theory of competition. Given his analysis of production for profit, and of the interaction of different capitals in which this idea of mobility of capital is set, it is clear why it cannot be adequately described by the label 'perfect liberty' – where that label denotes primarily an institutional environment without restrictive practices and legal inhibitions. For, that freedom or, more accurately, mobility that is relevant to the *competition of capitals* was defined by Smith in terms of technology, circulation and credit, and cannot be discussed or defined without reference to these.

What this brief survey of the steps by which Smith developed his theory of competition shows, is that Meek's idea that Smith developed a clear general conception of a specifically *capitalist* economic *system* is confirmed, not only by his clarification of the concept of profit and its inclusion in natural price (Meek, 1954 and 1959, p. 297), nor only by his 'new division of society into landlords, wage-earners, and captialists' (Meek, 1973b, p. viii), but also by his theory of competition – which was a remarkable investigation of competition *between different capitals*. Furthermore, the central role which production for profit (the form which pursuit of self-interest takes) played in his account of competition provides an initial link between his rudimentary surplus theory of the non-wage share and his theory of competition, profit and price. My concern in later chapters will be to investigate whether Smith succeeded in going beyond this initial link and establishing the ultimate link between surplus and price – a theory of value and distribution.

In Book I, Chapter vii, in explaining this tendency of prices to gravitate to their natural level, Smith based this on the response of capitalists, landlords and workers to deviations of profit, rents or wages from their natural levels (*WN*, I.vii.13 and 14). In explaining the same tendency Ricardo mentioned only the search of *capitalists* for the highest profits (Ricardo, *Works* I, p. 91; see also Marx, 1861–63, II, p. 210 and Eatwell, 1982, p. 208). The features of Smith's view of competition highlighted above are sufficient to demonstrate that too much significance should not be attached to this difference between Smith and Ricardo. In the *Wealth of Nations* taken as a whole a central role was attributed to *capital* and its mobility in the organisation of the economy (for a similar view see Bowley, 1975, pp. 365–6). This is conveyed in the remarkable statement by Smith which was placed at the head of this chapter. Furthermore, not only do employers, in their search for profits, regulate the economy, but in that search 'the proprietor of stock is properly a citizen of the world, and is not necessarily attached to any particular country' (*WN*, V.ii.f.6).

5 The Measure of Value

> The issue at hand, it is now generally recognised, corresponds to the modern 'index number' problem of estimating changes in 'real income' over space and time . . . Accordingly, the labour commanded by a commodity provides an index of its general purchasing power. (Hollander, 1973, p. 127)

> But though all things would have become cheaper in reality, in appearance many things would have become dearer than before, or have been exchanged for a greater quantity of other goods . . . Though it required five times the quantity of other goods to purchase it, it would require only half the quantity of labour either to purchase or produce it. (Smith, *WN*, I.viii.4)

Hollander is undoubtedly correct when he says that in recent years there has emerged a remarkable consensus concerning Adam Smith's measure of value. Smith's labour command measure is seen as an index of purchasing power designed to measure welfare; and the relationships between labour commanded and labour embodied, given so much attention by earlier commentators on Smith, are dismissed as having played no significant part in his thought. Yet there is a striking contradiction between the conventional view, as expressed by Hollander, and Smith's emphatic statement, quoted above, that the labour commanded (and labour embodied) value of a given commodity is *not* an index of its general purchasing power. In view of this, a re-examination of Smith's measure of value seems warranted.

This chapter presents a new interpretation of Smith's measure of value and demonstrates the weakness of the major traditional interpretations. It is argued that the key to understanding Smith's use of a labour commanded measure of value lies in identifying the purpose for which he intended his treatment of value and the assumptions upon which his measure was based. His main concern was with changes in the relative value of commodities brought about by changes in methods of production. His intention was, therefore, to find a standard 'by which we can compare the value of different commodities at all time and places' (*WN*, I.v.17). In Sections 1 to 3 it is argued, on the basis of detailed exegisis of Smith's text, that his choice of a labour command measure of value was predicated on a set of assumptions under which changes in value measured in labour commanded will, in general, be approximately proportional to changes in value measured in labour embodied. In Section 4 this interpretation is contrasted with the major interpretations available to date. The issues involved lie at the very heart of Smith's economic analysis. They include not only the meaning of the labour command measure itself, but also Smith's understanding of the differences between capitalist and pre-capitalist exchange, his approach to the analysis of capital accumulation, the relationship between labour command and a labour embodied measure and theory of value and, given the consensus in recent literature, the question of whether Smith saw his measure of value as a welfare index. Finally, in Section 5 the use which Smith made of his measure of value is shown to provide further evidence in support of the interpretation advanced here.

5.1 SMITH'S LABOUR COMMAND MEASURE

Smith addressed the task of showing 'what is the real measure of exchangeable value; or wherein consists the real price of all commodities' in Chapter v of the first book of the *Wealth of Nations*, 'Of the Real and Nominal Price of Commodities, or of their Price in Labour and their Price in Money'. This has been described as 'arguably . . . one of the most convoluted chapters ever to emerge from the pen of a great economist' (O'Brien, 1975, p. 82; and see Deane, 1978, p. 26; and Horner, quoted in Hollander, 1928, p. 38). However, it is argued here that when Chapter v is examined in the context of Smith's overall use of his measure of value, it admits of a relatively straightforward and consistent interpretation. At the heart of this interpretation lies the recognition of the fact that the early paragraphs of Chapter v refer to a pre-capitalist economy, while the rest of the chapter refers to a capitalist economy – a fact which is recognised by many commentators.[1] Indeed, it will be seen that several of the differences in interpretation of Smith's measure of value are closely linked to different views on the relative significance which should be attached to each part of Smith's famous chapter. For, it was in the first three paragraphs of the chapter that Smith initially defined labour as 'the real measure of the exchangeable value of commodities' (and equated this to the 'real price', 'real worth', 'first price' and the 'original purchase money'). Yet it was in later paragraphs that he indicated the *logic* of a labour command measure, and it was to a capitalist economy that he applied it. The problem is that the labour command measure has considerably different properties in each of these two cases and this makes it difficult to decide what Smith intended by his labour command measure.

5.1.1 The initial statement of labour as a measure of value

In the early paragraphs of the chapter, Smith adopted a definition of 'real price' which was effectively a measure of productivity. He defined 'the real price of everything, what everything really costs to the man who wants to acquire it, is the toil and trouble of acquiring it' (*WN*, I.v.2). It is clear that this refers both to labour embodied and labour commanded – or, more accurately, that at this stage of the chapter Smith did not distinguish between the quantity of labour expended in production of a commodity and the quantity of labour *embodied* in the *goods* which a commodity can purchase or command. In a pre-capitalist exchange economy these two quantities of labour will, of course, be equal.

> What is bought with money or with goods is purchased by labour, as much as what we acquire by the toil of our own body. That money or those goods indeed save us this toil. They contain the value of a certain quantity of labour which we exchange for what is supposed at the time to contain the value of an equal quantity . . . It was not by gold or by silver, but by labour, that all the wealth of the world was originally purchased; and its value, to those who possess it, and who want to exchange it for some new production, is precisely equal to the quantity of labour which it can enable him to purchase or command. (*WN*, I.v.2)

However, Smith pointed out that for several reasons labour is not commonly used as a measure of value (*WN*, I.v.4–6). Gold and silver, which are used, vary in their value due to changes in the quantity of labour used in their production, and a commodity which is itself continually varying in its own value can never be an accurate measure of the value of other commodities (*WN*, I.v.7).

Smith approached the problem of finding a commodity which is not continually varying in its own value in two ways. He considered production first from the point of view of the worker and asserted that labour *time* is indeed a good measure of difficulty of production:

Equal quantities of labour, at all times and places, may be said to be of equal value to the labourer . . . The price which he pays must always be the same, whatever may be the quantity of goods which he received in return for it . . . it is their value which varies not that of the labour which purchases them (*WN*, I.v.7).

Here Smith provided the first statement of constancy to justify his choice of labour as the measure of *value* or as the 'real price' of commodities. From this statement of constancy he inferred that 'At all times and places that is dear which is difficult to come at or which costs much labour to acquire' (ibid.). The choice of labour as a measure of value was, consequently, stated at this point;

Labour alone, therefore, never varying in its own value, is alone the ultimate and real standard by which the value of all commodities can at all times and places be estimated and compared. It is their real price; money is their nominal price only (ibid.).

Although no distinction was made at this stage between labour embodied and labour commanded, this passage can be understood to state that a constant quantity of labour expended in production creates a constant quantity of value.

5.1.2 An important switch in perspective

There followed a switch in perspective which is generally ignored by commentators and which seems to be the source of the view that Smith confused the 'sources' and 'measure' of value, and confused labour embodied and labour commanded. The switch involved abandoning the point of view of the worker and examining the exchange of labour for commodities as it is seen by those who hire labour. In addition to this change in perspective Smith extended the meaning of the term 'real price' from a reference to a quantity of 'toil and trouble', as outlined above, to a reference to a given 'quantity of necessaries and conveniences of life which are given for it [labour]'. It is of considerable importance to recognise this switch in perspective and in terminology; and equally important to recognise that Smith then made a number of assumptions which have the effect of rendering roughly equivalent 'real price' as measured by a *quantity of labour time* and 'real price' as measured by a quantity of '*subsistence of the labourer*'.[2]

Consider first the switch in perspective. Having argued that labour is the ultimate and real standard of value, Smith continued:

> But though equal quantities of labour are always of equal value to the labourer, yet *to the person who employs him* they appear sometimes to be of greater and sometimes of smaller value. He purchases them sometimes with a greater and sometimes with a smaller quantity of goods, and to him the price of labour seems to vary like that of all other things. It appears to him dear in the one case, and cheap in the other. In reality, however, it is goods which are cheap in the one case, and dear in the other. (*WN*, I.v.8, emphasis added)

This is perfectly consistent with what went before. But note how Smith immediately extended the meaning of the term 'real price'; and the explicit task in this chapter was to identify 'wherein consists the real price of all commodities' (*WN*, I.iv.15).

> In this popular sense, therefore, labour like commodities, may be said to have a real and a nominal price. *Its real price may be said to consist in the quantity of the necessaries and conveniences of life which are given for it*; its nominal price, in the quantity of money. The labourer is rich or poor, is well or ill rewarded, in the proportion to the real, not to the nominal price of his labour. The distinction between the real and the nominal price of commodities and labour, is not a matter of mere speculation, but may sometimes be of considerable use in practice. *The same real price is always of the same value*; but on account of the variations in the value of gold and silver, the same nominal price is sometimes of very different values. (*WN*, I.v.9–10, emphasis added)

It was in fact this latter, 'popular', idea of the 'real price' of commodities and labour that Smith developed and used. In particular, it was this idea of the *real price of labour* that he chose as his measure of the real price of all other commodities. By the real price of labour he explicitly now meant the *subsistence of the labourer* (*WN*, I.v.15).[3]

On the face of it there would seem to be a contradiction between Smith's initial statement that '*Equal quantities of labour, at all times and places, may be said to be of equal value to the labourer*' (*WN*, I.v.7) and his later statement that '*The same real price [subsistence of the labourer] is always of the same value*' (*WN*, I.v.10). However, it will be shown here that Smith developed and used his measure of value on the basis of a particular set of assumptions which render compatible these two statements of constancy. As stated above, he assumed that labour time was indeed a good measure of toil and trouble or difficulty of production. To understand how value, as represented by a *quantity of labour time*, will be equivalent to value, as represented by a *quantity of subsistence*, it is necessary to identify the two assumptions upon which Smith based his second statement of constancy; the 'same real price [quantity of subsistence] is always of the same value' (*WN*, I.v.10). First, he assumed that the corn wage of common labour is constant across long periods of time (*WN*, I.v.15). Second, he assumed that corn was produced at near constant cost (*WN*, I.xi.e.28). These assumptions not only allowed him to use the price of corn as a standard of value, as a proxy for the price of labour, but also provided a rational foundation for the use of a labour measure in the first place.

5.2 SMITH'S KEY ASSUMPTIONS

The passages in which Smith clearly adopted the two assumptions stated above confirm that his interest in value was primarily with changes in value due to changes in methods of production. These passages illustrate also Smith's view of the nature of the time priods over which the various influences that change money prices operate. As Sylos-Labini shows (1976, p. 202) Smith distinguished not only between the short run and the long run, but also between the long run and the 'stage of development' or 'condition'. Within a given stage of development methods of production may change, so changing relative natural prices; however, it is only in moving from one 'stage of development' or 'condition' to another that wages, profits and rents change (see *WN*, I.vii.34 and *WN*, I.viii.27). From the assumption of a constant corn wage Smith inferred that 'equal quantities of corn, therefore, will, at distant times, be more clearly of the same real value, or enable the possessor to purchase or command more nearly the same quantity of the labour of other people' (*WN*, I.v.15). This does not rule out changes in the corn wage as it may seem to do so. But while the prices of gold, silver, or any other commodity (except corn) may change due to changes in their method of production, it is only as society moves from one 'stage of development' or 'condition' to another that the corn wage will change (*WN*, I.v.15).

The second assumption upon which Smith based his statement that the same 'real price' (quantity of subsistence) is always of the same value was that corn is produced at constant cost. He made it quite clear that the money price of corn is determined by the relative methods of production of corn and silver (*WN*, I.v.16).[4] However, in this fifth chapter of Book I there was only an oblique reference to the assumed *constant* production cost of corn (ibid.). But when he came to *use* his labour command or corn measure of value, in the 'Digression Concerning the Variations in the Value of Silver' in Chapter xi of Book I, Smith made the assumption of a constant production cost of corn explicit. Furthermore, he stated clearly that this assumed constant cost, as well as the assumption of a constant corn wage, *were the basis upon which his measure of value was founded*. The relevant passage requires to be quoted in full:

> In every different stage of improvement, besides, the raising of equal quantities of corn in the same soil and climate, will, at an average, require nearly equal quantities of labour; or what comes to the same thing, the price of nearly equal quantities; the continual increase of the productive powers of labour in an improving state of cultivation being more or less counter-balanced by the continually increasing price of cattle, the principle instruments of agriculture. *Upon all these accounts, therefore*, we may rest assured, that equal quantities of corn will, in every state of society, in every stage of improvement, more nearly represent, or be equivalent to, equal quantities of labour, than equal quantities of any other part of the rude produce of land. Corn, accordingly, it has been observed, is, in all the different stages of wealth and improvement, a more accurate measure of value than any other commodity, or set of commodities. In all those different stages, therefore, we can judge better the real value of silver, by comparing it with corn, than by comparing it with any other commodity, or set of commodities. (*WN*, I.xi.e.28, emphasis added)

Besides illustrating Smith's assumption of a constant production cost of corn this passage is a key to Smith's treatment of value in general.[5] Given the role of the rising *price* of cattle in this account it should be clear that Smith did not assume that corn was produced by a constant *quantity of labour* (in the sense of 'direct' plus 'indirect' labour as used by Ricardo) – a point which is, in my opinion, confirmed by the very vagueness of his language in the above passage. My interpretation of the labour command measure is based solely on the approximately constant *money cost* and not on any constancy of labour embodied in corn.

5.3 THE OPERATION OF SMITH'S MEASURE

Smith's intention was to find a measure to study the changing value of commodities as a consequence of technical change. He adopted the money wage of common labour as his standard of value; his assumptions concerning the corn wage and the production conditions of corn implied that he could use the change in the labour command value of a commodity as a rough indicator of the change in the labour and other inputs required for its production. Some simple numerical examples can illustrate how this labour command measure worked and was actually used many times by Smith in the *Wealth of Nations*. Consider a manufactured commodity in the production of which improved techniques have halved both the labour and material inputs required.[6] A constant corn wage implies a constant money wage of 5, given an unchanged production cost of corn and an unchanged value of money. Assume the price of the material input is also unchanged (at 10). If the rate of profit is constant (100 per cent) then the change (fall) in the value of the manufactured commodity, measured in labour commanded, will be proportional to the change in its value measured in labour embodied (whether this refers to live labour performed or to the total physical requirements of production). Both labour commanded and labour embodied have been halved.[7]

Manufactured Commodity

	Labour input	Money wage	Material input	Material price	Cost	Profit rate %	Price	Labour command
Time 1	2	5	4	10	50	100	100	20
Time 2	1	5	2	10	25	100	50	10

In this example the constant money wage (representing a constant corn wage) implies a rising command by workers over manufactured commodities, as rising productivity makes manufactures cheaper in terms of corn. This is exactly what Smith envisaged – as is pointed out by Eltis (*WN*, I.viii.35; Eltis, 1975, p. 441).

It can be seen that Smith's use of a labour command or corn measure in this way depended not only on a constant corn wage but also on a roughly constant production cost of corn. Without this a change in the labour (or corn) command value of any given commodity could reflect not only a change in *its* value but also a change in the value of *corn*. It might be objected that the proportionality between the labour commanded and labour embodied measure of value could be maintained *even if* the price of corn had changed (thereby driving up the money wage – say, from 5 to 10), *so long as the share of labour in total price was constant.*[8] But to keep the share of labour constant in the face of changes in method of production *and* changes in the money wage (arising from changes in the production cost of corn) it is required that the *rate of profit* change in a particular way. A fundamental feature of Smith's approach to the study of price changes using his measure was that, in general, the rates of wages and profits were taken as given.

This point can be seen even more starkly if we construct a numerical example to illustrate Smith's assimption concerning *corn* production. Reductions in the quantity of labour required are offset by increases in the *price* of cattle, 'the principle instruments of agriculture'. As a result the labour command value of corn is constant. The *money* price of corn is also constant and will only change when the value of money changes – a most important element in Smith's overall analysis of value and changing relative values.

Corn

	Labour input	Money wage	Cattle input	Cattle price	Cost	Profit rate %	Price	Labour command
Time 1	10	5	5	10	100	100	200	40
Time 2	5	5	5	15	100	100	200	40

Here it may be objected that the assumption of a given corn wage alone implies a constant labour command price of corn – regardless of what assumption is made about the production cost of corn.[9] But if, contrary to Smith, the production cost of corn changes then the rate of profit must change or else the corn wage will change.[10,11]

5.4 CONTRAST WITH EXISTING INTERPRETATIONS

5.4.1 Labour command in capitalist and pre-capitalist exchange

Bladen adopted an interpretation of Smith's measure of value which is similar on many points to that presented above (Bladen, 1938, p. 33; 1974, 1975, p. 506). However, in the latter of these works his reading of the relation between the early paragraphs of Chapter v (which refer to a pre-capitalist economy) and the rest of that chapter (which refers to a capitalist economy) led him to a questionable interpretation of what Smith meant by 'labour command'. It was indicated above that in the early paragraphs of Chapter v Smith said that all commodities were initially 'purchased by labour'; here 'purchase' referred equally to labour expended in extraction of the commodity from nature, and to the exchange of two commodities – each containing the value of equal quantities of labour (*WN*, I.v.2). On the basis of this Bladen argued that *throughout Chapter v* (and, indeed, throughout the *Wealth of Nations*) 'labour command' referred to the quantity of labour *embodied in the goods which any given commodity can command* (1975, p. 510).

The issue involved here can be stated as follows. In a pre-capitalist economy labour command must equal labour embodied. Each commodity exchanges at one to one with commodities produced by an equal quantity of labour. But in a capitalist economy the idea of labour commanded no longer has an unequivocal meaning (Napoleoni, 1975, p. 70). The labour commanded by good A can refer either to; (a) the labour embodied in the commodities that A can purchase or command, or (b) the quantity of *live labour* that can be purchased directly with A. These two quantities of labour commanded will not in general be equal. Bladen's view was that for Smith labour command always referred to the first of these (Bladen, 1975, pp. 511–2). As a consequence of this interpretation Bladen was forced to dismiss Smith's assumption of a constant corn wage and of a constant production cost of corn (both of which can only refer to a command-over-live-labour measure) as ill-conceived attempts at *ex post* rationalisation. Although these assumptions imply that corn will command a constant quantity of *live* labour, Bladen dismissed their relevance, saying: 'But command means here hire, employ, and this, as I have said already, is a very different concept' (p. 516). But it seems clear that Smith's measure of value was indeed a command-over-live-labour measure, and that *in considering a capitalist economy* he invariably conceived of 'labour command' in the second of the two senses outlined above (Deane, 1978, p. 26).

5.4.2 Labour command and accumulation

If the argument of this chapter is correct then Smith's measure of value was designed to analyse changes in value resulting from changing methods of production. But being a measure of labour command it was also a measure of capital accumulation – where capital is understood in the classical sense (see *WN*, II.iii.5). Both Meek and Myint stressed this aspect of Smith's measure – and, in particular, that the labour commanded by the annual produce exceeded the quantity of labour used (embodied) in its production and, consequently, the *difference* was a measure of potential accumulation (Meek, 1973, p. 66; Myint, 1948, pp. 21-3; and see also Das Gupta, 1960; Garegnani, 1958; Napoleoni, 1975, p. 43; Bharadwaj, 1978a, p. 169; and Fine, 1982, p. 77).

Bladen objected to this view because of his rejection of the very idea that labour command refers to a quantity of *live* labour hired. But in dismissing this comparison of aggregate labour commanded and labour embodied he said 'Adam Smith proposed no such thing, and the proposition is nonsense . . . I can find no justification for attributing such a doctrine to Adam Smith' (Bladen, 1975, p. 512). This is surprising given Smith's clear comparison of these two quantities in the final paragraph of Book I, Chapter vi.[12]

On the other hand, in as much as neither Meek, Myint, nor Das Gupta related Smith's measure to the *changes* in value that result from changed methods of production then their accounts of Smith's measure of value were certainly incomplete. Indeed, the passage cited above was, to my knowledge, the *only* instance in which Smith used his measure to *compare* the relative magnitudes of the labour embodied in and the labour commanded by the annual produce; he did, of course, on many occasions refer to the labour command value of the annual produce (and changes in it) as a measure of potential productive employment (and accumulation) (see, for example, *WN*, II.ii.37 and *WN*, II.iv.11 and 12).

5.4.3 Labour commanded and labour embodied

It has frequently been said that Smith *confused* labour embodied and labour commanded. Two different allegations of confusion or inconsistency can be identified: first, that Smith confused the labour embodied and labour commanded *measure* of value; and second; that he put forward both a labour embodied and a labour commanded *theory* of value – although both are usually found together. Both the origin and significance of these allegations have been the subject of much confusion.[13] It should be clear that the interpretation of Smith's work presented here implies a definite rejection of the idea that Smith confused labour embodied and labour commanded.[14]

5.4.4 A price index?

I opened this chapter with a statement by Hollander of what is now the generally accepted interpretation. Smith's measure is seen as an attempt to construct a price index – to be used to deflate nominal quantities to yield 'real' quantities. Three versions of this view can be identified: first, that Smith wanted a measure of *general purchasing power* (Schumpeter, 1954, p. 193)[15]; second, that his was a measure of the purchasing power of individual commodities or incomes (Hollander, 1973); and third, that Smith chose labour command so that his price index would provide a special measure of *welfare* (Blaug, 1978, p. 51).[16] The basic idea of labour command as a measure of purchasing power was explained by Schumpeter as follows: that Smith first replaced nominal price by real price in the modern sense of price in *terms of all other commodities*. Then, 'in ignorance of the index number method already invented in his time', he replaced these real prices by prices expressed in terms of labour. 'In other words he chooses the commodity labour instead of the commodity silver as *numéraire*' (Schumpeter, 1954, p. 188).

As with other interpretations this is based on a particular reading of the relation between the early paragraphs of Chapter v and the later paragraphs. In the first three paragraphs of Chapter v Smith did indeed link labour command to purchasing power as follows. Everyone is rich or poor according to the extent that they can afford the necessaries and conveniences of life (v.1). After the social division of labour most commodities are purchased from others, and so a man 'must be rich or poor according to the quantity of that labour which he can command, or which he can afford to purchase' (v.1). So the *value* of any commodity 'to the person who possesses it . . . is equal to the quantity of labour which it enables him to purchase or command' (v.1). Since, in this sort of economy, commodities exchange in proportion to labour embodied he referred to the 'power of purchasing' as 'a certain command over all the labour, or over all the produce of labour which is then in the market' (v.3). It is from these paragraphs that Hollander deduces that 'the term "real value" thus applies to purchasing power over consumer goods, while command over labour serves as the indirect means thereto' (1973, p. 128). He, and others who adopt this interpretation, assume that the measure of value which Smith developed later in Chapter v, and used at various places in the *Wealth of Nations*, was intended to possess the same property.

This interpretation of Smith's measure of value is extremely dubious – for it is clear that changes in methods of production will rob the labour command measure of this property. (Recall that in the numerical example above a changing method of production changed the labour command value of the manufactured commodity and, what amounts to the same thing, changed the workers command over manufactured goods.) Hollander is, of course, aware of this difficulty but asserts, without evidence or explanation, that Smith simply assumed these problems away (1973, p. 128; and for some remarkable statements in the same vein see Barber, 1967, p. 35 and Kaushil, 1973, p. 36, n. 2). He cites only one of the applications made by Smith and that, at *WN*, I.xi.b.36, provides *no* evidence whatsoever of Smith having used labour commanded as an index of 'purchasing power over consumer goods'. Far from ignoring or abstracting from the relative price effects of 'secularly rising labour productivity' Smith actually *used his labour command (corn) measure to identify* these very effects – as will be shown below.[17] Indeed, Smith *explicitly* stated that differential rates of productivity growth will sever any connection between changes in the value of an individual commodity, as measured by labour commanded (or labour embodied), and changes in its purchasing power over other commodities in general. It is a wonder that his extremely clear statement of this, which has been partly reproduced at the head of this chapter, did nothing to halt the spread of the above interpretation.

Many modern commentators consider that Smith consciously chose to deflate nominal prices and nominal income by the price of *labour* rather than an *index* of prices because, as Hollander says, 'the particular choice of *numéraire* also has a normative significance' (1973, p. 127). Blaug, the dominant proponent of this view, considers that the value of an individual commodity, or of the national income, when measured by labour commanded was, in Smith's view, a measure *of welfare* (1978, p. 51). However, Blaug's account of the supposed *use* of this measure reveals the weakness of this view. For, as a measure of welfare it has two quite contradictory meanings. On the one hand, the 'burden of Smith's comments is that the labour-commanded standard provides a *positive* index of welfare: the higher the "real price" of a commodity measured in wage units, the better off we are for having it; the more labour the total product commands, the "richer" a nation is'. On the other hand 'if real wages are rising or prices are falling because of a rise in the productivity of labour, the number of current wage units commanded by the total product year after year may tend *downward*' (Blaug, 1978, p. 53 and see 1959, p. 152). But, of course, a study of his text as a whole reveals that Smith *almost invariably* used his measure of value to examine productivity improvements. Once it is recognised that he examines *changes* in relative prices it becomes clear that, for Smith, labour commanded was a measure of *value* and not a measure of welfare (Sylos–Labini, 1976, pp. 213–16).[18]

It will be noted that several of the interpretations which are criticised here are based on statements made by Smith in the first three paragraphs of Chapter v, while my interpretation views these statements in the light of the later paragraphs of Chapter v and of Smith's *use* of the labour command measure elsewhere in the *Wealth of Nations*. It may legitimately be asked what significance ought to be attached to those first three paragraphs of Chapter v. In my view two things can be said about this. First, most of the important statements in the early paragraphs of Chapter v are simply restatements of propositions found in the work of Cantillon, Harris, Hume, Mandeville and Hobbes (see the references to similar statements in the work of these writers cited by the editors of the Glasgow edition). This fact would allow us to conjecture, at least, that Smith attempted to base his new measure of value (for analysis of capitalist exchange) on some widely accepted basic propositions concerning wealth, labour, exchange and value.[19] Second, the single most important property that is found in Smith's discussions of the measure of value in *both* pre-capitalist and capitalist exchange is the *relationship between labour commanded and labour embodied*, and hence the relationship between labour commanded and value – without which no labour commanded measure could be taken very far. In the account of pre-capitalist exchange this relationship was established easily – as a direct equality of labour expended ('toil and trouble') to labour command (in the sense of labour 'contained' in goods commanded) – and this labour quantity was defined as the 'real price', 'value', 'real worth', 'real cost', 'first price', the 'original purchase-money' and 'real measure' (*WN*, I.v.1–3). It was of considerable importance that Smith be able to retain some relationship between difficulty of production and labour command, so that some consistent relationship between value and labour commanded could be posited. A relationship between labour embodied and labour command was carried over into Smith's discussion of capitalist exchange; but such a relationship could not be established simply. As was argued above, Smith would seem to have attempted to establish it by adopting his two crucial assumptions of a constant corn wage and constant production cost of corn.[20]

5.5   FURTHER EVIDENCE OF SMITH'S INTENTIONS

The use which Smith made of his measure of value in his 'Digression Concerning the Variations in the Value of Silver during the Course of the Four last Centuries' (*WN*, I.xi.e) provides compelling further evidence for the interpretation developed in this chapter. In order to demonstrate this it is necessary, as a preliminary, to provide the reader with a brief account of Smith's theory of evolution of the methods of production, and consequently of the value, of various commodities. As shown above Smith considered the price of corn to be roughly constant. He expected vegetable and garden produce to become cheaper as a result of technical improvements (*WN*, I.xi.n.10 and *WN*, I.viii.35). Live stock (cattle, poultry, dairy produce, rare birds, etc.). which were originally available in abundance in the wild, he expected to rise in price until, one by one, it became worthwhile to produce them for profit (*WN*, I.xi.1.1).[21] His views on the prices of silver, gold and other precious metals are of particular significance: although these have a natural price like all other commodities, this natural price has no definite trend that correlates with the 'progress of improvement' (*WN*, I.xi.d.4–7). This was because, unlike the method of production of other commodities, the 'fertility or barrenness of the mines, however, which may happen at any particular time to supply the commercial world, is a circumstance which, it is evident, may have no sort of connection with the state of industry in a particular country' (*WN*, I.xi.m.21). Finally, Smith considered that the 'real price' of manufactures would fall considerably due to improved methods of production (*WN*, I.xi.o.1).

Smith drew on this theory of the evolution of the methods of production of various commodities, and of the evolution of their relative prices, in his 'Digression Concerning the Variations in the Value of Silver during the Course of the Four last Centuries'. It is of the utmost importance to identify Smith's procedure in this

'Digression'. Recall that the course of the value of silver was effectively random in Smith's view (*WN*, I.xi.e.7). The 'Digression' was an attempt to establish its *actual* course (for a similar view see Bladen, 1974). At first sight his concern to discover the variations in the value of silver may seem excessive. However, what must be noted is that Smith did *not* bring a theory (or even knowledge) of the trend in the value of silver to bear on the historical data as a way of deflating actual prices to discover the evolution of various real prices. His procedure in the 'Digression' was exactly the reverse; he had an a priori theory of the development of the productive potential of the social system – hence he had an a priori theory of the evolution of various relative prices. He brought this theory to bear on the historical data in order to *discover the actual course of the value of silver*. As the editors of the Glasgow edition of the *Wealth of Nations* say when considering Smith's use of history: 'he worked from the system to the facts not from the facts to the system' (Campbell and Skinner, 1976, p. 56).

The content of the digression – and this is the point which I wish to stress – consisted of repeated application to the historical data of the concept of 'real price' (i.e. measurement of the change in the value of a commodity by its changing command over corn which has a constant value) and of the theory of the development of methods of production (with its implied view of how value is determined). For example, on the basis of these Smith challenged the prevailing view that 'from the invasion of Julius Caesar, till the discovery of the mines of America, value of silver was continually diminishing' (*WN*, I.xi.e.15). He acknowledged that cattle and poultry, etc. had a very low price in ancient times – 'but this cheapness was not the effect of the high value of silver, but of the low value of these commodities' (*WN*, I.xi.e.25). In Smith's opinion the prevailing view – that the value of silver was falling during this period – existed because other writers had adopted an a priori theory of the trend in the value *of silver* (i.e. that its value diminishes as its quantity increases *WN*, I.xi.e.15). His own procedure, based on his theory of the evolution of the value of commodities *other than silver*, contrasted sharply with theirs.

Smith also challenged the prevailing view on the direction of the value of silver in his own day. His argument of this point draws unambiguously on the features of his system which I have outlined in this chapter: the constant real price of corn (and the consequent idea that any change in the money price of corn reflected a change in the real price of silver), and a firm a priori view of the trends in the real price of cattle, poultry, etc. He argued that the value of silver was rising, and he insisted that any observed *fall* in the *money price of corn* was due to this deflation, and not a result of the corn export bounty, which, in his view, tended to *raise* the price of corn (*WN*, I.xi.g.3–5; 10,17).

Perhaps the most striking use to which Smith put his measure of value was in exploring the facts and causes of development. Consider first his chosen *indicator* of the stage of development. He noted that most writers who have collected information on prices seem to have considered the high value of gold and silver as a proof 'not only of the scarcity of these metals, but of the poverty and barbarism of the country at the time when it took place', and he added that 'this notion is connected with the system of political economy which represents national wealth as consisting in the abundance, and national poverty in the scarcity, of gold and silver' (*WN*, I.xi.n.1). For Smith the importance of his view that the real price of silver is effectively random (based on his firmly held *theory* of the trend of other prices), and of his ability to show how the actual history of the value of silver can be explained as a residual, lay in his being able to dismiss the value of silver *as an indicator of the stage of development* of an economy (*WN*, I.xi.n.2). For example, he contrasted the conventional view with his own *concept* of 'real price' and *theory* of relative real prices:

> But though the low money price either of goods in general, or of corn in particular, be no proof of the poverty or barbarism of the times, the low money price of some particular sorts of goods, such as cattle, poultry, game of all kinds, etc. *in proportion to that of corn*, is a most decisive one. (*WN*, I.xi.n.3, emphasis added)

It is clear, therefore, that here Smith's interest in relative real prices (i.e. prices in terms of labour or corn) was that they would indicate to him where a country lay in the developmental process.

But his ability to do that depended crucially on corn having a constant real price and the prices of other goods evolving in a predictable way as economic development proceeded. Smith's procedure can be visualised by reference to Figure 5.1 – which shows how the labour command value of corn, cattle and manufactures change as economic development proceeds.

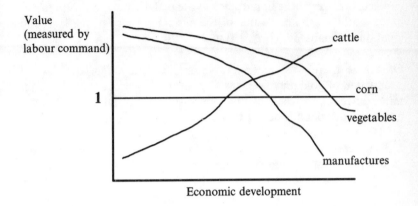

Figure 5.1   Smith's measure of the level of economic development

His procedure was to observe the relative price of cattle and manufactures to corn at a given time, or in a given country, and infer from that what stage of development the country was at.

It is clear from these passages that those commentators who said that Smith's labour command or corn measure was intended as a measure of *economic development* were half-right (e.g. Kaushil, 1973, p. 36). However, it is equally clear that the measure was not, as they claimed, *a measure of output* or of *purchasing power*. It was unequivocally a *measure of value*. But given the assumptions upon which it was based, and given the role which Smith assigned to changes in methods of production in changing value, and his theory of the evolution of the value of each commodity, it could serve as a measure of development.

Consider now the *causes* of development. Smith was anxious to defend his own theory of development – a theory in which the quantity and value of gold and silver play a negligible role. To do so he had to show that his own theory – based on the division of labour and capital accumulation – could explain the development of the various methods of production (and concomitant changes in prices). The method he chose was to show that the quantity and value of silver was a residual element, after the pattern of development had been determined by the persistent forces included in his own theory. Having explained that in the progress of improvement the production cost of silver may rise or fall he said:

Whether the one or the other of those two events may happen to take place, is of very little importance to the real wealth and prosperity of the world, to the real value of the annual produce of the land and labour of mankind. (*WN*, I.xi.m.2)

Of course there was, in fact, a dramatic *reduction* in the cost of production of gold and silver (as a result of the discovery of abundant mines in the Americas). In the 'Conclusion of the Digression' Smith evaluated the significance of this as follows:

The increase of the quantity of gold and silver in Europe, and the increase of its manufactures and agriculture, are two events which, though they have happened nearly about the same time, yet have arisen from very different causes, and have scarce any natural connection with on another. (*WN*, I.xi.n.1)

Smith's theory of economic development and the evolution of various methods of production (and of the influence of these on relative prices) was the foundation upon which this important conclusion rested, and his labour command measure of value (based on his very particular assumptions) was the instrument which he used to articulate that theory.

5.6   CONCLUSIONS

The chapter in the *Wealth of Nations* in which Smith introduced his labour command measure of value is notoriously difficult to understand. However, if we examine his *use* of the labour measure, and his treatment of value in general, then it becomes clear that the measure was designed for a specific purpose: to study the changes in the value of commodities brought about by changes in methods of production. Furthermore, Smith's studies of these reveal the properties that the labour measure was intended to have. The comparison of the changing value of a given commodity with the constant price of labour or corn was deemed to show the change in the difficulty of production of that commodity. It could do this because Smith assumed a constant corn wage and an approximately constant production cost of corn. If the famous Chapter v of Book I is approached with this in mind then several problems of interpretation are resolved. This reading of Smith raises serious doubts about the validity of the major interpretations available to date and, in particular, the now widely accepted view that Smith intended the labour commanded value of a commodity to be an index of its purchasing power over goods in general. This, and several other prominent interpretations, are based on misguided attempts to generalise from a few unrepresentative statements by Smith.

6 Value and Distribution

> The stock which must commonly be employed, the food, clothes, and lodging which must commonly be consumed in bringing them from the mine to the market, determine it. It must at least be sufficient to replace that stock, with the ordinary profits. (*WN*, I.xi.c.29)

> The natural price itself varies with the natural rate of each of its component parts, of wages, profit, and rent. (*WN*, I.vii.33)

The central questions which this chapter is designed to answer are: did Adam Smith succeed in developing a logically coherent theory of value and distribution and, if he did not, in what way did his analysis fall short of a solution to the problem of value? The identification of what he called the 'component parts of price' was central to his attempt to find such a theory. In Section 1 this analysis of the component parts of price is examined in great detail and some common misconceptions about it are cleared up. The resolution of price into wages, profits and rents brought Smith to a theory of value only in so far as he had a prior theory of these magnitudes – a theory of distribution. Consequently, in the second section of the chapter Smith's account of distribution is examined. It is shown that his explanation of profit and, in particular, of the falling rate of profit, was quite unclear – sometimes suggesting a theory of the rate of profit consistent with his surplus view of the *amount* of profit, at other times explaining profit by reference to other forces such as competition. Some neglected aspects of his discussion of both profit and rent are brought to light and, though these do not overcome the basic problem in the analysis, they do enhance our view of Smith's approach to distribution.

Drawing on all of this textual analysis Section 3 provides an assessment of the theory of value and distribution in the *Wealth of Nations*. It contains a precise statement of the way in which Smith's analysis fell short of a determinate theory of value and distribution by identifying an important dichotomy in the *Wealth of Nations*.

Not surprisingly, Smith's indeterminate theory of value and distribution provided an insufficient basis for the analysis of how changes in taxes and export subsidies influence prices and distribution.

This is demonstrated in Sections 4 and 5. It is also shown that his measure of value played an important role in his analysis of these issues – something that has not been understood by many of his critics. Finally, despite the indeterminate nature of his formal analysis of value there is plenty of evidence, in Smith's observations on actual price changes, of how he viewed the determination of value. This evidence is drawn upon in Section 6.

6.1 THE 'COMPONENT PARTS OF PRICE'

Clearly Smith's identification of the component parts of price was central to his attempt to find a logically coherent theory of value and distribution. There were three elements in Smith's analysis of the component parts which should be distinguished in assessing his contribution to value theory: the inclusion of profit in price, the inclusion of these profits at a uniform rate in natural price, and the resolution of production costs into wages, profits and rents. In this section we briefly consider each of these elements and then discuss how this part of Smith's analysis should be interpreted.

6.1.1 The inclusion of profits at a uniform rate in natural price

In order to explain the inclusion of profit in price Smith chose to compare capitalist and pre-capitalist production. He opened Chapter vi of Book I by stating that before 'the accumulation of stock and the appropriation of land' commodities exchange according to the quantity of labour necessary for acquiring them. In order to stress the relation between value and distribution he added, in the second and all subsequent editions, that 'in this state of things, the whole produce of labour belongs to the labourer' (*WN*, I.vi.4). Turning to capitalist production he explained that as soon as stock is accumulated its owners will use it to hire labourers 'whom they will supply with materials and subsistence, in order to make a profit by the sale of their work, or by what their labour adds to the value of their materials' (*WN*, I.vi.5). His inclusion of profit in price was based on his analysis of the nature of capitalist production and distribution – that is, on what I identified in Chapter 3 as his most basic surplus relation – the notion that 'the labour of a manufacturer adds, generally, to the value of the materials which he works upon, that of his own maintenance, and of his master's profit' (*WN*, I.iii.1; *WN*, I.vi.5; *WN*, I.viii.36; *WN*,

I.xi.b.4; *WN*, II.ii.35 and *WN*, II.v.11). It was in this context, of explaining the inclusion of profit in price, that Smith emphasised that profits are not simply the wages of a particular sort of labour (*WN*, I.vi.6). Again he drew attention to the relation between exchange and distribution by adding to the second edition the statement that, once capital has accumulated, 'the whole produce of labour does not always belong to the labourer. He must in most cases share it with the owner of the stock which employs him' – and he linked this with the fact that the quantity of labour used in production no longer regulates relative values (*WN*, I.vi.7). So, at the level of the *individual commodity* the new component parts of price corresponded to the new categories of income distribution – profits and rents.

This much alone signifies a major analytical achievement on Smith's part. Indeed, Meek considered that 'the most significant theoretical advance which Adam Smith made over the work of his predecessors was undoubtedly his inclusion of profit on capital as a constituent element of the supply price of commodities' (Meek, 1959, p. 297).[1] Meek based this conclusion on a study of the many obstacles which stood in the way of the physiocrats and early British economists developing a clear conception of the rate of profit. Profit had to be separated from rent and from the interest on money; it had to be identified as distinct from wages (see Skinner, 1966, p. lxx). Finally, to conceive of profit as a part of natural price it had to be seen to have a *normal* or natural rate on capital advanced – an insight that awaited Smith's outstanding analysis of competition. Meek concluded that 'it was the emergence of profit on capital as a new category of class income, sharply differentiated from other types of income, which cleared the way for the full development of classical political economy' (1954, p. 142).

The problem of value presented itself to Smith as the task of explaining how exchange values are determined once capital has accumulated, and of identifying the exact relationship between value and those component parts of price which are distributive categories (wages, profits and rent). His inclusion of profit (at a uniform normal rate) in price allowed him to state a more *exact* relation between price and the elements of production cost (labour, tools, materials – and now, profits) than his immediate predecessor Sir James Steuart had been able to do. Steuart could say only that price *must not be lower* than a sum sufficient to pay for the labour, tools and materials used up; on top of this 'real value' there would be 'profit upon alienation' which fluctuated and therefore could not be known (theoretically) beforehand (Steuart, 1767, p. 160).

6.1.2 The resolution of production costs into wages, profits and rents

However, like Steuart, Smith could see no other way of relating production costs to price than by evaluating labour, tools, materials, profits and rent, *in money terms*. This is a most important point in my argument and my overall interpretation of Smith's role in the development of classical economics. Those familiar with the work of Ricardo and Marx often wonder why, when relating price to production costs, Smith did not do his accounting in labour units, by reducing tools and material inputs to the labour embodied in them. In the Appendix to this chapter I demonstrate that Smith was not aware of the analytical device of reducing means of production to labour, and all the evidence suggests that Ricardo was the first economist to use this device. This is not to deny that Smith considered price to be determined by the physical requirements of production and the rate of profit – see, for example, the first statement quoted at the head of this chapter. Though this was a clear statement of *what* determines natural price, it offered no means of explaining quantitatively *how* these data determine it.

Thus, the third and most important element in Smith's analysis of the component parts of price was his simplification, or *resolution*, of this list of production costs into wages, profits and rents *only* – a procedure which we had cause to consider briefly in Section 3.2.4 above. This was based on Smith's argument that the prices of tools and raw materials used in production can themselves be resolved into wages, tool and material costs, profit and rent; and that these remaining tool and material costs can in turn be resolved into wages, profits and rents, and so on (*WN*, I.vi.10–16). When considering Smith's resolution of the price of any individual commodity into wages, profits and rent, it is important to note the sophistication of his procedure. First, he showed awareness of the fact that the use of commodities in production makes prices *interdependent* (*WN*, I.xi.o.2). Second, he had a clear conception of the mathematical form which each production cost equation would take. That is, he stated explicitly that wages enter the equation *arithmetically*, while profits enter *geometically* (*WN*, I.ix.24). Smith's resolution of prices into wages, profits and rent, is thus formally identical to the 'reduction to dated labour', or dated labour costs of Dmitriev and Sraffa. The correct interpretation of this fact will be considered in the final chapter of this book.

We may pause here to note a feature of Smith's approach. So far, Smith's introduction of wages, profits and rents, has been in an attempt to clarify the *nature and determination of exchange value* in a capitalist economy. Or, as Cannan put it, he has considered wages per head, profits per cent, and rent per acre, since it is these, in conjunction with the method of production, which figure in the natural price of any commodity (Cannan, 1929, p. 297). As has been noted by several authors the idea that price resolves into wages, profits and rents, brings one to a theory of value only in so far as one has a prior theory of the rates of wages, profits and rents. Cannan called the inquiry into wages per head, profits per cent, and rents per acre 'pseudo-distribution', to distinguish it from 'distribution proper', which he took to be theory about the *proportions* in which aggregate income is divided between classes and persons (Cannan, 1929, p. 301).

The next step in Smith's study of the component parts of price was to extend this idea that price ultimately resolves into wages, profits and rents, from the price of *individual* commodities to the price of any given *aggregate* of commodities, and then to the price of a particular aggregate – the annual produce:

> As the price of exchangeable value of every particular commodity, taken separately, resolves itself into some one or other or all of those three parts; so that of all the commodities which compose the whole annual produce of the labour of every country, taken complexly, must resolve itself into the same three parts, and be parcelled out among different inhabitants of the country, either as the wages of their labour, the profits of their stock, or the rent of their land. The whole of what is annually either collected or produced by the labour of every society, or what comes to the same thing, the whole price of it, is in this manner originally distributed among some of its different members. Wages, profit and rent, are the three original sources of all revenue as well as of all exchangeable value. All other revenue is ultimately derived from some one or other of these. (*WN*, I.vi.17)

In Chapter 3 we have considered how this extension served to obscure Smith's definition of annual produce and his distinction between necessary inputs and surplus. Here we are concerned with it as a contribution to a theory of value and distribution. At this point it may be useful to clarify a few points about Smith's resolution of prices into wages, profits and rents – that is, before introducing other complications.

6.1.3 Some comments on Smith's resolution

First, this resolution of the annual produce is quite valid, provided it is recalled that if fixed capital is in use it is only 'finally' or 'ultimately' that prices resolve into wages, profits and rent (*WN*, I.vi.10 and 11). Many scholars have taken Smith to have implied that the whole value of the annual produce resolves into wages, profits and rents *paid out in the current year* (see, for example, my discussion of Marx's criticism in Section 8.5). While there is no direct evidence that this is what Smith meant, it must be said that his statement that 'the whole of what is annually . . . produced . . . or what comes to the same thing, the whole price of it, is in this manner originally distributed among some of its different members', loses any real impact as a statement about distribution if the distribution in question is something that only takes place over several years (*WN*, I.vi.8 and see also *WN*, I.xi.p.7). Alternatively, one can take Smith to have referred, at least in these passages, to a circulating capital model – in which case the logic of the procedure is preserved (see Napoleoni, 1975, p. 43). But the important and interesting question remains – how far did this procedure bring Smith towards a coherent *theory* of value and distribution? It is to this question that the remainder of these comments are addressed.

Second, there is one aspect of this procedure that would seem to have been largely overlooked by scholars. The 'resolution' was used by Smith to identify *what variables* a theory of distribution (and ultimately a theory of value) would have to explain. It did this by distinguishing between 'original' and 'derivative' revenues. Having explained the resolution of individual exchange value into wages, profits and rents, he introduced the resolution of the whole annual produce. From this he inferred that 'wages, profit and rent, are the three original sources of all *revenue* as well as of all exchangeable value. *All other revenue is ultimately derived from some one or other of these*' (*WN*, I.vi.17, emphasis added). It was this *latter* point which he developed, explaining that all taxes, salaries, annuities and interest 'are ultimately derived from some one or other of these original sources of revenue' (*WN*, I.vi.18).

The clarification of this point was a necessary step in any application of a surplus theory to the price and income phenomena of a capitalist economy – but, logically, it is *not dependent* on the resolution of annual produce into wages, profits, and rents.[2] Indeed, Meek did focus on this aspect of Smith's procedure: 'As I see it, the really central element in that work was Smith's new division of society into landlords, wage-earners, and capitalists', but without noting that, in Smith's case at least, it would seem to have been arrived at by means of the resolution of annual produce into wages, profit and rent (Meek, 1973b, p. viii).

Third, Sraffa focused on the latter part of Smith's statement that 'wages, profit and rent, are the three original sources of all revenue as well as *of all exchangeable value*' when stating his view that in Smith 'the price of commodities is arrived at by a process of *adding up* the wages, profit and rent' (Sraffa, 1951, p. xxxv). It will transpire that this 'adding up' view of Smith's treatment of value has a certain validity, but it should be noted that Smith was evidently somewhat unhappy with the statement that profits and rent are 'sources of value'. For, in several passages in which he originally said this, he subsequently removed the words 'are a source of value' and replaced them by 'constitute a component part', in the second and all subsequent editions of the *Wealth of Nations* (*WN*, I.vi.6 and 8). Further light is thrown on this 'adding up' view in my discussion of causation in Smith's resolution of price (see Section 6.1.4 below). In addition, there may be a more general benefit from adopting the view that Smith's analysis of the component parts of price should not be seen, at least in the first instance, as a *theory* of the *determination* of value. Commenting on Chapter vi Deane has said: 'This and similar passages have often been adduced as evidence that Smith had a pure cost of production theory of value. However, it can be regarded as no more than a breakdown of the components of value, with taxonomic rather than explanatory significance' (Deane, 1978, p. 28, and see also Bharadwaj, 1980, p. 351). Anything which undermines the idea that Smith had a 'cost of production theory of value' will serve to reduce misunderstanding of his work. For that interpretation, by focussing on the contrast between *cost* and *demand* rather than on the relationship between *value* and *distribution*, fosters a quite incorrect view of the nature of the indeterminacy in Smith's theory of value (see Chapter 10 below).

Fourth, both Cannan and Buchanan considered that Smith's application of the resolution of price (into wages, profit and rent) *to the value of the whole annual produce* was an attempt by him to use his theory of price (such as it was) as a theory of *distribution* (Cannan, 1898, p. 146; 1929, p. 292; Buchanan, 1929, p. 605). Note that the resolution of *individual* prices into wages, profits and rents involved wages per head, profits per cent and rent per acre – what Cannan called 'pseudo-distribution'. But the resolution of the value of the annual produce involved its '*division*' or 'parcelling out' as *aggregate* wages, *aggregate* profits and *aggregate* rents – that is, 'distribution proper' (*WN*, I.vi.18; *WN*, I.xi.p.7; *WN*, II.ii.1). Furthermore, Cannan considered that the passage in which Smith applied the resolution to the annual produce was 'an afterthought inserted when the dissertation on prices which forms the bulk of Book I was already far advanced, if not quite completed' (Cannan, 1929, p. 295). This formed part of his more general case that only after his contact with the physiocrats did Smith become interested in distribution. In support of these points Cannan cited the fact that the last four chapters of Book I do not deal with 'distribution proper' but with 'pseudo-distribution' – indeed their stated purpose was to explain the causes of *variations* in the natural *rates* of wages, profits and rents since 'the natural price varies with the natural rate of each of its component parts' (*WN*, I.vii.33; Cannan, 1929, p. 292).

This observation concerning Smith's 'resolution', first of individual price and then of the annual produce, has much to commend it.[3] However, it ignores the fact that *had Smith succeeded*, in the last four chapters of Book I, in presenting a consistent theory of the *rates* of wages, profits and rents (i.e. 'pseudo-distibution') then his theory of value and distribution would have been complete (including 'distribution proper'). For the resolution of *each individual price* to wages, profits and rents, involves the use of the data on inputs and outputs. Given these data then value and distribution are determinate once the rate of wages, profits and rents, are known.

6.1.4 Causation in Smith's resolution

Smith's views on the determination of value cannot be understood without a clear appreciation of the way in which he structured the various forces which influence the value of commodities (Sylos-Labini, 1976, p. 202). We have seen in Chapter 5 that Smith distinguished not only between the short period and the long period, but also between the long period and the 'stage of development'. In Smith's analysis these related to the determination of value as follows. In the short period 'market prices' were determined by the 'proportion between the quantity which is actually brought to market . . . and the effectual demand' (*WN*, I.vii.8). In the long period the 'natural price' is determined by the method of production of each good and the prevailing 'ordinary or average' rates of wages, profits and rents (*WN*,

I.vii.11). These natural prices change if methods of production change; but *for the purposes of determining natural prices* the rates of wages, profits and rents *are taken as given* (*WN*, I.vii.14). Only as the society moves from one 'stage of development', or 'condition', to another in the 'progress of improvement' do the rates of wages, profits and rents vary. Smith identified three different stages: progressive, stationary, and declining (*WN*, I.vii.34; *WN*, I.viii.27). It is the rate of progress, and changes in it, that Smith considered to determine the natural rates of wages, profits and rents.

Smith's identification of this hierarchy of forces was a statement of the direction of causation in the determination of value – a crucial step towards a logically coherent theory of value. Recognition of this hierarchy, and of the separability of the theories of market behaviour, technical change, and accumulation, which were posited to explain market price, natural price and distribution, respectively, is necessary if Smith's work is to be correctly placed in the development of economic science.

Failure to consider the analytical structure of Smith's explanation of value has led many commentators to miss the significance of the context in which Smith said that natural prices *vary* with variations in wages, profits and rents (see the second quotation at the head of this chapter). The statement came at the end of Chapter vii, after Smith had finished with the relation of natural to market price, when he pointed forward to his chapters explaining 'distribution'. Furthermore, the statement, when considered in its entirety, made quite clear that the rates of wages, profits and rents are taken as *given* in the determination of natural price, and are themselves determined by a different set of forces.

> The natural price itself varies with the natural rate of each of its component parts, of wages, profit, and rent; and in every society this rate varies according to their circumstances, according to their riches or poverty, their advancing, stationary, or declining condition. I shall, in the four following chapters, endeavour to explain, as fully and distinctly as I can, the causes of those different variations. (*WN*, I.vii.33)

Now that we have completed our study of Smith's understanding of the relation between price and the distributive variables we must examine his attempt to determine the natural rates of wages, profits and rents.

6.2 DISTRIBUTION

Smith's discussion of value in Chapters vi and vii of Book I of the *Wealth of Nations* indicates that he considered natural prices to be determined by methods of production and the state of distribution. As it stands, this statement says little about what his theory of the determination of value was. In Section 6 of this chapter I use Smith's study of several practical problems to infer his views on the determination of prices, and thereby infuse some content into this statement. Specifically, I show that he considered prices to be determined by methods of production and took *as given* the prevailing rates of wages, profit and rents. Here we ask to what extent Smith succeeded in giving *analytical* content to his account of the component parts of price, by developing a consistent *theory* of distribution. We do this by asking whether he succeeded in deriving a precise theory of distribution from his statements about the determinants of the non-wage share – profits plus rents – which we have surveyed in Chapter 3.

Smith's treatment of wages was considered in Chapter 3. There it was concluded that his theory of wages could be considered as a version of subsistence theory. At any rate, it is not in this theory of wages that the major difficulties arise.

However, Smith's theory of the rate of profit is by no means clear and presents considerable problems of interpretation. Consequently, this examination of the nature and extent of a theory of distribution in Smith will concentrate on his account of the rate of profit.

6.2.1 Surplus and profit

In places Smith can be considered to have taken the initial steps towards developing a theory of the rate of profit consistent with his surplus view of the *amount* of profits and rents and his subsistence theory of wages (as documented in Chapter 3 above). A fundamental feature of his account was that he related the rate of profit to the *same* dynamic forces which determine the rate of wages. He opened his chapter on 'The Profits of Stock' by saying that 'the rise and fall of the profits of stock depend upon the same causes with the rise and fall in the wages of labour, the increasing or declining state of the wealth of the society; but those causes affect the one and the other very differently' (*WN*, I.ix.1). In the course of this chapter he considered various cases of progressive, stationary and declining countries. In comparing Scotland, France, England and Holland he consistently said that those growing slowest have high wages and low profits and *vice versa* (*WN*, I.ix.8–10). Of course, his belief in an inverse relation between the wage and the rate of profit is, of itself, not a theory of profit nor evidence of a surplus theory of profit. Indeed, as will become apparent, it is precisely Smith's *explanation* of the falling rate of profit which is unclear, and on which there are many different opinions.

One explanation of the falling rate of profit which certainly was consistent with a surplus view of the *amount* of profits and rents was his account of why the North American colonies are an exception to the general rule that 'high wages of labour and high profits of stock . . . are things which, perhaps, scarce ever go together' (*WN*, I.ix.11). This was because in a new colony, what stock they have 'is applied to the cultivation only of what is the most fertile and most favourably situated lands' which 'must yield a very large profit'. But:

> As the colony increases, the profits of stock gradually diminish. When the most fertile and best situated lands have all been occupied, less profit can be made by the cultivation of what is inferior both in soil and situation. (*WN*, I.ix.11)

And he stressed that 'the wages of labour do not sink with the profits of stock'. This has often been seen, with some justification, as an anticipation of Ricardo's theory of profit but, as Tucker notes, it was not applied generally nor developed by Smith (Tucker, 1960, p. 90).

Another hint of a surplus theory of the rate of profit may, perhaps, be found in Smith's definition of the maximum and minimum rate of profit. He defined the maximum rate as follows:

> The highest ordinary rate of profit may be such as, in the price of the greater part of commodities, eats up the whole of what should go to the rent of land, and leaves only what is sufficient to pay the labour of preparing and bringing them to market, according to the lowest rate at which labour can anywhere be paid, the bare subsistence of the labourer. The workman must always have been fed in some way or other while he was about the work; but the landlord may not always have been paid. (*WN*, I.ix.21)[4]

Most significant of all is that passage, from which I quoted in Chapter 3 above, in which Smith explained the fall in the rate of profit by reference to the increased proportion of capital to output (see p. 42

above). I shall have more to say presently about the possibility that this was what underlay Smith's expectation of a falling rate of profit.

At this point, however, two facts should be noted which necessarily qualify any hypothesis that Smith developed a surplus theory of the rate of profit.

First, and most fundamentally, even in those passages where he gave hints of surplus theory of the rate of profit, Smith did not *consistently* formulate the problem in such a way as to relate the rate of profit to the ratio of aggregate profits to aggregate capital. Furthermore, he did not focus on the relation of wages to the rate of profit in such a way as to identify a precise determinate relationship between the two variables, which might have been used to close his theory of value. To some extent this may be explained by the fact that his theory of *rent* was not such as to throw the relation of wages to the rate of profit into sharp relief. His theory encompassed both absolute and differential rent (*WN*, I.xi.b.3). Although he made clear that rent left all capitals with a uniform rate of profit (*WN*, I.xi.6), and although he considered the possibility of no-rent production of several products (*WN*, I.xi.c.13), he did not in general treat the determination of value at the no-rent margin.

6.2.2 Competition and Profit

In addition to Smith's failure to consistently relate the rate of profit to the ratio of aggregate profits to aggregate capital advanced, his work contained many references to the determination of the rate of profit by a force other than the prevailing subsistence wage and the requirements of production. The rate of profit was influenced by *competition* (*WN*, I.ix.2).

There has been much discussion on how this idea of Smith's should be understood. Tucker notes that 'Joseph Massie and David Hume had argued that the growth of stock tends to depress profits by increasing the intensity of competition', and, in his view, 'Smith's explanation of the long-run fall of the average rate of profit in England was *more detailed*, but *the principle was the same*' (Tucker, 1960, p. 60, emphasis added). The extra detail to which Tucker refers was Smith's explanation of *how* intensified competition reduces the rate of profit. A sudden increase in capital *increased the wage* (*WN*, I.ix.7–10, 13–14; and see *WN*, II.iv.8 and 12), and *reduced the price* which capitalists could charge (*WN*, I.ix.13–14; *WN*, IV.vii.c.9, 26 and 33; and *WN*,

V.i.e.26), so that 'the profits which can be made by the use of capital are in this manner diminished, as it were, at both ends' (*WN*, II.iv.8).

Clearly, in the absence of some fall in underlying profitability, the rise in wages will last only as long as it takes population to respond – a point which Ricardo made repeatedly (e.g. *Works*, VI, p. 226; Tucker, 1960, p. 112) and which there is no reason to believe Smith overlooked. The downward pressure on prices created by increased output will also be temporary, unless the position prior to extra accumulation was not fully competitive – a possibility which will be considered presently. If these wage and price changes were, as Tucker says, 'the details' added by Smith to the traditional view of Massie and Hume, what was 'the principle' which in Tucker's view, he shared with them?

Tucker says it is to be found in Smith's famous statement:

> When the stock of many rich merchants is turned into the same trade, their mutual competition naturally tends to lower its profit; and when there is a like increase of stock in all the different trades carried on in the same society, the same competition must produce the same effect in them all. (*WN*, I.ix.2)

Ever since West's pamphlet of 1815 this view has been considered a *fallacy of composition* (Hollander, 1973, p. 61; Tucker, 1960, p. 60; Napoleoni, 1975, p. 49). Alternatively, it can be seen as a, perhaps badly phrased, expression of a consistent belief that demand sets a limit to production. This is the interpretation preferred by Bowley (1973, pp. 220–2; and see Tucker, 1960, pp 60–1). There can be no doubt that in general Smith attributed considerable importance to the extent of the market (see *WN*, II.v.7; *WN*, I.x.c.26; *WN*, IV.i.31; *WN*, IV.vii.c.6, 21, 51, 80 and 102). But Corry doubts that limited demand could have been Smith's explanation for the falling rate of profit, noting that it was he who formulated the important classical maxim 'what is annually saved is as regularly consumed as what is annually spent' (*WN*, II.iii.18; Corry, 1962).

Some deny that Smith's theory of accumulation really incorporated a continuously falling rate of profit at all. For example, Lowe argues that Smith's theory of growth was essentially one of continual accumulation 'until the full utilisation of the natural environment prevents further expansion of aggregate and per capita income' – a 'threat of exhaustion of natural wealth [which] is *regarded as far distant*' (Lowe, 1954, pp. 135 and 139, emphasis added; for a similar view see Spengler, 1959b, p. 8; West, 1974, p. 329, and Corry, 1962).

Heilbroner would seem to accept this, yet notes that 'evidently the process *cannot* be "hitchless", since it ends in decline'. He says: 'Nowhere does Smith actually explain the mechanism that leads him to the conclusions so unequivocally spelled out . . . there is only one behavioural force that Smith must have reckoned on to produce this result. This is a rate of population growth that . . . we must assume . . . proceeds relentlessly until it reaches a point at which the increase in productivity stemming from the continuing division of labour is finally overwhelmed by the decreasing productivity of the land and resources available to the nation' (Heilbroner, 1975, pp. 529–30; see also Barkai, 1969, p. 404).

Bliss links Smith's falling rate of profit with what he calls 'the orthodox vision of capital accumulation' – that is 'an ancient idea [that] the accumulation of capital is accompanied . . . by a continuous decline in the rate of interest' (Bliss, 1975, p. 279). If we put aside any idea that Smith's adherence to this 'ancient idea' implies his use of an essentially neoclassical theory of distribution – for Bliss provides no explicit argument to that effect – this observation may be accorded a possible validity. For, Corry seems to conclude that Smith's belief in a falling rate of profit, despite his unambiguous adherence to the 'saving is spending' theorem, is to be explained by his adoption of a *traditional* view from Hume and others (Corry, 1962). Tucker also stresses the continuity of belief and, in addition, the influence of the empirical evidence on interest rates through time and across countries (Tucker, 1960, pp. 62–3) and *passim*).

Clearly there is little possibility of finding in the *Wealth of Nations* evidence of a consistent rationale for the path of the rate of profit and thereby limiting the range of interpretations. However, there are two points which would seem not to have received sufficient attention to date.

Gravitation to the natural rate of profit

The first point that has been neglected is that many of Smith's statements, to the effect that increased competition reduces the rate of profit, would seem to refer to movements of profit *to* its natural rate, rather than to downward movements *of* the natural rate itself. It was stated above that the downward pressure on prices created by intensified competition will be purely temporary *unless the position prior to extra accumulation and production was not fully competitive.* In the latter case, increased production and competition would indeed lower prices towards their natural level and reduce profits.

There can be no doubt that in many cases in which Smith referred to increased (or decreased) competition lowering (or raising) the prices at which capitalists can sell, and consequently lowering (or raising) their profits, he had in mind just such a movement *towards* (or away from) a fully competitive situation (Sylos-Labini, 1976, p. 220). For example, in the long chapter 'Of colonies' he explained that the effect of increased or decreased competition on profits arose because Britain's monopoly of the colony trade (established by the acts of navigation) reduced (or increased) the 'whole quantity of capital employed in that trade *below what it naturally would have been in the case of free trade*' (*WN*, IV.vii.c.25 emphasis supplied; see also 33 and 102). Indeed, the whole thrust of the *Wealth of Nations* was for the *establishment* of competition in areas hitherto subject to restrictions. It remains true that Smith did not always make clear the distinction between the effect of competition in creating a tendency *toward* a uniform rate of profit, and the effect of accumulation in *changing* that normal rate.

6.2.3 The ratio of capital to output

It has frequently been overlooked that in explaining the fall in the *natural* rate of profit Smith explicitly distinguished between the influences of supply and demand on *market* prices and the forces which determine the natural rate of profit:

> As the quantity of stock to be lent at interest increases, the interest . . . necessarily diminishes, not only from the general causes which make the market prices of things commonly diminish as their quantity increases, *but from other causes which are peculiar to this particular case*. As capitals increase in any country, the profits which can be made by employing them necessarily diminish. It becomes gradually more and more difficult to find within the country a profitable method of employing any new capital. There arises *in consequence* a competition between different capitals. (*WN*, II.iv.8, emphasis added)

In this passage it was made clear that the reduction of profits because of intensified competition is a *consequence* of the *independent* fact that 'it becomes gradually more and more difficult to find within the country a profitable method of employing any new capital' – and, furthermore, that this downward path of interest is not equivalent to the movements of *market price* as a result of competition. It follows that we should not look to Smith's account of intensified competition *per se* for his ultimate explanation of the falling rate of profit. Looking back to those hints at a surplus theory of profit, which were reported above, it can be seen that there is one possible explanation for the falling rate of profit which is seldom cited but which surely deserves consideration.

Recall that in Book II, Chapter iii, on the accumulation of capital, Smith put aside the resolution of the annual produce into wages, profit and rent, and considered its division into capital and revenue (where revenue meant profit and rent). There he explained that as a country develops the ratio of capital to output increases, so reducing the share of profits and rents – see passage quoted on p. 42 above. Although he was not primarily concerned, in that chapter, with determination of the *rate* of profit he did note the implications of the trend in question:

> Though that part of the revenue of the inhabitants which is derived from the profits of stock is always much greater in rich than in poor countries, it is because the stock is much greater: in proportion to the stock the profits are generally much less. (*WN*, II.iii.10)

In fact arguments of this sort can be found throughout Smith's account of profits – *including* those passages where the dominant theme seems to be the effect of competition.

For example, in Chapter ix of Book I, having explained the ways in which increased competition reduces the rate of profit, he said 'the acquisition of new territory, or of new branches of trade may sometimes raise the profits of stock' (*WN*, I.ix.12). It is made clear that this counteracting force does not rely entirely on these new markets and branches being 'understocked' with capital, since this would only be temporary.[5] Rather, in the new territory and branches, capital 'is applied to those particular branches only which afford the greatest profit' (ibid.). The initial scarcity in the new territory is removed by capital flows in response to profit differentials, 'till the profits of all come *to a new level*, different from a *somewhat higher* than that at which they had been before' (*WN*, IV.vii.c.19, emphasis added).

Likewise, Smith's concern with the extent of the market did not arise primarily from consideration of the effect of intense competition on selling prices in markets of limited size, nor from an interest in the acquisistion of large new markets which would be 'understocked' for a long period. Rather, it arose from his view of the *structure of production* and *its effect on profitablity and accumulation*. Smith considered that there was far more scope for division of labour in industry than in agriculture (*WN*, I.i.4) and consequently industry would show increasing returns to scale; this rising proportion of output to capital would raise the proportion of surplus (profits and rents) to capital advanced (Eltis, 1975, p. 444). However, these increasing returns could only be reaped at large scale: the 'perfection of manufacturing industry, it must be remembered, depends altogether upon the division of labour; and the degree to which the division of labour can be introduced into any manufacture, is necessarily regulated, it has already been shown, by the extent of the market'(*WN*, IV.ix.41). It is clear, therefore, from the passages cited that the *ratio of capital to output* remained under consideration, even where Smith's topic seems to be the influence of *competition* on profits.

Eltis adopts a similar interpretation of Smith's explanation of profits. He points out that if one adopts this view then 'the rate of profits may rise or fall in the course of development'. This will depend on whether the returns to scale are sufficient to outweigh the increased capital requirements per worker – which will in turn depend on the mix of manufacturing and agriculture (Eltis, 1975, p. 444). This interpretation has the considerable advantage of being able to incorporate several of the other interpretations outlined above. For example, it implies that Smith was not necessarily inconsistent in believing in ultimate decline and at the same time predicting long epochs of rapid growth if correct policies were adopted.[6]

6.2.4 Summary on profits

In Book V, Chapter ii, in preparing to examine the effect of a tax on profits, Smith summarised his theory of profit in a most interesting way:

> The ordinary rate of profit, it has been shown in the first book, is everywhere regulated by the quantity of stock to be employed in proportion to the quantity of employment, or of the business which must be done by it. (*WN*, V.ii.f.3)

On the one hand, this can be read as referring to the influence of the ratio of capital to output on the rate of profit and, hence, as further evidence for my interpretation. Indeed Eltis, without citing this particular summary, says 'the crucial factor is stock in relation to the business that is transacted, or in modern terms, the ratio of capital to output' (Eltis, 1975, p. 440). Viewed in this way, Smith's summary can be seen to foreshadow Ricardo's famous summary of his theory of profit: 'The rate of profit and interest must depend on the proportion of production to the consumption necessary to such production' (*Works*, VI. p. 108).

It is a remarkable fact that Smith's summary (and many other statements to the same effect) can equally be seen to be very similar to the *traditional* idea, which was expressed by Massie as follows: 'That the Profits of trade in general, are governed by the Proportion which the Number of Traders bears to the Quantity of trade' (quoted in Tucker, 1960, p. 40). Tucker notes that this idea is to be found in the work of Child, Hume and Hutcheson, and is the basis of the notion that profits depend on the intensity of competition (Tucker, 1960, pp. 40–5).

Moreover, it is the *latter* argument which was used most frequently throughout the *Wealth of Nations*. There is no doubt that Smith was aware that increased capital will imply intensified competition *only if there is some reduction in underlying profitability* – he explicitly described the intensified competition as a '*consequence*' of the fact that 'as capitals increase . . . the profits which can be made by employing them necessarily diminish' (*WN*, II.iv.8). But there seems to be no possibility of identifying, with any certainty, the basis of this fall in profits, and hence the forces which he considered to determine the *natural rate* of profit.

6.2.5 Rent

In examining Smith's treatment of distribution the focus here has been on his explanation of *profits* – largely because it is this which is most relevant to an assessment of his contribution to the development of the classical theory of value and distribution. On rent, I confine my discussion to the following brief comments.

Given the importance of Smith's assumption of a constant production cost of corn, and his belief that, even in Europe, 'much good land remains to be cultivated' (*WN*, II.v.37) Gee seems justified in doubting the accuracy of those interpretations which see Smith's rent as the result of diminishing returns or absolute land scarcity (Gee, 1981). Second, despite its clarification of several points, there must also be some doubt about the validity of Buchanan's argument that whenever Smith described rent as *price determining*, rather than price determined, he was concerned with a situation in which there was *alternative* land *use* (Buchanan, 1929). For, however unsatisfactory, Smith's ultimate explanation of rent would seem to have been the *surplus* created on food-producing land, as explained in his comparison of corn, potatoes, and rice production – from which I quoted in Section 3.4.2 above (*WN*, I.xi.b.37). There he made clear that rice fields, though they have *no alternative use*, nevertheless yield a rent determined by the surplus over input requirements and profits at the natural rate (*WN*, I.xi.b.39, and see Fine, 1980, for a similar view).

Third, Campbell and Skinner are surely misleading when they say that, although Smith considered both increases and decreases in wages and profits, he 'was quite clear in respect of rent however, arguing that rent payments would increase over time' (Campbell and Skinner, 1982, p. 180). The existence in the *Wealth of Nations* of contradictory predictions concerning rents was noted by Cannan (1898, p. 277, and see also Hollander, 1973, pp. 147–8). Despite this, there are two aspects of this contradiction which would seem not to have been highlighted to date. To begin with, although the reader is undoubtedly left with two *different* predictions concerning the share of rents, a study of Smith's arguments shows that the two predictions were derived on the basis of very different *assumptions*.[7] Second, Smith's prediction of a *falling* share of rents, which receives much less notice in the secondary literature than his opposite prediction, was stated in conjunction with his prediction of a falling share and rate *of profit*, and was based on that argument concerning the increased ratio of *capital* to *output* to which I have drawn attention above (*WN*, II.iii.9). The chapter in which he linked falling profits and falling rents was precisely Chapter iii of Book II, in which Smith put aside *price* and its component parts, deducted from annual *produce* all that was required for 'replacing a capital', and related accumulation to the magnitude of the residual – profits plus rents.

6.3   ASSESSMENT

6.3.1 The theory of value and distribution

Two aspects of Smith's approach to value and distribution remain to be examined: his analysis of taxes and export subsidies and his observations on various price changes. However, these examinations will be easier if an assessment is now made of how far his component parts of price and his analysis of wages, profits and rents, brought Smith towards a determinate and coherent theory of value and distribution. This examination of Smith's treatment of distribution has shown that, although he adhered consistently to his particular 'subsistence' theory of wages, he failed to explain the determination of the rate of profit and, in particular, he did not identify a clear analytical relation between the *rates* of wages, profits and rent. When we combine this finding with our observations concerning surplus in Smith's work (see Chapter 3 above) we can identify the following dichotomy in the *Wealth of Nations*. On the one hand, there is in the *Wealth of Nations* a surplus theory of the *amount* of profits plus rent, based on the distinction between productive and unproductive labour and the ranking of industries according to their surplus producing potential. Smith consistently related the rate of *accumulation* to the magnitude of aggregate profits plus rents. However, in general, he did not use these changes in the amount of profits plus rent (brought about by changes in the extent of the market, the pattern of production, or the inputs to production) to calculate changes in the *rate* of profit. Indeed, he did not consistently relate the rate of profit to the ratio of aggregate profits to aggregate capital advanced. On the other hand, there is also in the *Wealth of Nations*, in the component parts of price, a 'theory' of price which relates prices to the *rates* of wages, profits and rents, but which does not provide or draw on an adequate explanation of the rate of profit.

Smith dealt with *aggregate* profits, but on very few occasions, and then only vaguely, did he relate the *rate* of profit to that magnitude. Precisely what was needed, to give theoretical content to his component parts of price, was a *combination* of the approach which related individual prices to the rates of wages, profit and rent, and the approach which related aggregate profts plus rents to aggregate output and capital. This observation will prove useful when evaluating the theoretical significance of the analytical identity between Smith's resolution of individual prices into wages, profits and rents and the 'reduction to dated labour' of Dmitriev and Sraffa – and hence when evaluating the similarities between Smith's work and the surplus theory of value and distribution in its modern form (see the final chapter of this study).

It was presumably because Smith did not determine the rate of profit, and identify an analytical relation between the rates of wages, profits and rents, that Sraffa described his theory of value as one in which 'the price of commodities is arrived at by a process of adding-up the wages, profit and rent' (Sraffa, 1951, p. xxxv). (While Sraffa's description would seem to be justified I will argue in Chapters 7 and 10 that Dobb was not sufficiently careful in inferring just what Smith's 'adding-up' approach to value did and did not imply.) The implication of Smith's indeterminate theory of distribution is that his statement that 'the natural price itself varies with the natural rate of each of its component parts' is effectively an assertion – it is unsatisfactory not because it is incorrect, but because it remains unanalysed. The inadequacy of Smith's theory of value and distribution would seem, therefore, to be accurately characterised by Sylos-Labini when he says 'Smith's theory of prices, however, would seem to be indeterminate rather than wrong' (1976, p. 204). As a consequence of this, his theory of value provided an insufficient basis for the analysis of how *changes* in the rates of wages, profits and rents, influence prices.

6.3.2 The theory of distribution and the measure of value

Indeed, as we will see presently, it is in his analysis of such changes, and of the effects of taxes and bounties, that Smith's theory of value was at its weakest. The analysis of how changes in wages, or changes in taxation, influence profits, rents and prices, required both a coherent theory of distribution and a suitable method of measuring changes in these variables. Subsequent classical economists struggled with the *Wealth of Nations* in their effort to develop each of these. It has been shown in the previous chapter that Smith's labour command measure of value was designed in order to measure changes in price due to changes in *methods of production*. For this reason alone it was likely to be unsuitable for measuring changes in value due to changes in *distribution* or changes in taxes and subsidies. On top of this must be placed the fact that he did not develop a determinate theory of distribution or identify analytical relationships between the rates of wages and profits. Since the *design of a measure of value* suitable for analysing changes in taxes, etc., would necessarily draw heavily on the theory of distribution it is, therefore, not surprising that Smith's measure of value was not adequate for conducting such an analysis. This is what will be demonstrated in my discussion of Smith's analysis of taxes and the corn export bounty.

The analytical point can be illustrated by comparing Smith's measure of value with that of Ricardo – which *was* designed to assist in the analysis of changes in distribution and taxation. Smith's measure of value was based on the invariance of the price of corn, which was in turn based on the idea that the falling quantity of labour required to produce corn was roughly offset by the rising price of cattle (see Chapter 5 above). The invariance of Ricardo's measure was based on the idea that rising wages were exactly offset by falling profits – which was in turn based on the notion that the measuring commodity was produced by a very particular combination of labour and means of production. It is interesting that at one place Smith did mention the possibility that high wages and low profits might exactly offset one another (*WN*, I.xi.23). What is significant is that he nowhere related this property to either corn, or labour – 'the only accurate measure of value, or the only standard by which we can compare the values of different commodities' (*WN*, I.v.17). What Smith's theory lacked was an examination of the *relevance* of the structure of the inputs of labour and means of production *to the properties of an invariant standard of value*. But it is most important to see that the absence of such an examination is *simply a symptom* of his failure to develop a theory of the rate of profit and, more specifically, an analytical relation of wages to profit. For, without an analytical relation between the rates of wages and profits the *relevance* of the structure of the 'layers' of inputs *to specification of a measure of value* will not emerge – since, when wages rise there will be no definite fall in profits, and hence there could be no suggestion of the idea of 'balancing commodity' whose value stayed the same when wages rose and profits fell.

Smith paid no attention to the structure of the layers of inputs in designing or choosing his measure of value. There are two aspects of this structure that are relevant, that were taken account of by Ricardo, and that should be kept in mind when considering the details of Smith's analysis of the effects of taxes and the corn bounty on prices. First, the measure of value should be a commodity in the production of which labour and means of production are used in 'average' proportions. Second, it is useful to have a particular relation between the structure of production of the measuring commodity, the money commodity, and the wage commodity. In Smith the measuring commodity was the wage commodity, corn; but no relation between the methods of production of corn and silver was specified. In Ricardo, the measuring commodity was the money commodity, and besides being produced by an 'average' proportion of labour to means of production, it was also assumed to have the same 'structure' as the wage commodity (O'Brien, 1975, p. 88). Consequently, as used by their respective authors the two measures have diametrically opposite properties. For Smith, *any change in the money price of corn indicated a change in the value of money*; no change in the production cost of corn was possible. For Ricardo, no change in the value of money was possible; *any change in the money price of corn indicated a change in the physical production cost of corn.*

Smith's measure of value was not designed to be invariant with respect to changes in wages, profits and rents. In a sense, this can be seen as a consequence of his treatment of profits. As has been demonstrated in Chapter 5, his primary use of the measure was to examine *changes* in the value of specific commodities, or groups of commodities, as a result of changes in methods of production (Section 6 below). For this task his corn measure was relatively well-suited. However, the limitations of his measure, and of the theory of distribution that lay behind it, were shown when he turned instead to analyse the effects of various taxes and the corn export bounty.

6.4 TAXES

When considering taxes Smith made use of his analysis of the component parts of price to insist that 'every tax must finally be paid from some one or other of those three different sorts of revenue' (*WN*, V.ii.b.1). In Chapter 3, I noted Smith's view that a general tax on rent will fall on landlords and a general tax on profit will fall on interest. Recall that the profits of the undertaker seem to have been considered a necessary payment and therefore 'a subject not directly taxable' (*WN*, V.ii.f.2). If this were true of aggregate profits (of undertakers) then it was doubly true of the profits in one particular industry. In considering a 'tax upon the profit of particular employments' Smith introduced an argument which, for a reason that will emerge presently, was of considerable importance in his treatment of value and distribution.

That argument went as follows. Employers in manufacturing pass on a tax on their particular profits by raising their price, 'in which case the final payment of the tax would fall altogether upon the consumers of those goods' (*WN*, V.ii.f.2 and see *WN*, V.ii.g.8). But employers in agriculture cannot raise their price, and so must pass on a tax on their particular profits by paying less rent, so that 'the final payment of the tax would fall upon the landlord' (*WN*, V.ii.f.2 and *WN*, V.ii.g.8). It would seem that, in this context, by 'agriculture' Smith meant, in fact, the production of *corn* and that he was adhering to his general assumption of a constant price of corn.

Smith's analysis of a general tax on wages also mirrored his rudimentary surplus theory of value and distribution – both in the clarity of his fundamental conclusion (such a tax *must* raise money wages – *WN*, V.ii.i.1), and in the weakness of his detailed analysis of the effects on prices and distribution. The general tax on wages will again fall initially on employers. However, it is very striking and completely puzzling that, in examining how employers will pass on the tax, Smith invoked his analysis of a tax on the profits of *particular* employments (as outlined above) and not his analysis of a tax on profits *in general* (which indicated that it would reduce interest). Thus, he again distinguished between manufacturing (where prices rise) and agriculture (where rents fall) in explaining that in the case of a general tax on wages 'the final payment would in different cases fall upon different persons' (*WN*, V.ii.i.2). This can be seen as an important error in Smith's analysis.

This treatment of a tax on wages (or wage goods), as analogous to a tax on *particular* profits rather than to a tax on profits *in general*, when combined with his adherence to the assumption of a constant price of corn, led Smith into some of his least satisfactory discussions of value and distribution.

6.4.1 Smith's analysis of a tax on wages or wage goods

In the first edition of the *Wealth of Nations* Smith said that a 'tax upon the wages of country labour does not raise the price of the rude produce of land; for the same reason that a tax upon the farmer's profit does not raise that price' (*WN*, V.ii.4). However, he was evidently somewhat unhappy with this assertion that the price of rude produce *does not rise at all*; for, in the second and subsequent editions, he qualified this by saying that a tax on country labour 'does not raise the price of the rude produce of land *in proportion to the tax*; for the same reason that a tax upon the farmer's profit does not raise that price *in that proportion*' (emphasis added). He did not, however, go back and alter his account of the effects of a tax on the farmer's profit, and thereby bring it into conformity with his qualification.

Furthermore, he noted that taxes on necessaries *raise the price* of manufactures and *reduce rent* in agriculture, thereby falling on consumers and landlords – the employers not only retaining their profits but earning profit on the amount of tax they initially advanced. But some manufactured commodities 'are real necessaries of life', and their increased price 'must be compensated to the poor by a *further advancement of their wages*' (*WN*, V.ii.k.9, emphasis added). Further rounds of wage and price increases would therefore follow. Smith showed considerable insight when he said 'how far the general enhancement of the price of labour might affect that of every different commodity, about which labour was employed, could never be known with any tolerable exactness' (*WN*, IV.ii.34). But the idea of rounds of wage and price increases continuing until all the burden had been passed from workers and employers-as-capitalists, to landlords and rich consumers, lacks plausibility and raises doubts about the analytical refinement of the theory of distribution upon which it is based (Hollander, 1973, p. 180).

Although the ultimate problem lay with his *theory of distribution*, the immediate weakness in his analysis of the effects on value and distribution of tax changes arose from his corn measure of value. This measure, as specified by Smith, is of limited use in examining the effects of taxes on prices, because a tax on labour or on the primary wage commodity, corn, *violates the very assumptions upon which the corn measures was premised.* Smith's detailed analysis of the effects of taxes on prices and distribution, which has been outlined here, appears in Chapter ii of Book V; it is interesting to note that in an earlier brief reference to taxes on necessaries, in Chapter ii of Book IV, Smith identified exactly the real nature of such taxes:

> taxes upon the necessaries of life have nearly the same effect upon the circumstances of the people as a poor soil and an bad climate. Provisions are thereby rendered dearer in the same manner as if it required extraordinary labour and expense to raise them. (*WN*, IV.ii.35)

This fact would seem to have been neglected or unavailable to Smith when he came to treat the effect of taxes, and the corn export bounty, in more detail. For there, because of his adherence to the fundamental assumptions which underlay his measure of value, the *real value of corn cannot be increased.*

6.5   THE CORN EXPORT BOUNTY

The nature of Smith's treatment of value and distribution is further revealed in his analysis of the effects of the corn export bounty. Like his analysis of taxes this chapter, 'Of Bounties' (IV.v.), highlights the indeterminate nature of his theory of distribution and the associated limitations of his measure of value. Smith's argument concerning the corn export bounty provides further evidence in support of an important element of the interpretation of his theory of value and distribution outlined in this study – namely, the view that he adhered resolutely to the assumption of a constant price of corn. Furthermore, consideration of the details of Smith's argument is necessary if an evaluation is to be made of the characterisation of Smith's theory of value offered by Dobb (1973, 1975) and Meek (1973a).

Smith challenged the view that the corn export bounty or subsidy had led to a fall in the price of corn – and insisted that any observed fall in its price was merely a result of 'the gradual and insensible rise in the real value of silver' (*WN*, IV.v.a.5).[8] In his view the bounty caused a *rise* in the price of corn on the home market and a slight fall in the price on the export market. A crucial part of Smith's analysis was his denial that this increased price offered any stimulus to production (*WN*, IV.v.a.9). This he explained as follows:

> The real effect of the bounty is not so much as to raise the real value of corn, as to degrade the real value of silver; or to make an equal quantity of it exchange for a smaller quantity, not only of corn, but of all other home-made commodities: for the money price of corn regulates that of all other home-made commodities. (*WN*, IV.v.a.11)

Smith's defence of this proposition relied on a combination of arguments that were typical of his treatment of value and distribution: the subsistence wage and strategic position of corn in agricultural production, the international specie-flow mechanism, and the definitional relation between the money price of corn and the value of silver.

First, the subsistence wage implied that workers must be fully compensated for the effect of the bounty on the price of corn (*WN*, IV.v.a.12). Also, since other agricultural commodities 'in every period of improvement, must bear a certain proportion to that of corn, though this proportion is different in different periods', their prices must rise with that of corn (*WN*, IV.v.a.13). As a result of this feed through of the initial price increase 'the money price of labour, and of everything that is the produce either of land or labour, must necessarily either rise or fall in proportion to the money price of corn' (*WN*, IV.v.a.14).

It will be noted that this differs from his account of the effect of a tax on agricultural necessaries – there *all* prices did *not* rise; instead rent was squeezed and *only* manufactured prices rose. In the case of the bounty, Smith could defend a *general* inflation by resource to the international specie-flow mechanism.[9] The increased export of corn would initiate an increased inflow of specie which would raise all prices on the home market and reduce the value of silver.

It can be argued, and indeed it was by Ricardo, that this fall in the value of silver will only be *temporary*, since the rising prices will change the trade balance and thereby create an inflow of goods and an outflow of silver (*Works*, I, p. 310). In fact, Smith noted that the country imposing the corn export bounty will be undersold 'not only in foreign, but even in the home market' (*WN*, IV.v.a.17) – although he did not say that this mechanism would re-establish the original distribution of specie, despite the bounty. Rather, he based the reduced value of silver, and higher price level, primarily on the fact that the corn bounty alters the specie points – and these are, of course, persistent and not temporary.[10] To explain this, Smith cited the cases of Spain and Portugal, which supplied the rest of Europe with gold and silver; 'these metals ought naturally, therefore, to be somewhat cheaper in Spain and Portugal . . . the difference, however, should be no more than the amount of freight and insurance' (*WN*, IV.v.a.18). But Spain by taxing, and Portugal by prohibiting, the exportation of gold and silver, *widen these specie points* and lower the value of silver in their countries (*WN*, IV.v.a.19). Although no law can actually stop the export of metals they 'load that exportation with the expense of smuggling' and detain a larger quantity than would otherwise remain. It was to this *persistent* effect that he *compared* the corn export bounty:

> The bounty upon the exportation of corn necessarily operates in exactly the same way as this absurd policy of Spain and Portugal. Whatever be the actual state of tillage, it renders our corn somewhat dearer in the home market that it otherwise would be in that state, and somewhat cheaper in the foreign; and as the average money price of corn regulates more or less that of all other commodities, it lowers the value of silver considerably in the one, and tends to raise it a little in the other. (*WN*, IV.v.a.20)

It can be said, therefore, that Smith's famous statement that 'the money price of corn regulates that of all other home-made commodities' had a certain rational foundation in the case of the corn export bounty – where an inflow of specie would, indeed, occur. Ricardo accepted the point which Smith made here (*Works*, I. pp. 130, 316).

However, in the passage quoted above there are hints that Smith had in mind *two distinct* processes: the effect of the bounty on the money price of corn, and an *autonomous* effect of the money price of corn on the money price of all other commodities. And his subsequent comments confirm the presence of a third element in his account of the bounty, and of the relations of value to distribution in general, namely, the *definitional relation* between the money price of corn and the value of silver, arising from the assumption of a constant cost of corn.

This emerges most starkly in his comparison of the effects of the corn export bounty with the effects of other bounties or legally granted monopolies. When the 'country gentlemen' of Britain established import duties and an export bounty on corn 'they did not perhaps attend to the great and essential difference which nature has established between corn and almost every other sort of good' (*WN*, IV.v.a.23). Bounties or monopolies for other goods do actually raise their *real price*, 'render them equivalent to a greater quantity of labour and subsistence', and consequently 'really encourage' their manufacture.

Smith's explanation of why this is not true of the corn export bounty should be quoted in full, since it illustrates the extent to which he adhered to his assumption of a constant cost of corn.

The nature of things has stamped upon corn a real value which cannot be altered by merely altering its money price.[11] No bounty upon exportation, no monopoly of the home market, can raise that value. The freest competition cannot lower it. Through the world in general that value is equal to the quantity of labour which it can maintain, and in every particular place it is equal to the quantity of labour which it can maintain in the way, whether liberal, moderate, or scanty, in which labour is commonly maintained in that place. Woollen or linen cloth are not the regulating commodities by which the real value of all other commodities must be finally measured and determined; corn is. The real value of every other commodity is finally measured and determined by the proportion which its average money price bears to the average money price of corn. The real value of corn does not vary with those variations in its average money price, which sometimes occur from one century to another. It is the real value of silver which varies with them. (*WN*, IV.v.a.23)

Parts of this argument are perfectly plausible. If the 'real price' of corn is *defined* as the ratio of its money price to the money wage rate then, provided the money wage rate rises in line with the money price of corn (as it must, given Smith's subsistence theory), the 'real price' of corn will not change.[12] If the 'real price' of any other good is *defined* as the ratio of its money price to the money price of corn, then this will only remain constant if its money price rises with that of corn. It is clear that Smith *assumed* that money prices would indeed rise. In seeking the foundations for this assumption it has been shown that it depends, first, on the general relation between wage costs and price spelled out by Smith. Secondly, it depends also on the international specie-flow mechanism. However, it has to be recognised that there was a third element in Smith's argument: he would seem to have implicitly invoked the *inverse relation between the price of corn and the general value of silver* that is embodied in his chosen measure of value. The basic assumptions of Smith's model (adopted for valid analytical reasons) led him to the axiom that a rise in the price of corn was *synonymous* with a fall in the value of silver. No other interpretation can account for the final sentence of the passage quoted above.

But this property of Smith's measure (that any change in the money price of corn indicates a change in the value of money) cannot validly be invoked in an analysis of a tax on necessaries or a corn export bounty. A more concrete theory of the rate of profit, and a measure of value consonant with such a theory, were required for analysis of these problems.

6.6   OBSERVATIONS ON ACTUAL PRICE CHANGES

It has been shown that Smith did not provide a sufficiently precise theory of distribution to render his analysis of the 'component parts of price' a determinate theory of value. In this situation his analytical account of value and distribution may usefully be supplemented by a study of his empirical observations on prices and price changes. Such a study does, indeed, yield further information on Smith's view on the determination of value.

There are three things relevant to this: the structure of causation in Smith's account, his observation and analysis of actual price changes, and the question of the labour theory of value. The first two of these have already been discussed and can be dealt with briefly.

6.6.1 The structure of causation

We have seen that Smith's statement of the component parts of price must be judged indeterminate as a theory of value and distribution, because Smith did not provide a convincing explanation of the rate of profit nor an analytical relation of wages to the rate of profit. But is it only formally that the resolution of price was indeterminate or circular. Smith's thinking about the relation of production cost to price and about the relation of wages and profits to price was, most emphatically, neither circular nor indeterminate. The proof of this lies in the way in which he structured the forces which determine and change natural prices. This has been outlined in Section 6.1.4 above.

6.6.2 The evolution of prices and methods of production

In Chapter 5 I drew attention to Smith's extensive analysis of actual price changes in his 'Digression Concerning the Variations in the Value of Silver', in order to demonstrate his use of his measure of value. But Smith's analysis there also provides extensive evidence of how he understood prices to be determined and, most significantly, changed over time. The account in that 'Digression', and elsewhere in the *Wealth of Nations*, leaves absolutely no doubt that his view was that given the rates of wages, profits and rents, prices were determined by methods of production. Furthermore, it is clear that he almost invariably took the state of distribution as given and consequently explained changes in prices by reference to changing methods of production (see Section 5.5 above).

6.6.3 The labour theory of value

It is shown in the Appendix to this chapter that in relating production cost to value Smith was, in all probability, not aware of the device of expressing means of production in terms of labour embodied, and that in general he expressed production costs in money terms, denominated in wage units. On occasion he did express costs in physical terms – as, for example, in the passage quoted at the head of this chapter, when he explained the 'principles which fix the lowest ordinary price' of commodities (which, in the case of commodities which are reproducible and not monopolised, is the *natural* price). However, this can only be read as a *theory* of value when placed in an analytical structure which relates value to distribution. The relation of value to distribution, or the explanation of distribution, is the primary question. Contrary to what is implied in much of the secondary literature, the units in which inputs are calculated is secondary – although a given theory of value and distribution may influence the choice of calculation method.

In explaining changes in value brought about by changes in methods of production Smith frequently related the change in value to the change in the quantity of *labour* used in production.[13] For example, in explaining the reduced price of manufactures, he said:

> The consideration of these circumstances may, perhaps, in some measure explain to us why the real price both of the coarse and of the fine manufactures, was so much higher in those ancient, than it is in the present times. It cost a greater quantity of labour to bring the goods to market. When they were brought thither, therefore, they must have purchased or exchanged for the price of a greater quantity. (*WN*, I.xi.o.13)

This passage, and the similar ones cited in the footnote, raise the question of the labour theory of value in Smith's work. Two points can be stated with certainty at this stage. First, Smith's treatment of exchange in 'that early and rude state of society which precedes both the accumulation of stock and the appropriation of land' cannot properly be considered an instance of the labour theory of value, since any theory of value would predict the same exchange ratios in this situation (Schumpeter, 1954, p. 310). In addition, it should be recalled that there is no evidence that Smith considered it possible to reduce means of production to labour embodied (see Appendix).

Second, there is no foundation to the view that those passages in which Smith related *changes* in value to changes in the quantity of labour used in production are evidence of confusion or inconsistency on his part. Such a view has been taken by several writers who wish to stress Smith's contribution to the surplus theory – and who consider that contribution to lie primarily in his use of a labour theory of value (even if only for a pre-capitalist economy) (see the detailed discussion of Dobb's interpretation in Chapter 10 of this study). It is precisely those writers who attribute to Smith a fully developed labour theory of value for the 'early and rude state of society', and a *rejection* of a fully developed labour theory of value for a capitalist society, who consider the passages under consideration as evidence of confusion. Thus, Hunt considers passages which relate changes in value to changes in labour quantity as 'perplexing ambiguities' in Smith's work (Hunt, 1979,

p. 50). Meek said that 'Smith not infrequently forgot that he had rejected' the labour theory of value (1977, p. 7). Bharadwaj argues that because Smith's labour command measure of value did not possess the property of invariance which he sought he 'often lapsed into a labour approach' (1980, p. 351; see also Douglas, 1928, p. 90; and Viner, 1968, p. 327).

These interpretations contain both analytical and exegitical errors. Analytically, to relate changes in value to changes in the quantity of labour used in production does not imply belief in a labour theory of value (Bladen, 1975, p. 516). In addition, these interpretations ignore the properties of Smith's labour command measure of value – in particular those properties which make it a good measure of changes in value due to changed methods of production. Recall that Smith considered that the labour command measure of value could be used not only to measure natural price, but also to measure each of its component parts (*WN*, I.vi.9). When natural price and its component parts are measured in labour command (money wage units) the first of those component parts (wages), so measured, gives the *quantity of labour* used in production to the commodity. The price of the commodity will vary in proportion to variations in this quantity of labour used in production so long as the shares of wages and non-wage revenues do not vary much (Garegnani, 1958). The relationship between Smith's treatment of value and the use of the labour theory of value as an analytical device by Ricardo and Marx will be considered in later chapters.

APPENDIX: ABSENCE OF REDUCTION OF MEANS OF PRODUCTION TO LABOUR IN SMITH'S WORK

It was stated above that Smith could see no other way of relating production costs to price than by evaluating labour, tools, materials, profit and rent in money terms. This is so because he was not aware of the analytical device of evaluating tools and materials in terms of the quantity of labour embodied in them - he did not have available the concept which has become known as 'indirect labour'. This hypothesis is of some significance in evaluating Smith's treatment of value; it is shown in the course of this essay that it helps to make available a simpler and more consistent interpretation of Smith's theory of value, and of its relation to the subsequent history of the surplus approach to value and distribution, than that traditionally presented. It should be stressed that what is being discussed here is not a *theory* of value, but simply a *technique of analysis*: the reduction of commodities used as means of production to the quantity of labour required for their production (Roncaglia, 1978, p. 101).

It would require a separate study to consider all the evidence in defence of the proposition that Smith did not reduce tools and materials to 'indirect labour', and that the first clear use of this procedure was in Ricardo's *Principles*. Some of this evidence is briefly summarised here. In Book I, Chapter v of the *Wealth of Nations*, when constructing his measure of value, Smith stated that in a pre-capitalist economy commodities exchange in proportion to the quantity of labour used in production – but even in this context he said that goods 'contain the *value* of a certain quantity of labour which we exchange for what is supposed at the time to contain the *value* of an equal quantity' (*WN*, I.v.2). When he outlined the difficulties involved in ascertaining 'the proportion between two different quantities of labour' he considered only the difficulty in measuring *direct* labour (*WN*, I.v.4). In his statement: 'that is dear which it is difficult to come at, or which it costs much labour to acquire', he seems to refer only to *direct* labour (*WN*, I.v.7).

In Book I, Chapter vi, Smith explicitly related value to labour quantities; the first instance of this referred to an 'early and rude state of society', and the 'labour necessary for acquiring different objects' is unequivocally direct labour only (*WN*, I.vi.1). Turning to a capitalist economy, Smith said that the 'quantity of labour commonly employed in acquiring or producing any commodity' no longer regulates the 'quantity which it ought commonly to purchase, command, or exchange for' (*WN*, I.vi.7). Smith's explanation of this may, perhaps, be considered to refute the hypothesis that he did not use 'indirect labour' calculation; for, he said, 'An additional quantity, it is evident, must be due *for the profits* of the stock which advanced the wages and furnished the materials of that labour' (emphasis added). It may be considered that, without the method of reducing means of production to indirect labour, Smith would have had to say that in addition (to wages) something must be given *for the materials used in production*, plus the profits on these, and on the wages advanced. However, Smith's avoidance of any such statement provides no evidence against the hypothesis that he did not use 'direct labour' calculation. The explanation which Smith did adopt is perfectly consistent with, and deducible from, his resolution of the *price* of tools and materials to wages, profits and rent.

In this essay great significance is attached to Smith's assumption of a constant production cost of corn. Examination of the passage in which Smith spelled out this assumption provides further evidence that, although he made extensive use of the property of a constant quantity of labour embodied in corn, he did not have available to him the concept of reducing instruments of production to 'indirect labour':

> In every different stage of improvement, besides, the raising of equal quantities of corn in the same soil and climate, will, at an average, require nearly equal quantities of labour; *or what comes to the same thing, the price of nearly equal quantities*; the continual increase of the productive powers of labour in an improving state of cultivation being more or less counterbalanced by the continually increasing price of cattle, the principal instruments of agriculture. (*WN*, I.xi.e.28, emphasis added)

Likewise, Smith frequently referred interchangeably to the 'produce' and the 'value of the produce' as, for example, when he said the 'whole of what is annually either collected or produced by the labour of every society, or what comes to the same thing, the whole price of it' (*WN*, I.vi.18). In comparing inputs and outputs he frequently used the device of referring simply to the *value* which the worker, or all workers, add to the materials upon which they work (*WN*, II.iii.1). When explaining rent, he frequently reverted to the physiocratic method of comparing the quantity of *corn* produced with the quantity of *corn* necessary to 'maintain all the labour for bringing it to market' (e.g. *WN*, I.xi.b.4).

The nearest which Smith came to treating means of production as accumulated labour was in the opening paragraph of Book II, Chapter iii, of the *Wealth of Nations*, when defining productive and unproductive labour. But consideration of this passage confirms that Smith did not reduce means of production to the quantity of labour embodied in their production, and did not conceive of means of productions transferring their value (or a part of their value) to products.

> But the labour of the manufacturer fixes and realises itself in some particular subject or vendible commodity, which lasts for some time at least after that labour is past. It is, as it were, a certain quantity of labour stocked and stored up to be employed, if necessary, upon some other occasion. That subject, or what is the same thing, the price of that subject, can afterwards, if necessary, put into motion a quantity of labour equal to that which had originally produced it. (*WN*, II.iii.1)

For Smith, capital was stored-up labour in the sense that it can *command* labour at some future date. However, Marx, in his *Economic and Philosophical Manuscripts*, having asked 'what is capital?', quoted the words 'a certain quantity of *labour stocked* and stored up' from Smith, and stated that 'Capital is *stored up labour*' (Marx, 1844, p. 295). It is clear that Marx meant 'stored up labour' in a different sense than Adam Smith.[14] It has been seen in Section 6.6.3 that Smith frequently related changes in value to changes in the quantity of labour used in production; in none of these instances either did he use 'indirect labour' calculation. Finally, it may be significant that instead of referring to machines, etc. as 'dead *labour*' as, for example, Marx did, Smith referred to workers as 'living *instruments of trade*' (*WN*, IV.viii.44).

The hypothesis that Smith did not have the device of reducing means of production to accumulated labour receives indirect support from an examination of the development of the labour theory of value in pre-Smithian literature. Petty posed the problem of finding a 'par and equation between lands and labour', and of finding a 'par and equation between art and simple labour', but did not propose to reduce stock to labour. Furthermore, in reducing 'art' to a quantity of 'simple labour', he proposed to reduce the contribution of 'art' to the number of *days' labour saved*, not the number of days' labour *embodied* in acquiring the 'art' (Johnson, 1937, p. 270).

Locke would seem to have come closer to the idea of means of production as 'past labour', but in the one passage in the *Wealth of Nations* which echoes this aspect of Locke's work, Smith was unequivocally referring to the great *variety* of *types* of labour that go into making the woollen coat of the most common artificer, and not to the total *quantity* of past labour embodied in it (*WN*, I.i.11). Likewise, Cantillon proposed a 'par or relation between the value of land and labour' but did not reduce means of production to past labour (1755, p. 31). Smith makes no reference to the attempt by Petty and Cantillon to find such a 'par'. Finally, in the pamphlet published in 1738 by William Pulteney (who was considered by Marx to be 'much nearer the mark' than Smith where the labour theory of value was concerned) there is no reduction of means of production to past labour (Pulteney, 1738, pp. 17–19; Marx, 1867, p. 137n).[15]

Turning from the predecessors of Adam Smith to his *successors*, the hypothesis presented here is again indirectly confirmed. There is no evidence of the use of indirect labour calculation, or that they took Smith to mean by 'quantity of labour' both direct *and indirect labour*, in either Buchanan's editions of the *Wealth of Nations*, or in Lauderdale's criticism of the labour theory and measure of value as found in the work of Petty, Harris and Smith (Lauderdale, 1804, pp. 24–38).

Nothing in Ricardo's work indicates that he attributed the device of indirect labour calculation to Smith. He explained the idea of treating means of production as quantities of labour in considerable detail in his *Principles*. Indeed, in the third edition he changed the title of the relevant section of the chapter, 'On Value', in order to make quite explicit that 'Not only the labour applied immediately to commodities affect their value, but the labour also which is bestowed on the implements, tools and buildings, with which such labour is assisted'. Furthermore, he added a sentence in which he explained how value is transferred from an implement to a commodity (*Works*, I, pp. 22–3). It is clear, therefore, that Ricardo did not consider the concept and method of indirect labour calculation as sufficiently obvious or established to be understood without considerable explanation. Finally, it is shown in Chapter 8 of this study that Marx, although he considered Smith to have, on occasion, determined value by labour time, nowhere explicitly attributed the device of indirect labour calculation to Smith.

The verdict of more recent historians on the hypothesis presented here can be summarised. Only two historians explicitly support this view. Cannan said that Smith 'knows of no way of "converting" two of these into the third. He does not, like Petty, search for a par between labour, capital and land' (1929, p. 171).[16] Blaug argues that Smith considered it possible to add labour, capital and land only in terms of *money*, 'and, in particular, there is no suggestion that the value of capital goods can be reduced to labour expended on their production in the past; . . . it is this reduction which constitutes the *pons asinorum* of the labour theory of value' (1978, p. 41). In addition, Skinner *may* lend support to this hypothesis – because he interprets Smith's statement that labour commanded exceeds labour embodied to refer to *direct* labour embodied (1974, p. 51).

Several commentators explicitly attribute indirect labour calculation to Smith: Wieser (1888, p. 200), Hunt (1979, p. 91), and Christensen (1979, p. 101) positively; Bladen (1975, p. 516), hesitatingly – and none on the basis of detailed evidence from Smith's work. Most commentators do not explicitly consider the issue at all; many seem to implicitly *assume* that Smith reduced means of production to past labour (e.g. Böhm-Bawerk, 1884, p. 242; Gordon,

1959, p. 462) while most seem to imply that Ricardo was the first economist to do this (e.g. Taussig, 1896, p. 169; Weisskopf, 1955, p. 69).

Part II
Interpretations

7 Ricardo's Development of Smith's Theory

> Smith's peculiar theory of value . . . was refashioned by Ricardo so as to make conditions of production, and in particular quantities of labour expended in production, the basic determinant . . . In doing so he rejected the Adding-up components Theory, and by implication rejected the possibility of treating the sphere of exchange relations as an 'isolated system', and anchored the explanation of these exchange-relations firmly in conditions and circumstances of production. (Dobb, 1973, p. 115)

In presenting the view that Smith contributed to the development of *both* classical and neoclassical theory – a view which we can call the two-streams view of Smith – Dobb placed great emphasis on Ricardo's theoretical departure from Smith's treatment of value and distribution (1973, pp. 47, 49, 72, 76–8, 80, 97, 112–16, 118–19, 122; 1975). These departures, and Ricardo's criticisms of Smith, were considered of such a kind as to warrant the conclusion that Smith and Ricardo belonged, at least in part, to two different 'streams of theory' (see, for example, the statement quoted above). However, given that the interpretation of Smith's treatment of value spelt out in the previous chapter, differs significantly from that adopted by Dobb (in ways which were indicated in passing in previous chapters and will be examined in detail in Chapter 10) a re-examination of the relation of Ricardo's work to that of Smith is in order.

This chapter takes as its point of departure Sraffa's demonstration, in his 'Introduction' to Ricardo's *Principles*, that Ricardo was concerned throughout the rest of his work to defend the theory of the rate of profit that he had set out first in his *Essay on Profits* of 1815 (Sraffa, 1951, pp. xxx–xlix). Attention is drawn to certain aspects of this new theory of profits and it is shown that the differences between the conclusions reached by Smith and Ricardo on the relation of wages, taxes and bounties to prices and distribution were a result of this new theory of profits *in combination with* a new set of assumptions adopted by Ricardo. This allows a distinction to be drawn between what is theoretically significant and what is incidental (arising purely from particular assumptions) in the differences between Smith and Ricardo. Ricardo's *theoretical difference* from Smith is seen to consist in his theory of profit, combined with the theory of differential rent – and in the closure of the theory of value which these facilitated. Since this theory of profits was a development of Smith's surplus theory, based firmly on his subsistence wage theory, then Smith and Ricardo can be seen to have contributed to the development of the *same* stream of theory.

7.1 THE NEW THEORY OF PROFITS

Sraffa's account of the development of Ricardo's thought is sufficiently well known not to require a detailed restatement. However, in this section several points in that account will be highlighted in order to provide historiographical support for an important analytical proposition. The analytical point is as follows: it is well known that Smith and Ricardo reached quite different conclusions on the effects on prices of wage rises, taxes and bounties. However, reference to the analytical definitions set out in Chapter 2 will confirm that their respective view on these questions cannot be used as criteria in order to classify their work as belonging to a classical or 'supply and demand' tradition of theory. It is the structure of their explanations of value and distribution which place them in one or other, or neither, of the two streams of theory. It is argued here that, historically, Ricardo's significant theoretical departure from Smith consisted of his new theory of profits and *not* of his new views of the relation of wages, taxes or bounties, to prices. These latter views (the exact sources of which are identified later in this chapter), and the extent to which they contradicted those of Smith, were both *analytically* and *chronologically* secondary.

It need scarcely be pointed out that Ricardo's theory of subsistence wages, upon which his theory of profits was predicated, was a direct development of Smith's theory that population responds to capital accumulation (*Works*, II, pp. 264–5, 383; I, pp. 78, 96, 292; Tucker, 1960, pp. 95, 112).[1]

Along with his new theory of profits Ricardo's theory of differential rent was of great significance in leading him to views contradictory to those of Smith on the relation of wages, taxes and bounties, to prices. Yet it is of interest that Ricardo developed his theory of profits *before* and *independently* of his adoption of the differential theory of rent. (Sraffa, *Works*, IV, pp. 3–6; Ricardo, *Works*, VI, pp. 94–5, 102; Dobb, 1973, p. 68).

Sraffa's aim in examining in detail the development of Ricardo's thought was to establish the presence of a consistent purpose in his adoption, in turn, of a corn model, a labour theory of value, and an invariant standard of value (Sraffa, *Works*, I, pp. xxxii–xlix). For the purpose of identifying the theoretical difference between Ricardo and Smith, what this sequence (and the interpretation of it provided by Sraffa) reveals is that Ricardo's labour theory of value (and, of course, the corn model and invariant standard in their turn) was primarily an *analytical device* designed to facilitate a statement of his new formulation of the surplus theory of the rate of profit, and only secondarily a theory of the determination of the exchange value. It follows that *historically*, as well as *analytically*, it was Ricardo's new theory of the rate of profit which constituted his *theoretical* difference with Smith, and that any particular set of results concerning the effect of wages, taxes or bounties, on prices, were consequential. To see this, note that he developed the new theory of profits *prior to* his challenge to Smith's views on the relation of wages and taxes to prices (Sraffa, *Works*, I. p. xxxiv).

Indeed, it can even be said that although, as Sraffa (p. xxii) showed, Ricardo had *no* theory of value (in the sense of a logical solution of the relation of value to distribution) in his *Essay on Profits*, he had formed his views on *what forces determine value* before he identified the assumptions necessary to a general demonstration of his theory of the rate of profit. In the *Essay* he said that 'the difficulty or facility of their production will ultimately regulate their exchangeable value' (*Works*, IV, p. 20), and in saying this he can be considered to have adopted Smith's view (recall the account of Smith's views on the determination of value in Chapter 6 above).[2] Indeed, as Sraffa pointed out, Ricardo retained this view in the *Principles* (Sraffa, *Works*, I, p. xxxiv). Of course, too much should not be made of this continuity from Smith to Ricardo, since the proposition in question forms only a small part of a solution to the problem of value; however, it serves as a reminder that the proposition that value is determined by methods of production, was a feature of the classical approach, in general, and not merely of the *particular results* generated by Ricardo's *analytical devices* of the 'corn ratio theory', the labour theory of value, and the invariant standard of value – all of which render distribution independent of value.

One final aspect of Sraffa's account is relevant to the identification of the theoretical difference between Ricardo and Smith. By December 1815 Ricardo was aware of the need, if his theory of profit was to be demonstrated in a general framework, to make prices independent of changes in wages (Sraffa, *Works*, I, p. xxxiv; Ricardo, *Works*, VI, p. 348). Sraffa focused on this realisation and on Ricardo's successive attempts to establish this property (*Works*, I, pp. xxxv–xlix). He pointed out that throughout these attempts Ricardo adhered to his two central substantive propositions or theories: that 'profits depended on wages' (*Works*, VII, p. 78), and that the value of commodities is regulated by the 'difficulty or facility of their production' (Ricardo, *Works*, IV, p. 20). Sraffa described this as follows:

> All these elements of the *Essay* are taken over into the chapter On Value in the *Principles* with the addition of several new ones, *some of which have come to be regarded as the most characteristic of Ricardo's theory*, and are there built into a systematic theory of Value, on which are now based the Theories of Rent, Wages and Profit. (Sraffa, *Works*, I, p. xxxiv, emphasis added)

These 'new elements' derived from Ricardo's identification (in December 1815) of an assumption which was necessary for a general demonstration of his theory – an assumption which he described as the 'sheet anchor on which all my propositions are built', and which Sraffa considered to be 'the turning point in this transition from the *Essay* to the *Principles*' (Ricardo, *Works*, VI, p. 348; Sraffa, p. xxxiv). What Ricardo had identified was the importance of the supposition of the invariability of the precious metals as a standard of value (the remaining new elements can be considered to be the series of alterations made to the specification of the production conditions of the measure of value; see Sraffa, op. cit. p. xxxix). What is of interest in the present context is Sraffa's statement that these new elements 'have come to be regarded as the most characteristic of Ricardo's theory'. For, given the basic theory of distribution, it is the adoption of a particular specification of a measure of value which generates a particular set of results relating wages, taxes and bounties, to prices. And concentration on *these results*, rather than on Ricardo's two main *substantive propositions*, as for example by Dobb (1973, pp. 46–7, 76–7; 1975, pp. 326–8), quite apart from obscuring the true *theoretical* significance of Ricardo's work, has led to exaggeration of the differences between the *theories* of Smith and Ricardo. Particular results concerning the relation of wages (taxes or bounties) to prices should not be used as criteria of theoretical classification.

Finally, given the interpretation of the relation of Ricardo to Smith implicit in Dobb (1973, 1975) it needs to be stated explicitly that the labour theory was *not* Ricardo's theory of relative price or, put another way, that his theory of value and distribution was very definitely a development of Smith's analysis of the *component parts of price*, that is, a development based on Smith's analysis of value in a *capitalist* economy, and *not* on Smith's analysis of a pre-capitalist economy. By contrast, the implication of Dobb's view is that Smith's essential contribution to classical theory was his use of a labour theory of value in certain circumstances (1975, p. 330). I am concerned throughout this study to question a corollary of this view, namely, that Smith's treatment of value in a capitalist setting – his component parts of price – was *not* a contribution to the surplus approach, and that it was, instead, *inherently* a contribution to another, opposed, stream of theory. The weakness of the analytical classification which underlies this view is considered in Chapter 10; what has been shown here is that this view is also *historically* inaccurate.

7.2 ASSUMPTIONS AND THEIR CONSEQUENCES

The different conclusions reached by Ricardo and Smith on the effects of wage changes, taxes and bounties, on prices and distribution are a result of Ricardo's adoption of a firm analytical relation between wages and profits, *in combination* with the fact that his basic assumptions differed in important respects from Smith's. Before considering these differences an important similarity between their respective analyses should be noted.

7.2.1 Ricardo adopted Smith's structure of analysis

Ricardo adopted Smith's theory of competition and consequent analysis of the relation between natural and market price – saying 'In the 7th Chapter of the *Wealth of Nations*, all that concerns this question is most ably treated' (*Works*, I, p. 91). He made two modifications to Smith's method. First, because he recognised the difficulty of observing or describing the details of the process of adjustment of the productive potential of the economy he introduced the *financial system* as the key to movements of capital (ibid., p. 89; see

Marx's approval of this point, 1861–63, II, p. 210). Second, he concentrated on the actions of *capitalists* in explaining the adjustments which occur when, for whatever reason, market price is not equal to natural price (ibid., p. 91). However, as indicated in Chapter 4, the extent to which this latter point constituted a departure from Smith's view should not be exaggerated (see *WN*, I.xi.p.10; *WN*, II.iii.28; *WN*, II.v.37; *WN*, IV.ii.9; *WN*, V.ii.f.6).

Like Smith, Ricardo's concern with value was almost exclusively with *changes* in value (Sraffa, op. cit. p. xlix); furthermore, like Smith, Ricardo focused on changes in value due to changes in methods of production (*Works*, I. p. 36). Also, analysis of these changes was conducted by reference to an *a priori* theory of the production methods of the most important agricultural and manufactured commodities *(Works*, I, pp. 97, 117, 313, 373; IV, p. 20; VI, p. 179). Of course, the *content* of this theory differed somewhat from that adopted by Smith (see Section 7.2.2 below).

Ricardo also adopted Smith's view of how the forces which change value should be structured. This structure, which was in essence *analytical* (as shown in Section 6.1.4), defined natural prices in terms of given methods of production, but allowed these methods to change within a time period in which the underlying real wage was constant. For example, Ricardo said:

> An alteration in the permanent rate of profits, to any great amount, is the effect of causes which do not operate but in the course of years; whereas alterations in the quantity of labour necessary to produce commodities, are of daily occurrence. (*Works*, I, p. 36)

Of course, Ricardo's more detailed consideration of the ratio that forms the rate of profit revealed that a constant level of subsistence did not imply a constant rate of profit, if changes in methods of production of wage goods were occurring.

7.2.2 Ricardo rejected Smith's assumptions

Recall that Smith assumed a constant production cost of corn, a rising production cost of most other agricultural products, a falling production cost of manufactures (except where more expensive agricultural inputs counteract this), and an unpredictable path in the production cost of precious metals (recall Section 5.5 above). On top of these purely *technical* assumptions he made the analytical choice of a corn measure of value. This was more or less adequate for analysis of changes in methods of production but offered no handle on the effects of taxes on wages or necessaries, or of the corn export bounty.

Ricardo's purely technical assumptions were as follows: a rising production cost of corn and of other agricultural commodities (*Works*, IV, p. 13; I, pp. 70, 373), and a falling production cost of manufactures (*Works*, I, pp. 36, 97; VI, p. 179; Sraffa, *Works* IV, p. 20 n.) – except where more expensive agriculture inputs counteract this (*Works*, I, p. 118). From December 1815 onwards he made the analytical assumption of the invariability of precious metals as a standard of value (Works, VI, p. 348; I, pp. 28, 44; Sraffa, op. cit. I, p. xxxiv). The rejection of Smith's constant price of corn was clearly of major significance (Stigler, 1952, p. 185; Corry, 1962, p. 15). Ricardo considered that 'No point in political economy can be better established, than that a rich country is prevented from increasing in population, in the same ratio as a poor country, by the progressive difficulty of providing food' (*Works*, I, p. 373). The idea of diminishing returns in agriculture was familiar to Ricardo from 1810 and was adopted by him *prior* to his formulation of his new theory of profits (Hollander, 1979, pp. 112, 117, 124).

It has been shown above that on the basis of his assumptions about technical change and his chosen measure of value Smith considered that every change in the price of corn was indicative of a fall in the value of money (see Section 5.3 and 3.2). In contrast to this, on the basis of his new assumptions about technical change and the availability of land, and his new measure of value, Ricardo considered that every rise in the price of corn was indicative of an increase in the quantity of labour used in its production. In effect, the introduction of the possibility of a changing price of corn (independent of a falling value of money) forced the corn rate of profit into centre-stage; Ricardo's new theory of profit purported to explain it; and his measure of value (initially, and in all its subsequent variations) was chosen to highlight the new theory.

Many of the differences between the conclusions reached by Smith and Ricardo are explained by their different assumptions – the remainder by Ricardo's new theory of profits in combination with his different assumptions. The following four sections outline the implications of their different assumptions.

7.2.3 Labour commanded and labour embodied measures of value

In the secondary literature, the most widely cited of Ricardo's criticism of Smith is that concerning the labour embodied and labour commanded measures of value.[3] This is partly because it pertains to the question of whether or not Ricardo adopted a labour theory of value; and great, perhaps excessive, weight has been attached to this as the single theoretically significant issue in comparison of the work of Smith and Ricardo.[4] However, secondary discussion of Ricardo's criticism of Smith has not paid sufficient attention to their respective assumptions. Just as Smith's use of the labour command measure depended on his adoption of a set of assumptions which, to the best of his knowledge, rendered changes in labour commanded proportionate to changes in labour embodied (see Section 5.2 above), so Ricardo's rejection of Smith's central assumption of a constant price of corn necessitated abandonment of the labour commanded measure (Sylos-Labini, 1976, p. 209)

His criticism of Smith makes this quite clear; commenting on Smith's measure of value he said:

> Sometimes he speaks of corn, at other times of labour, as a standard measure; not the quantity of labour bestowed on the production of any object, but the quantity which it can command in the market: *as if these were two equivalent expressions. (Works*, I, p. 14, emphasis added)

The final clause has, almost universally, been taken to be an accusation that Smith *confused* labour embodied and labour commanded (Macdonald, Douglas, Schumpeter, Dobb, Blaug, Kaushil, Sylos-Labini, Meek, – all as cited above; O'Brien, 1975, p. 83; Hunt, 1979; Robbins, 1958, p. 67; Bladen, 1975, p. 513). But, in my opinion there is no evidence for that view. Ricardo was *not* dismissing Smith's measure as *self-evidently* absurd; the scholars cited above would seem to ignore the remainder of the sentence in question:

> as if these were two equivalent expressions, and as if because a man's labour had become doubly efficient, and he could therefore produce twice the quantity of a commodity, he would necessarily receive twice the former quantity in exchange for it. (ibid.)

Ricardo's *objection* came only in the *next* paragraph – and it was clearly an objection to Smith's assumptions:

> *If* this indeed were true, if the reward of the labourer were always in proportion to what he produced, the quantity of labour bestowed on a commodity, and the quantity of labour which that commodity would purchase, *would be equal*, and either might accurately measure the variations of other things: but they *are not* equal. (*Works*, I, p. 14, emphasis added)

Why are they not equal? The example which Ricardo used to show the non equivalence of the labour embodied and labour commanded measures illustrates clearly the importance of the difference between his and Smith's assumptions concerning the production conditions of corn:

> In the same country double the quantity of labour may be required to produce a given quantity of food and necessaries at one time, than may be necessary at another, and a distant time; yet the labourer's reward may possibly be very little diminished . . . Food and necessaries in this case will have risen 100 per cent if estimated by the *quantity* of labour necessary to their production, while they will scarcely have increased in value, if measured by the quantity of labour for which they will *exchange*. (*Works*, I, p. 15)

To show that the labour embodied in corn was not equal to, or even proportional, to the labour it can command, Ricardo had explicitly to draw on the idea of *diminishing returns in agriculture*. But, as I have shown, Smith did *not* consider that there was diminishing returns in corn production. To point out these facts is in no way to diminish the *analytical* significance of the labour embodied measure in Ricardo's attempt to generalise his own theory of the rate of profit.

While Ricardo was clearly aware of Smith's assumption of a *constant value* of corn and, as will be seen below, while he several times drew attention to it as the source of Smith's erroneous results, he nowhere commented on Smith's underlying supposition of a *constant labour cost of production of corn*. In Chapter 28 of the *Principles* he said 'corn, according to him, is always of the same value because it will always feed the same number of people' (p. 374). It should be clear, in view of the evidence cited in Chapter 5, that this does not fully account for Smith treating the value of corn as constant.

7.2.4 Gold and corn in rich and poor countries

Different assumptions underlie the different views of Ricardo and
Smith on what happens to the relative prices of corn and gold as society
becomes richer (MacDonald, 1912, p. 568). It is necessary to show that
their difference on this question is of no *inherent analytical importance*
because Dobb has said 'Ricardo may well have considered this chapter
of the *Wealth of Nations* as an example of misleading use of general
supply – demand reasoning to the neglect of the rooting of "natural
value" in conditions of production' (1975, p. 334). Smith's view that
corn is dear relative to other agricultural goods and to silver in a poor
country, and cheap relative to these goods in a well-developed country,
was a *direct result* of the assumptions he adopted in Book I, Chapter xi
(these were set out in Section 5.5 above). Ricardo was explicit about the
source of his disagreement with this view. He accepted Smith's view
that 'cattle, poultry, game of all kinds, the useful fossils and minerals of
the earth, etc., naturally grow dearer as the society advances' (*WN*,
I.xi.i.3) but asked:

> Why should corn and vegetables alone be excepted? Dr. Smith's
> error throughout his whole work, lies in supposing that the value of
> corn is constant; that though the value of all other things may, the
> value of corn never can be raised. (*Works*, I, p. 374)

The more general point in Dobb's remark, that Ricardo considered
Smith to have used 'supply-demand relations . . . as the vehicle and
framework of determination' (Dobb, 1973, p. 119; 1975; p. 334), is
shown to be without foundation in Section 7.5 below.

7.2.5 Rent

It has been shown that the different conclusions reached by Smith and
Ricardo arose from Ricardo's development of a new theory of profit,
in combination with the different assumptions adopted by the two
writers. This is nowhere more true than on the question of rent and the
issues which are affected by it. Clearly abandonment of Smith's
constant cost of corn opened the door the differential theory of rent.
This in turn threw into relief the relation between wages and profits, as
Ricardo noted when he said 'By getting rid of rent, which we may do
on the corn produced with the capital last employed, and on all
commodities produced by labour in manufactures, the distribution

between capitalist and labourer becomes a much more simple consideration' (*Works*, VIII, p. 194). The significance of their different assumptions, and Ricardo's awareness of this significance, is indicated by his comment on Smith's analysis of the rent of mines (where Smith recognised differential productivity) – the 'whole principle of rent is here admirably and perspicuously explained, *but every word is as applicable to land as it is to mines*' (*Works*, I, p. 330, emphasis added).

This question of rent, influenced as it was by assumptions concerning the method of production of corn, in turn influenced the views of Smith and Ricardo on the relative interests of the classes. In grappling with Smith's views on this Ricardo said:

> Adam Smith never makes any distinction between a low value of money, and a high value of corn, and therefore infers, that the interest of the landlord is not opposed to that of the rest of the community. (*Works*, I p. 336)

In the light of my detailed study of the *Wealth of Nations* it can be seen that this characterisation of Smith's position was perceptive; and it confirms the importance of underlying assumptions in forming their different opinions on whether or not landlords have an interest in restrictions on the import of corn (*Works*, I, p. 337).

7.2.6 Effects of a tax on wages

Different assumptions also played a role in bringing Smith and Ricardo to quite different conclusions on the effect of a tax levied on wages. This was, perhaps, the most significant divergence between the two; for, it was on this question that Ricardo's transformation of Smith's surplus *view* of rent and profit into a precise *theory* of the *rate* of profit had its greatest impact. Recall that in Smith's view a tax on wages was paid ultimately by the landlords (and rich consumers), since manufacturing capitalists could pass it on in higher prices but farmers could not raise the price of corn (*WN*, V.ii.i.4). This was a conclusion to which he was led not only by his continued adherence to his measure of value in a context in which it was inappropriate, but also by his unfortunate step of analysing a tax on wages as if it were analogous to a tax on *particular* profits, rather than a tax on profits *in general*. Sharing Smith's theory of wages, Ricardo accepted that wages must rise: 'Thus far we fully agree, but we essentially differ in our views of the *subsequent operation* of such a tax' (*Works*, I, p. 222, emphasis added).

Ricardo's approach was first to expose Smith's argument by pushing it to its logical conclusion. He pointed out that, on Smith's assumptions, every rise in the price of manufactures would raise wages further, 'without any assignable limits', and he cast doubt on the plausibility of such a view (*Works*, I, p. 225). He then revealed the more fundamental weakness in Smith's position, his lack of an analysis of the relation between wages and profits, by introducing the minor correction that a tax on wages was analogous to a rise in the price of wage goods due to 'increasing difficulty of production'. That is, the tax would increase the real value of those necessaries – a view which Smith himself had stated at one point but had ignored when analysing a tax on wages (see Section 6.4). The result of introducing this correction, which of course amounted to an abandonment of Smith's constant value of corn, was that if the price of corn rose (as well as manufactures) then 'it is obvious that the tax could never be paid' (*Works*, I, pp. 225–6). The way was then open for a statement of his own alternative theory, based as it was on the use of an analytical device that held all prices constant in the face of a tax on wages.

This case demonstrates clearly the general points of this section, that the different results of Smith and Ricardo were generated by different assumptions concerning methods of production, and by Ricardo having recast Smith's surplus view as a theory of profit. Furthermore, this new theory of profit *seemed to Ricardo to require for its presentation* the use of an analytical device which made prices invariant to changes in wages. But Ricardo's own comments confirm that it was the *new theory* of profit, and *not* a particular set of wage-price relations, that constituted the substance of his theoretical difference with Smith. He said, for example:

I hope, then, that I have succeeded in showing, that any tax which shall have the effect of raising wages, will be paid by a diminution of profits, and, therefore, that a tax on wages is in fact a tax on profits.

This principle of the division of the produce of labour and capital between wages and profits, which I have attempted to establish, appears to me so certain, that excepting in the immediate effects, I should think it of little importance whether the profits of stock, or the wages of labour, were taxed. (*Works*, I, p. 226, emphasis added)

In fact, as will be shown in detail in the following section, this 'principle of the division of the produce' remained Ricardo's central theoretical proposition despite several alterations in his view of how changes in wages affect prices (Sraffa, op. cit., p. xxxix).

7.3   THE RELATION OF WAGE CHANGES TO PRICES

This section offers an assessment of the importance of the different views of Ricardo and Smith on the effect of changes in wages on prices. Analytically, it is clear that their conflicting results on this question cannot be used to classify them as belonging to either classical or 'supply and demand' theory. Indeed, the theoretical work of Sraffa has shown that Ricardo's 'principle of the division of the produce of labour and capital between wages and profits' does not depend on the validity of *any* particular relations between wage changes and prices; in particular, it does not depend on the complete independence of value and distribution (1960, p. 6). Recall that in the section on 'interdependence' in Chapter 2 it was made clear that it is the *nature* of the relationship between value and distribution, and not the extent to which changes in wages change prices, that is theoretically significant.

It will be shown here that this is historically true also. Thus, what Sraffa has described as Ricardo's 'preoccupation with the effect of a change in wages', and the fact that 'the problem of value which interested Ricardo was how to find a measure of value which would be invariant to changes in the division of the product', do not in any way indicate that the interdependence between value and distribution implicit in Smith's account of the effect of wage changes on prices, and against which Ricardo argued, was *of the sort found in 'supply and demand' theory*. It has been indicated in the preceding chapter that this was not the case.

This interpretation contrasts most sharply with the 'two streams' view of Smith, which distorts Smith's treatment of value, and distorts Ricardo's criticisms of Smith, and then combines these to identify a much greater theoretical difference between the two writers than is warranted. For example, Dobb, by conflating Smith's analysis of *taxes on wages* with his analysis of the *corn export bounty*, attributed to Smith the view that a tax on wages would raise *all* prices. He then explained Ricardo's criticism of Smith as a response to the fact that 'the Adam Smith theory leads to an absurd conclusion that the value of everything can rise simultaneously whenever one of the "components" rises for any reason' (Dobb, 1973, p. 76; see also p. 47). This concentration on wage-price relations, and distortion of Smith's actual views on that question, had the effect first, of portraying Smith and Ricardo as having *two different theories* of value, and second, of implying that Ricardo in some way disputed Smith's view of *how wages enter into the price* of a commodity, as part of a more general rejection of his conception of the *relation between cost and price*. It should be clear from the preceding chapter that *Smith* never reached the 'absurd conclusion' attributed to him by Dobb. This section deals with Ricardo's treatment of the effect of wage changes on prices.

7.3.1 Ricardo accepted Smith's view

Ricardo's comments on the effect of an increase in cost of production in specific trades make it clear that he accepted Smith's view of how wages and the other elements of cost feed into prices. He said, for example, 'On the same principle that a tax on corn would raise the price of corn, a tax on any other commodity would raise the price of that commodity' (*Works*, I, p. 243; see also p. 156).[5]

His acceptance of Smith's view of how wages and taxes feed into prices – with the major innovation that the rates of wages and profits are firmly bound together – can be somewhat obscured by his statements of the following sort:

> It appears, then, that the rise of wages will not raise the prices of commodities (*Works*, I, p. 105).

and

> In the chapter on Wages, we have endeavoured to show that the money price of commodities would not be raised by a rise of wages . . . (*Works*, I, p. 126).

What he meant , of course, was that a rise of wages will not raise the price of *all* commodities.[6] These statements are cited merely to show that Ricardo's concern in criticising Smith was not the relation between cost and price but the theory of the rate of profit. It is necessary to show this because of the widespread influence of Dobb's interpretation of Smith's role in the development of classical political economy.

7.3.2 Ricardo ignored many effects

In order to demonstrate 'the principle' he consistently *ignored* some of the effects of changes in wages and changes in cost of production on prices. This can serve to create the incorrect impression that he rejected the relation between cost and price spelt out by Smith, and could, mistakenly, be taken as evidence in support of a two-streams interpretation of Smith's work. In Chapter V, 'On Wages', Ricardo gave a numerical example to illustrate the effect of a rising price of corn; in the numerical example he assumed that the prices of all other goods in the wage basket would remain unchanged in the face of both the increased price of corn and the increased money wage (*Works*, I, pp. 103; see also pp. 118, 122, 214–15, 308) – although he acknowledged that some effect was likely (*Works*, I, pp. 104, 117). Even where he allowed that 'the probable effect of a tax on raw produce, would be to raise the price of raw produce, and of all commodities in which raw produce entered' he ignored certain price effects: 'to simplify consideration of this subject, I have been supposing that a rise in the value of raw produce would effect, in equal proportion all home commodities' (*Works*, I, pp. 169, 171).

His defence of this procedure reveals again the primacy of the theory of the rate of profit and the theoretical insignificance of the details of the wage-price changes: 'In all these calculations I have been desirous *only to elucidate the principle*, and it is scarcely necessary to observe, that my whole basis is assumed at random, and merely for the purpose of exemplification' (*Works*, I, pp. 121–2, emphasis added; see also Groenewegen, 1972, p. 59, n. 2).

7.3.3 Ricardo modified his results

In December 1815 Ricardo recognised the need for a measure of value as 'the sheet anchor on which all my propositions are built' (*Works*, VI, p. 348; Sraffa, 1951, p. xxxiv). As Sraffa has explained, Ricardo made a series of alterations in the specification of his *measure* of value (Sraffa, op. cit. p. xl–xlv; Ricardo, *Works*, I, pp. 63, 17, n. 3. pp. 43–7; II, p. 64; VIII, p. 193; IV, p. 405) – 'modifications which were designed to minimise the extent of such price-changes in either direction as, in terms of the newly adopted standard, do occur when wages rise' (Sraffa, p. xxxix). The effect of these alterations to the measure of value was to alter the results relating wages to prices in Ricardo's text, but not, and this is the crucial point, *the relation of distribution to value* in

Ricardo's *theory*.[7] The theory of the rate of profit, and indeed, the theory of what determines exchange value, remained constant throughout these changes (Sraffa, op. cit. pp. xxxvii–xlix).

7.3.4 Ricardo's account of Smith's results

Recall that the only place in the *Wealth of Nations* where Smith invoked the maxim that 'the money price of corn regulates that of all home-made commodities' was in the chapter on the corn export bounty (*WN*, IV, v.a.11; and see Section 6.5 above). Put another way, Smith did not combine this view, that the price of corn regulates all prices, with an assumption of diminishing returns in agriculture. This is not true of the contemporary orthodoxy after 1815 – although that orthodoxy was considered then, and is considered by many still, to have been 'Smithian' (Ricardo, *Works*, IV, p. 21n; VI, pp. 105, 348; I, p. 46). Dobb's view that Smith and Ricardo belonged in two different streams of theory was based on his supposition that Ricardo's criticism of Smith was that 'the Adam Smith theory unqualified leads to an absurd conclusion: that the value of everything can rise simultaneously whenever one of the "components" rises for any reason' (Dobb, 1973, p. 76). It is necessary, then, to examine this supposition.[8]

At first sight it does *seem* that Ricardo did accuse Smith of having reached the 'absurd conclusion' mentioned above. In Chapter 1 of his *Principles*, when discussing the invariable measure of value, he said:

> Before I quit this subject, it may be proper to observe, that Adam Smith, and all writers who have followed him, have, without an exception that I know of, maintained that a rise in the price of labour would be uniformly followed by a rise in the price of all commodities. (*Works*, I, p. 46; and see also IV, p. 19, n.; VII, p. 105)

It is of the utmost importance, if Smith's economics is to be correctly understood, to recognise that in this passage Ricardo referred simultaneously to the contemporary orthodoxy (which shared his belief in diminishing returns in agriculture) and to Smith's position – without acknowledging that it was *in his analysis of the corn export bounty* that the latter had said that 'the money price of corn regulates that of all home-made commodities'. Ricardo's pathbreaking refutation, in the preceding pages, of the commonly held view was a logical consequence of his new theory of profits, and did not deal with the case of the bounty (*Works*, I, p. 46).

However, when Ricardo turned to examine various policy issues, in the later chapters of the *Principles*, he paid meticulous attention to Smith's particular assumptions and the details of his arguments.[9] He confined reference to Smith's statement that 'the price of corn regulates...' to his own chapter on bounties – where he challenged the underlying idea of a constant value of corn (*Works*, I, p. 313; see also pp. 228, 315). Indeed, he stressed that 'perhaps in no part of Adam Smith's justly celebrated work, are his conclusions more liable to objection, than in the chapter on bounties' (p. 304). On this subject he disputed Smith's argument that there would be a specie inflow to raise all prices and lower the value of money (pp. 104–5, 169); he contended that if there was such an inflow it 'cannot possibly be permanent' (pp. 310–11; see also 168–9); and he conceded that 'the tendency of a bounty on the exportation of any commodity is to lower in a small degree the value of money' (p. 316; see also p. 229).[10]

It is probable that Ricardo paid greater attention to the details of Smith's case in the later chapters of his *Principles* than he did in the earlier one, or in the *Essay on Profits* or the *pre-Principles* correspondence, because he re-read Smith in December 1816, *after* having sent a draft of the first seven chapters to Mill in October of the same year (*Works*, VII, pp. 88–9; 100, 107–8; 115; Sraffa, 1951, pp. xv–xviii).

Attention to the details of Ricardo's criticism of Smith shows that Dobb was not correct in attributing to Ricardo his own view that 'Adam Smith's theory leads to an absurd conclusion that the value of everything can rise simultaneously whenever one of the "components" rises for any reason' (Dobb, 1973, p. 76)

7.3.5 Ricardo allowed that all prices may rise

Final confirmation that the effect of wage changes on prices was secondary to the new theory of profit is provided by the number of instances in which Ricardo, while adhering to his theory of profit, allowed that all prices might rise in money terms. Finishing his chapter on profits, he said 'But if it were otherwise, if the price of commodities were permanently raised by high wages, the proposition would not be less true, which asserts that high wages invariably affect the employers of labour' (*Works*, I, pp. 126–7).[11] It is clear that in general Ricardo regarded these effects on the general price level as temporary, if there was 'free trade in the precious metals' (p. 229; see also pp. 214, 316).

In addition to these allowances Ricardo subsequently qualified his more general view that 'corn and *all* home commodities could not be materially raised in price without an influx of the precious metals' (*Works*, I, pp. 168, 213). In the third edition he added the following footnote: 'It may be doubted whether commodities raised in price, merely by taxation, would require any more money for their circulation. I believe they would not' (p. 169n; and see a second, more lengthy, footnote explaining his reversion to the view he had held in 1811, pp. 213–4 n.).[12]

In this section I have re-examined the relation of wages to prices in Ricardo's *Principles*. This is necessary because Dobb's interpretation of Adam Smith had as its foundation a particular reading of the relation of wages to price in Ricardo's work, and of Ricardo's criticism of Smith's ideas on this question. It has been shown that Dobb's view of Smith involved a misreading of Smith's treatment of value, a misreading of Ricardo's criticism of Smith, and a combination of these to identify a much greater difference between the theories of the two men than was in fact the case.

7.4 VALUE AND RICHES

In Chapter 20 of his *Principles*, 'Value and Riches, Their Distinctive Properties', Ricardo surveyed Lauderdale's and Say's criticisms of Smith on the question of the measure and source of value. In as much as Say's work was a rudimentary version of the supply and demand theory (a question on which historians have differed), that is, in as much as there were *two* competing streams of *theory* in existence in his day, Ricardo unambiguously considered his own theory as founded on Smith's, and defended him against the criticisms of Say and Lauderdale. This is demonstrated in this short section.

Early in his economic work Ricardo had remarked 'I like the distinction which Adam Smith makes between value in use and value in exchange. According to that opinion utility is not the measure of value' (*Works*, III, p. 284; the significance of this derivation from Smith was noted by Meek, 1973, p. 88). Then, having opened his *Principles* by quoting Smith's original statement of the distinction, he went on to say 'Many of the errors in political economy have arisen from errors on this subject, from considering an increase of riches, and an _ncrease of value, as meaning the same thing, and from unfounded notions as to what constituted a standard measure of value' (p. 274; see also Cannan, 1929, p. 173).

Although he was critical of Smith's actual choice of corn as a measure of value,[13] his targets in this chapter were Lauderdale, who defined value in such a way that riches were measured by value,[14] and Say who, in addition to that, considered that *utility* was the measure and foundation of value (*Works*, I, pp. 276–7, 280–5, 287, n.1).[15] Ricardo considered both writers to have abandoned Smith's distinction between *value in use* and *value in exchange*. But he noted that 'although Adam Smith has given the correct description of riches', he had, in the early paragraphs of Book I, Chapter v, defined value in terms of *purchasing power* over commodities in general, and had thereby confounded value and riches (*Works*, I, pp. 227–8). He had, by the same token, laid the basis for immense and prolonged misunderstanding of his measure of value, as was shown in Chapter 5 of this study. In general, however, it is clear that in discussing the work of those who, to use Wieser's phrase, derived value from utility, Ricardo considered that they had abandoned Smith's approach – an approach to which he himself adhered.

7.5 SUPPLY AND DEMAND

Dobb defended the view that Smith contributed to the development of neoclassical theory by asserting that Ricardo considered him to have explained value by supply and demand. Two passages from Ricardo's *Principles* were cited in support of this interpretation: Chapter 28, on the comparative value of gold and corn, and Chapter 30, 'On the Influence of Demand and Supply on Prices' (Dobb, 1973, p. 119; 1975, p. 334). The first of these has been examined in Section 7.2.4 and shown to have nothing to do with supply and demand – the difference between Smith and Ricardo being explained by their different assumptions. On Chapter 30 Dobb said:

> On a number of occasions Ricardo, in controversy with the position of Smith and of Malthus, criticised and dismissed explanations in terms of 'supply and demand' . . . What Ricardo had in mind was the use of the notion of supply-demand relations by Smith in his system as a whole – as the vehicle and framework of determination. Ricardo was using it, in other words, as a label for the rival theory of value and distribution that he was combating. (Dobb, 1973, p. 119)

There is no evidence whatsoever that Ricardo included Adam Smith among those who held 'the opinion that the price of commodities depends solely on the proportion of supply to demand' (Ricardo, *Works*, I, p. 382). Indeed, all the evidence points in the opposite direction.

First, in Chapter 30 Ricardo did not mention the *Wealth of Nations*; Dobb acknowledged this but said 'it seems likely that general reference to the latter was not altogether out of mind' (1975, p. 334). Second, the view which Ricardo was criticising, and which he considered to have become 'almost an axiom in political economy' (p. 382), was quite plainly the direct opposite of Smith's view. For example, Ricardo said, 'It is this opinion which has made Mr Buchanan maintain that wages are not influenced by a rise or fall in the price of provisions, but solely by the demand and supply of labour' (ibid.). The same is true of the views of Say and Lauderdale criticised by Ricardo (pp. 382–3).

Third, and most important, *all* of Ricardo's *actual*, as distinct from *inferred*, comments on Smith's treatment of supply and demand *were approving*. For instance, in 1814 in a dispute with Malthus on the 'effects of the wants and tastes of mankind', he wrote that 'Adam Smith in Book V, Chapter I, page 134 concisely expresses what appears to me correct, of the effects of demand on the price of commodities' (*Works*, VI. p. 184). Several years earlier he had written to Mill explaining that 'As to the use of the word demand, I follow Dr Smith's rule, which is to call it effectual demand, as often as it means the will to purchase combined with power' (VI, p. 58). There is further evidence in his *Notes on Malthus* of 1820 that he considered his view of supply and demand to be the same as that of Smith. When Malthus distinguished between 'the two systems' of 'cost of production' and 'demand and supply', which 'have an essentially different origin', Ricardo's 'note' said 'By cost of production I invariably mean wages and profits. Adam Smith includes rent . . . *In this sense only do I differ from Adam Smith*' (*Works*, II, pp. 42–5, emphasis added). Furthermore, when Malthus said that 'the great principle of demand and supply is called into action to determine what Adam Smith calls natural prices as well as market prices', Ricardo *cited Smith* in his own defence: 'The author forgets Adam Smith's definition of natural price, or he would not say that demand and supply could determine natural price' (*Works*, p. 46). Indeed, Dobb quoted this 'note' on Malthus at length in order to demonstrate the theoretical differences between Ricardo and Malthus – yet it is puzzling that what it reveals about *Ricardo's view of Smith* was ignored (for a similar view to that presented here see Bharadwaj, 1978a, p. 168).[16]

7.6 CONCLUSION

Such was the dominance of Ricardo in nineteenth century economics that much of what is commonly believed about Adam Smith's economic ideas derives not from study of the *Wealth of Nations* but from Ricardo's criticism of it in his *Principles*. This seems to be nowhere more true than in Dobb's interpretation of Smith's role in the development of economic theory – which placed great emphasis on Ricardo's supposed rejection of Smith's theoretical approach. This chapter has tried to establish two things. First, that not everything Ricardo said about Smith's ideas was accurate. Second, and much more important, that once we have paid meticulous attention to Smith's text much of Ricardo's criticism of Smith appears in a subtly different light. But this subtle difference is crucial in accepting or rejecting Dobb's view of the way in which, and the extent to which, the theoretical approaches of Ricardo and Smith differed. And, precisely because Ricardo was such an historically significant figure, this is, in turn, central in determining the validity or invalidity of Dobb's view of Adam Smith's role in the development of theories of value and distribution.

8 Marx on Smith

[Adam Smith] has no immanent law to determine the *average profit* or its amount. (Marx, 1861–63, III, p. 69)

Science, unlike other architects, builds not only castles in the air, but may construct separate habitable storeys of the building before laying the foundation stone. (Marx, 1859, p. 57)

8.1 MARX'S 'TWO STREAMS' PROPOSITION?

In restating the view of Dobb and Meek that 'Smith would be included as a theorist of both "distinct and rival traditions in nineteenth century economic thought" ' Bradley and Howard add 'Marx seems the first to have explicitly noted this aspect of Smith's work' (1982, p. 34). What these authors have in mind are a number of statements by Marx, of the following sort:

Adam Smith's successors, in so far as they do not represent the reaction against him of older and obsolete methods of approach, can pursue their particular investigations and observations undisturbedly and can always regard Adam Smith as their base, whether they follow the esoteric or the exoteric part of his work or whether, as is almost always the case, they jumble up the two. (Marx, 1861–63, II, p. 166; see also 1861–63, I, pp. 88, 151; and III, p. 20)

This statement could, at first sight, be seen as a two streams proposition. In order to assess whether such a view is justified it is necessary to examine Marx's many comments on Smith's work in more detail.

Such an examination shows, first and foremost, that Marx regarded Smith as a surplus theorist (Section 2 below). However, his definition of the surplus theory yielded a distinction between what he called 'esoteric' (initiated) and 'exoteric' (ordinary) aspects of Smith's work (as in the passage quoted above). In his view the presence of these two elements in his work meant that Smith was 'the source, the starting point, of diametrically opposed conceptions' (1861–63, III, p. 20). In addition, Marx considered that Smith alternated between a labour embodied and labour commanded explanation of value. Furthermore, given the crucial role of the labour theory of value in his own (and Ricardo's) attempt to advance the surplus theory, he formed the very definite view that Smith's transition from 'esoteric' ideas (which embody the implications of the surplus view of distribution) to the 'exoteric' (which merely describe economic phenomena as they appear in everyday life) was *caused by*, and is to be *found in*, his transition from a labour embodied to a labour commanded approach to value.

It is shown in this chapter that Marx's identification of a labour embodied and labour commanded explanation of value in the *Wealth of Nations* is questionable (Sections 3 and 4 below). What then of his distinction between the 'esoteric' and 'exoteric' elements in Smith's work – and his trenchant criticism of the latter? It transpires that all these criticisms, despite their apparent diversity, had a single motivation – Smith's failure to embed his surplus *view* of distribution in a logically coherent *theory* of price (Sections 3, 4 and 5). This central point was undoubtedly correct – despite the inaccuracy of many parts of Marx's account of Smith's work. Consequently, the distinction between 'esoteric' and 'exoteric' has to be judged as valid (and can, indeed, be restated to accord with modern theoretical definitions) but, without the touchstone provided by the clarity of the labour embodied/labour commanded dichotomy, it cannot be used to divide Smith's work neatly into two independent or easily identifiable parts (Section 6).

Finally, it is also shown in Section 6 that, quite independent of the modifications to Marx's account which are called for, his statement quoted above was not equivalent to the modern 'two-stream proposition' concerning Smith's role in the development of economics. His distinction between 'esoteric' and 'exoteric' ideas was related, but not identical, to his distinction between 'classical' and 'vulgar' political economy; these were the 'diametrically' opposed conceptions of which Smith was the source. A study of this aspect of Marx's account leaves no doubt that the distinction between 'classical' and 'vulgar' political economy was not equivalent to the modern distinction between classical and marginalist theory. In order to use Marx's account of Smith's work as support for the two streams view of it, a much more detailed set of historical and analytical connections linking these 'vulgar' writers with Smith (on the one hand) and with neoclassical theory (on the other) would have to be illustrated, than has hitherto been done by any proponent of that view.

8.2   SMITH AS A SURPLUS THEORIST

In *Theories of Surplus Value* Marx traced the history of the concept of economic surplus; it will be shown here that he unequivocally counted Adam Smith as a surplus theorist. In identifying the basic analytical elements of the surplus theory he argued that 'the foundation of modern political economy, whose business is the analysis of capitalist production, is the conception of the value of labour-power as something fixed, as a given magnitude – as indeed it is in practice in each particular case' (1861–63, I, p. 45). He opened his account of Smith's contribution by saying: 'Adam Smith, like all economists worth speaking of, takes over from the Physiocrats the conception of the average wage, which he calls the natural price of wages' (ibid., p. 69).

Marx pointed his readers to Smith's view that once stock has accumulated 'in the hands of particular persons' it will be used to employ 'industrious people . . . in order to make a profit by the sale of their work, or by what their labour adds to the value of the materials' (*WN*, I.vi.5). It was Smith's analysis of this added value which Marx considered of greatest significance; he quoted Smith's statement that 'the value which the workman adds to the materials, therefore, resolves itself . . . into two parts, of which one pays their wages, the other the profits of their employer' (*WN*, I.v.5). He commented 'Here therefore Adam Smith explicitly states: the profit which is made on the sale of the complete manufacture originates not from *the sale* itself, not from the sale of the commodity *above* its value, is not profit upon alienation'. Marx continued:

> Indeed, on the contrary, he traces the profit of the capitalist precisely to the fact that he has not paid for a part of the labour added to the commodity . . . Thereby he traces the true origin of surplus value. (1861–63, I, p. 80)

In addition, he stressed the fact that Smith refuted the view that profits were the 'wages of a particular sort of labour', and adopted Smith's description of them (and rent) as a 'deduction' from the value which the workmen have added to the materials of labour (*WN*, I.viii.8).

Marx considered that a surplus theory of the economy must be based on a physical analysis of the creation of surplus in production and, consequently, he laid great stress on the fact that 'Adam Smith conceives *surplus-value* – that is, surplus-labour performed and realised in the commodity over and above the paid labour . . . – as the *general category*' (1861–63, I, p. 82). He noted Smith's distinction between 'original' and 'derivative' revenues and praised Smith's demonstration that all interest on money, taxes, salaries, pensions, and annuities of every kind, in 'so far as they are not deductions from wages themselves – are merely shares in profit and rent, which are themselves in turn reducible to surplus-value, that is, unpaid labour time'. 'This', he said, 'is Adam Smith's general theory of surplus value' (1861–63, I, p. 84). It was this analysis of economic surplus that Marx considered to be the 'esoteric' part of Smith's work.

Smith's great *original* contribution to the development of the surplus theory was, in Marx's view, his *generalisation* of the concept of surplus from agriculture to all spheres of production (1859, p. 209; 1861–63, I, p. 85). But a rejection of the view that only agricultural labour produces a surplus necessitated a new formulation of the concepts of productive and unproductive labour. Marx commented as follows on Smith's definition:

> Productive labour is here defined from the standpoint of capitalist production, and Adam Smith here got to the very heart of the matter, hit the nail on the head. This is one of his greatest scientific merits . . . that he defines productive labour as labour *which is directly exchanged with capital*. (1861–63, I, p. 157)

In addition, despite his own criticism of Smith, he strongly defended Smith's distinction against its many critics, saying that 'the distinction between productive labours and unproductive labours is of decisive importance for what Smith was considering: the production of material wealth, and in fact one definite form of that production, that capitalist mode of production' (1861–63, I, p. 284; II, p. 414).[1]

Indeed, throughout his commentary Marx credited Smith with having identified the specifically *capitalist* features of the economic system under investigation – from its fundamental characteristic, the purchase of labour by capital (1861–63, I, pp. 78, 87), to its most important price phenomenon, the inclusion of profit, at a uniform rate, in the natural price of commodities (1861–63, III, p. 83). This judgement, that Smith gave a general characterisation of the capitalist economy, is neatly conveyed in his statement that 'Real political economy *à la* Smith treats the capitalist only as personified capital, M-C-M, agent of production'. Note also his description of 'the essence of the *Wealth of Nations* – namely, the view that the capitalist mode of production is the most productive mode' (1861–63, I, pp. 270 and 199).[2] It is not surprising therefore, that should he have considered Smith an 'original thinker' (1885, p. 394) – 'the Luther of political economy' – and named him as 'the best representative of classical political economy' (1867, p. 174n), and said that it was with Adam Smith that political economy 'reached a certain stage of development and . . . assumed well-established forms' (1861–63, III, p. 501).

8.2.1 Marx's criticism of Smith

In reporting Marx's identification of Smith as a surplus theorist I have omitted to mention his criticisms. In order to assess to what extent, and *in what way*, Marx qualified this identification his criticism of Smith's work must be examined. Since these criticisms are scattered through the *Economic and Philosophical Manuscripts* (1844), the *Grundrisse* (1857–58), *A Contribution to the Critique of Political Economy* (1859), the three parts of *Theories of Surplus Value* (1861–63) and the three volumes of *Capital* (1867, 1885, and 1894) it is helpful to consider them under three headings: first, those criticisms which were concerned with Smith's rejection of the labour theory of value; second, Marx's comments on Smith's use of a labour commanded measure of value; and third, his criticisms of Smith's famous 'resolution' of prices into wages, profits and rent (these latter criticisms can in turn be subdivided – as will be seen below).

It will be shown that these seemingly different criticisms in fact boil down to one central point: Smith's failure to provide a theory of the rate of profit. For Marx, this meant that Smith had failed to develop his surplus *view* of distribution into a logically sound *theory* of value and distribution. Despite various inaccuracies in Marx's account of Smith's work, and consequently some unjustified criticism, this fundamental point was correct.

8.3   THE LABOUR THEORY OF VALUE

Marx considered that the labour theory of value provided the possibility , indeed the only possibility, of a solution to the problem of linking the surplus theory of distribution to a correct theory of relative prices (Garegnani, 1984; Eatwell, 1974). It was from that perspective that he examined the work of Smith and Ricardo. His most prominent criticism of Smith was that he initially held, but then abandoned, a labour theory of value. In this section this criticism of Smith is examined and evaluated. It turns out that although Marx's interpretation of Smith was inaccurate on a number of points, the purpose of his criticisms of Smith can be identified and has to be judged to have been correct.

Early in his chapter on 'Adam Smith', in Part I of *Theories of Surplus Value*, Marx said that in his *Contribution to the Critique of Political Economy* (1859), he had already shown how Adam Smith:

> sometimes confuses, and at other times substitutes, the determination of the value of *commodities* by the quantity of labour required for their production, with its determination by the quantity of living labour with which commodities can be bought. (1861–63, I, p. 70; see also 1859, p. 59)

These statements by Marx would seem to have done much to establish the view that Smith confused labour embodied and labour commanded (Schumpeter, 1954; Blaug, 1978; Douglas, 1928).

In evaluating the accuracy of Marx's statement little attempt is usually made by scholars to identify to what he was referring when he said that Smith did, at least intermittently, determine value by labour time. However, there is much to be gained from exploring Marx's argument in some detail. An important and recurring theme in his account of Smith's work was the view:

> that this vacillation and the jumbling up of completely heterogeneous determinants of value do not affect Smith's investigations into the nature and origin of surplus-value, because in fact, without even being aware of it, whenever he examines this question, he keeps firmly to the correct determination of the exchange-value of commodities – that is, its determination by the quantity of labour or the labour time expended on them. (1861–63, I, p. 71; see also pp. 74–5; 79–80; 85, 96–7).

In what sense did Smith 'keep firmly' to the correct determination of value? In explaining this Marx cited Smith's statement that the value which the workmen add to the materials resolves itself into two parts, one of which pays their wages, the other the profits of their employer (1861–63, I, p. 79). This implies, said Marx, that 'the value, that is, the quantity of labour which the workmen add to the materials, falls . . . into two parts'; and he considered that Smith had hereby 'himself refuted' the idea that the existence of capitalist production 'invalidates the law' that commodities exchange in proportion to the labour-time materialised in them (1861–63, I, pp. 79–80). Later Marx said that:

> In yet another passage Adam Smith sums up his view on the whole question, making it all the more clear how far he is from even attempting in any way to prove that the value added by the labourer to the product . . . is no longer determined by the labour-time contained in the product, because the labourer does not himself appropriate this value in full, but has to share it – the value or the product – with the capitalist and the landowner. (1861–63, I, p. 84; see also p. 80 and II, p. 232)

The passage in question is that in which Smith said that rent and profit are 'deductions from the produce of labour', and that the master 'shares in the produce of their labour, or in the value which it adds to the materials'. Marx stressed that the deductions are from 'the workman's product or the *value* of his product, *which is equal to the quantity of labour* added by him to the material' (1861–63, I, p. 85, emphasis added; and see p. 82).

It is clear, therefore, that when Marx said that Smith, in analysing surplus value in general, 'keeps consistently to the correct determination of value', he had in mind Smith's idea that the value-added by the labourer is divided between wages and profits.[3] It is clear also that Marx took Smith to have used the word 'value' in the same sense that he himself always used it – to denote of a quantity of *labour time*. In interpreting these statements by Smith as adherence to a labour theory of value, or as refutation of his idea that once capitalism prevails commodities no longer exchange in proportion to labour embodied (*WN*, I.vi.7), Marx was surely stretching a point. For, Smith's habit of tracing wages and profits (the value added) to the labour applied by the workmen was not really equivalent to the determination of value by labour time – though it does seem to indicate that, in some imprecise way, he considered labour the *source* of value.[4]

Marx backed up this reading of Smith by arguing that Smith's analysis of changes in value due to *changes* in methods of production was based on a labour theory of value:

> Many examples can be given to show how often in the course of his work, when he is explaining actual facts, Smith treats the quantity of labour contained in the product as value and determining value.

Some of these are quoted by Ricardo. His whole doctrine of the influence of the division of labour and improved machinery on the price of commodities is based on it. (1861–63, I, p. 71, and see p. 96)

Marx cited several passages from Smith in defence of this view (1861–63, II, pp. 226, 371). It has been shown, in Chapter 6 above, that although Smith unequivocally put forward the view that prices are determined by methods of production, and that changes in value are in general attributable to technical changes, these views should not be seen as evidence of adherence to a labour theory of value. Consequently, these passages cited by Marx fail to provide backing for his view that Smith's treatment of surplus was based on the determination of value by labour time.

In fact, it should be noted that Marx himself strongly qualified the view that Smith had a labour theory of value. Three examples of this can be cited. To begin with, on several occasions in *Theories of Surplus Value*, he acknowledged the distinction between Smith's view of surplus labour and the labour theory of value *per se*. For example, in distinguishing between Smith and Ricardo he said 'Adam Smith, however, had already stated the correct formula. Important as it was, to resolve value into labour, it was equally important to resolve surplus value into surplus-labour, and to do so in explicit terms' (1861–63, II, p. 405; see also p. 217; III, p. 239; and 1894, p. 830).

Second, apart from the argument cited above, Marx attributed a labour theory of value to Smith in the following minimal sense. He considered that Smith had mistakenly attempted to explain natural price by the addition of the natural rates of wages, profits and rents (e.g. 1861–63, I, p. 97). Smith was quite definite that the natural rate of wages was determined by the natural price of the means of subsistence. Marx considered that in determining the latter price 'in so far as he determines it at all, he comes back to the correct determination of value, namely, the labour-time required for the production of these means of subsistence' (1861–63, I, p. 96). Besides being a labour theory only in an indirect sense, this only brings us back to Smith's explanations of the changing relative value of the various agricultural commodities which constitute the wage – explanations which should not be read as evidence of a labour theory of value.

Third, Marx qualified his interpretation by saying that, in analysing surplus, Smith kept firmly to the correct determination of value 'without even being aware of it'. Furthermore, in Part II of *Theories of Surplus Value* he wrote for himself a thumbnail sketch of the contents of Book I of the *Wealth of Nations*. There he noted, with considerable justification, that in Chapters i to iv 'as in the following chapters, *value is determined in passing*' (p. 344, emphasis added).

In assessing Marx's commentary, too much significance should not be attached to any single statement by him concerning Smith's adherence to a labour theory of value (or switching between a labour 'embodied' and labour 'commanded' theory). Apart from the diversity in his comments which has been illustrated above, there are two general reasons for caution. First, most of these comments come from his unpublished notebooks. Second, Schumpeter has argued that '*criticism of Ricardo was his method in his purely theoretical work*' (1954, p. 390), and this must be extended to his criticism of Smith also. Consequently, his criticism of Smith should be read as an exercise in economic theory and not just an historical account of Smith's work (see O'Brien, 1976b, p. 66). To date, in identifying the 'Marxist interpretation of Adam Smith', too much attention has been paid to isolated statements, taken out of context, and not enough to the underlying drift of Marx's commentary (see, for an example, Blaug, 1978). Marx noted that in a purely agricultural model the creation and disposition of surplus could be analysed in physical terms – and he was quite content with such an approach. But he was aware that outside of that context 'the process is mediated through purchase and sale . . . and the analysis of value in general is necessary for it to be understood' (1861–63, I, p. 46). His anxiety was that a departure from the labour theory of value would necessarily imply a loss of the surplus view of distribution.

In particular, he was concerned that without the labour theory it would be impossible to determine the rate of profit independently of, and prior to, the determination of natural prices (1861–63, II, p. 190; III, p. 517; 1894, p. 817). This was the role which the labour theory played in his own analysis. And it was precisely a failure to explain the rate of profit that he identified as Smith's essential analytical weakness – hence the first quotation placed at head of this chapter. Marx said:

> But the task set was not to compare the levels of actual rates of profit, but to determine the *natural level of the rate of profit*. Adam Smith seeks refuge in a subsidiary investigation into the level of the rate of interest in different periods, which in no way touches upon the problem he has set himself. (1861–63, II, p. 228)

It was to this failure and not, as will be shown below, to Smith's *idea* of natural price that Marx objected. It was to this omission that he attributed Smith's subsequent failure to correctly analyse the effects of changes in wages, taxes on necessaries, or the corn export bounty, on prices. And, despite certain inaccuracies and exaggerations in his account of Smith's work, this point has to be judged to have been correct.

8.4 LABOUR COMMAND

8.4.1 Labour command as a theory of value

Consider first Marx's interpretation of Smith's labour command measure as a *theory* of value. On introducing Smith's measure Marx said 'Here value is made the measuring rod *and the basis for the explanation* of value – so we have a vicious circle'; and he said repeatedly that Smith *switched between* the labour theory of value and the 'determination of value by the value of labour' (1861–63, I, p. 71, emphasis added, and p. 76).

Strictly speaking, there is little justification for this view. As I have stressed in Chapter 5, adoption of a labour command measure of value does *not* necessarily imply adoption of a labour command *explanation* of value. Indeed, it seems likely that Sraffa had these statements by Marx at least partly in mind, when he said that it was incorrect to believe that 'to every theory of value there corresponds an appropriate "invariable standard" ' and , in particular, 'there would not seem to be such a relation between the theory that wages determine prices and the "labour commanded standard" ' (Sraffa, 1951, p. xli).

It has to be said, in Marx's defence, that what concerned him was the idea that a rise in wages could raise all prices. It was shown in Chapter 5 that this idea was, and indeed still is, widely attributed to Smith. Indeed, Marx considered that this idea 'corresponds to *Adam Smith's second explanation of value*, according to which it is equal to the quantity of labour a commodity can purchase' (1861–63, II, p. 200, emphasis added). Again, strictly speaking, this was not an accurate account of Smith's work.

What was true was that Smith quite failed to provide a satisfactory solution to the problem of relating wages to prices. And his treatment of value (based on the labour command measure) was especially ill-equipped to deal with one question in particular: the effects of changes in wages (due to taxes or the corn export bounty) on prices and profits (see Sections 6.4 and 6.5 above). It was this incorrect analysis of the role of wages in the determination of price that preoccupied Marx in his criticism of, what he took to be, Smith's determination of value by wages (1861–63, II, p. 226; 1857, p. 326). This is made abundantly clear when Marx said:

> the fact that he had also made the value of labour, or the extent to which a commodity (or money) can purchase labour, the *measure of value*, has a disturbing effect on Smith's argument when he comes to the *theory* of prices, shows the influence of competition on the rate of profit, etc.; it deprives his work of all unity, and even *excludes a number of essential questions from his inquiry.* (1861–63, I, p. 74, emphasis added; see also p. 97)

This insightful comment shows that Marx was clearly aware that his use of a labour command measure of value was the *proximate* cause of Smith's failure to analyse the effects of wage changes on prices. His comments on this aspect of Smith's work confirm my central hypothesis concerning his criticisms of Smith – that fundamentally they were all concerned with Smith's failure to provide a theory of the rate of profit.

8.4.2 Labour command as a measure of value

What of Marx's understanding of the rationale behind Smith's *measure* of value itself? Here two things are of note. First, there is clear evidence that Marx did not fully grasp the assumptions upon which Smith's measure was predicated; in particular, he was not aware of the consistency with which Smith adhered to the assumption that corn would require a constant quantity of labour for its production (1861–63, II, p. 370). He repeatedly argued that in adopting a labour command measure Smith was illegitimately claiming invariance 'for this *changing* value of labour itself' (1861–63, I, p. 77). For example, he said:

> Yes, says Adam Smith: However much the value of the quarter of corn, determined by labour-time, may change, the worker must always pay (sacrifice) the same quantity of labour in order to buy it . . . The value of the corn too changes only in so far as we are considering the labour required for its production. If, on the other hand, we examine the quantity of labour against which it exchanges,

which it sets into motion, its value does not change. And that is precisely why the quantity of labour, against which a quarter of corn is exchanged, is the *standard measure of value* (1861–63, II, p. 402).[5]

The invariance of the given corn wage was, indeed, *part* of the rationale of Smith's measure; however, another part, which was clearly not perceived by Marx in this and similar passages, was the assumption that the labour embodied in the corn wage was roughly constant.[6] In addition, Marx held the somewhat surprising view that 'Smith never used' his labour command measure of value 'when he was really analysing his subject matter' (1861–63, III, p. 14; see also II, pp. 402–3).

The second thing that can be said about Marx's comments on Smith's measure of value is that, notwithstanding the above point, there is some evidence that Marx at least *sensed* the true nature of Smith's measure. This evidence is contained in Marx's survey of Smith's chapter on rent (Book I, Ch. xi) – the chapter in which Smith actually *used* his measure to analyse the changing relative value of various agricultural and manufactured commodities. There Marx quoted at length the passage in which Smith said that in the process of economic development the production of corn would 'require nearly equal quantities of labour'. Marx's primary purpose in doing this was to show 'the peculiar manner in which Adam Smith mixes up the measure of value by the quantity of labour with the price of labour or the quantity of labour which a commodity can command' – the meaning of which alleged mix up will be revealed presently. But he added, significantly, that this passage 'also shows *how it has come about that at times he elevates corn to the measure of value*' (1861–63, II, p. 366, emphasis added).

In explaining how Smith 'mixes up' labour command and labour embodied Marx showed further insight into Smith's measure. Recall that Smith considered that several agricultural commodities, other than corn, would become dearer in the process of economic development, and he typically expressed this as follow: 'As it cost a greater quantity of labour and subsistence to bring them to market, so when they are brought thither, they represent or are equivalent to a greater quantity' (*WN*, I.xi. 1.13). Marx's comment on this was that:

Here it is once more evident, how Smith is only able to use value as determined by the quantity of labour it [value] can buy, in so far as he confuses it with value as determined by the quantity of labour required for the production of the commodities. (1861–63, II, p. 369)

Once allowance is made for the inaccuracies in Marx's interpretation which have been outlined above, it should be clear that here he had sensed the exact nature of Smith's measure of value: Smith could only use a labour commanded measure (Marx mistakenly refers to 'determination' of value) *of changes in relative value* due to changes in methods of production, in as much as these changes in labour commanded were roughly proportional to changes in labour embodied. Although he mistakenly attributed this proportionality to confusion on Smith's part, it can nevertheless be said that Marx came nearer than any other major economist to identifying Smith's particular train of thought.

8.5 THE RESOLUTION OF PRICE INTO WAGES, PROFITS AND RENT

Next I consider a number of criticisms which Marx made of Smith's idea that the price or exchangeable value of every commodity resolves itself into wages, profits and rents. A number of distinct but related points can be identified in Marx's many comments on this 'incredible blunder in analyis, which pervades all political economy since Adam Smith' (1894, p. 836). These will be examined in turn. This examination yields a vantage point from which it can be seen, once again, that Marx was primarily concerned with a particular theoretical limitation of Smith's work – his failure to embed the *content* of his surplus theory of distribution in his account of natural price.[7]

8.5.1 The 'inner connection' between wages and profits

Marx's primary objection to the resolution of price into revenues was that in the process of doing this Smith effectively *reversed* the direction of causation between value and the revenues into which it is divided, and thereby lost sight of the central implication that the surplus view of distribution has for the theory of price. Commenting on Smith's statement that 'wages, profit and rent, are the three original sources of all revenue, as well as of all exchangeable value' (*WN*, I.vi.17) he said:

> Adam Smith . . . first correctly interprets value and the relation existing between profit, wages, etc., as component parts of this value, and then he proceeds the other way round, regards the prices of wages, profit and rent as antecedent factors and seeks to determine

them independently, in order then to compose the *price of the commodity* out of them. The meaning of this change of approach is that first he grasps the problem in its *inner relationship*, and then in the reverse form, *as it appears in competition*. (1861–63, II, p. 106)

This idea, that the resolution of price into revenues was an occasion of error, was one to which Marx returned again and again.[8]

The 'inner connection' to which he referred is the inverse relationship between wages and profits (1861–63, III, p. 503; see also II, pp. 217, 165). Marx considered that in Chapter vi of Book I of the *Wealth of Nations* 'the resolution of value into wages, profit and rent [to which he had no objection, as will be shown below] is still dominant', and that 'it is only in Chapter vii, on natural and market price, that the compounding of the price from their constituent elements wins the upper hand' (1861–63, II, p. 346, emphasis added). The danger, in his view, was that with such an approach to price 'the vulgar conception . . . that wages arise from labour, but profit and rent – independently of the labour of the worker – arise out of capital and land as separate sources . . . evidently creeps into Adam Smith's writing . . .' (1861–63, II, p. 347)

These two conceptions of distribution and its relation to value are so different that it might be inferred that Marx considered Smith to have expounded an approach to distribution which was actually opposed to his own approach. However, on closer examination it seems that no such inference is warranted. It will be shown here that Marx's criticism of Smith's 'adding up' of wages, profits and rents, was in fact a criticism of Smith's failure to present a clear theory of the *rate of profit* (and of rent), and this reflected Smith's limited success in the difficult task of formulating his surplus view of distribution as a coherent theory of profit. Consequently, Marx's trenchant criticism of Smith's treatment of natural price is quite consistent with his view of him as an important contributor to the development of surplus theory. In order to appreciate this it is necessary to distinguish between the several arguments presented by Marx.

It has been stated above that his primary objection to Smith's 'resolution' was the danger of *reversing* the direction of causation and so losing the implications of the surplus view. When Marx said that Smith had sought to determine wages, profits and rent 'independently' he in fact meant this in two slightly different senses. On several occasions he said that Smith had attempted to determine the natural rates of wages, profits and rent 'independently of the *value* of the commodity' (1861–63, II, pp. 235, 347); in other places he said he had tried to determine these revenues 'independently *of one another*' (e.g. 1885, p. 387). I will consider each of these in turn.

It is easy to show that the first of these statements refers to Smith's theory of profit and price, and in no way places Smith in a different stream of fundamental theory than Marx. Summing up his section on 'Adam Smith's Theory of the "Natural Rate" of Wages, Profit and Rent' Marx said that he 'tries to establish these separately and independently of the *value* of the commodity – rather as elements of the natural price' (1861–63, II, p. 235). By 'value' Marx meant, of course, *labour embodied*. The comment reflects his view that the rates of wages and profits are themselves *price* phenomena and the determination of one of them (and hence of prices) required reference to some data outside the price domain. His objection to the idea of 'revenues as the source of commodity value instead of the commodity value being the source of revenue' was always based on the fact that such a view provides no guide to 'how to determine the value of each of these revenues'. And he considered that 'here Adam Smith has but empty phrases to offer' (1885, p. 387). It was this failure concerning the determination of distribution, and hence of price, that made Smith's correct *description* of natural price and its component parts seem like an 'adding-up' proposition.

The second charge, that in Smith's work 'these revenues are determined independently of *one another*' (1885, p. 387, emphasis added) is potentially much more serious, for it is the basis of the view that 'the vulgar conception . . . that wages arise from labour, but profit and rent . . . arise out of capital and land as separate sources . . . evidently creeps into Smith's writing' (1861–63, II, p. 347). Before evaluating the validity of this criticism it is important to identify exactly what Marx's view was. First, it should be noted that, once again, he considered that Smith vacillated between the correct and incorrect positions: first *dividing* price into wages, profit and rent, and then '*compounding*' it out of these revenues (1861–63, II, p. 347; III, p. 515). Second, and most important, despite holding this view Marx did *not* consider that Smith had *independent theories of wages, profits and rent*. In other words he did not consider that the 'adding-up' of revenues was a *theoretically formulated* position of Smith's.[9]

Marx's reading of Smith's theory of profit, wages and rent

This can be seen by briefly examining Marx's views on Smith's explanation of the rates of profit, rent and wages. On his natural rate of profit Marx felt that 'he does not tell us at all what it is or how it is determined although we are supposed to determine the natural price of the commodity by means of this natural rate of profit' (1861–63, II, p. 229). Recall his view that rather than determine the *natural level* of the rate of profit, 'Adam Smith, seeks refuge in a subsidiary investigation into the level of interest in different periods' (1861–63, II, p.228, italics in original). And, elsewhere he said emphatically that 'he has no immanent law to determine *average profit* or its amount' (1861–63, III, p. 69, italics in original).

What of Smith's idea that the rate of profit is reduced by intensification of competition? In interpreting this idea Marx paid attention to various strands of Smith's argument and the different contexts in which they were used. He noted, of course, that Smith's explanation of the high rate of profit in new colonies was 'one of the foundations of the Ricardian explanation of why profits fall' (1861–63, II, p. 228; and see Section 6.2.1 above). In many other instances, when confronted with elements of Smith's argument, he did *not* consider Smith's view that competition lowers profits to be his *theory* of the *natural* rate. Rather, he frequently viewed this idea as referring to the *gravitation* of profits from an 'arbitrary', 'excess', or non competitive level *to their natural rate*.

For example, he believed that Ricardo was wrong to assert, in criticism of Smith, that 'no overproduction in one country is possible', *no* overabundance of capital is possible, and *no* international movement of capital could alter the natural rate of profit (1861–63, II, pp. 468, 496 and 436). In another instance he focused on a different part of Smith's argument: against 'the Ricardians [who] insist that profits can only fall . . . because necessaries rise in price', he stated that 'Ricardo himself admits that profits can also fall when capitals increase faster than population, when the competition of capitals causes wages to rise. *This corresponds to Adam Smith's theory*' (Marx, 1861–63, III, p. 106, emphasis added).[10]

If Marx seems here to have let Smith off the hook, concerning the effect of competition on profits, it should be noted that on occasion he did acknowledge that Smith's argument – elements of which were valid if applied in the correct sphere – had, by design or default, served as his *explanation* of the *natural* rate of profit. For example, while criticising

Ricardo on crises he noted that 'when Adam Smith explains the fall in the rate of profit from an overabundance of capital, an accumulation of capital, he is speaking of a *permanent* effect and this is wrong' (Marx, 1861–63, II, p. 497n). Nevertheless, on viewing his account as a whole the definite impression is created that, in criticising Smith's treatment of profit, Marx focused less on Smith's argument concerning competition, than of the fact that he had *no theory* of average profit – and focused less on either of these than on the *result* that in the *Wealth of Nations* natural price 'is supposed to be calculated and discovered by adding together the natural prices of wages, profit, and rent' (Marx 1861–63, I, p. 97). Possible reasons for this will be suggested presently.

Turning to Smith's ideas on rent, it is clear that Marx did not consider him to have presented a coherent theory of the rental rate and, in particular, that he did not believe that Smith attempted to explain rent independently of wages and profits (1861–63, II, p. 358). In his view, when explaining rent, Smith 'forgot altogether that it is a question of *price*, and derives rent from the ratio between the amount of *food* yielded by agriculture and the amount of *food* consumed by the agricultural worker', thus reverting to an essentially physiocratic outlook (1861–63, II, pp. 55–8).

Finally, Marx did not consider that Smith had produced a clear theory of the *money* wage rate. He was unequivocal that the 'basis from which he determines the natural rate of wages is the value of labour-power itself, the *necessary* wage', but asks: 'how does he propose to determine the value of the necessary means of subsistence – and therefore of commodities in general?' (1861–63, II, pp. 222–3). Smith's theory was unable to determine 'the *natural price* of labour' and so resulted in a 'vicious circle'.[11] Again, Marx considered that Smith had investigated the *deviations* around the natural rate without determining that rate itself. Finally, however, it is perfectly clear that Marx did not consider Smith to have presented a theory in which the wage was unconnected to the rate of profit. Indeed, his very criticism was that Smith, by failing to investigate the value of the commodity, had failed to disentangle the simultaneous influences of wages, profits and the rate of accumulation on one another (1861–63, II, p. 223).

Summary and assessment

It is clear, therefore, that when Marx said that in parts of Smith's work natural price 'is supposed to be calculated and discovered by adding together the natural prices of wages, profit and rent' he did not, in fact, mean that Smith had actually produced, or even attempted to produce, independent theories of each of these rates (1861–63, II, p. 97).

At one point Marx does seem to have implied that the invalid *determination* of price by the natural rates of wages, profits and rents, was antecedent, in Smith's thought, to the, correct, idea that price could be *resolved* entirely into wages, profit and rent. He said that Smith may have resolved price in this manner in order to *avoid* having to *determine value* independently of wages, profits and rents (1861–63, II, p. 219).[12] Here Marx would seem to be using Smith's formulation rhetorically, in order to highlight the need to determine the size or value of total product prior to the analysis of distribution.

In the work of both Marx himself, and of Ricardo, it would seem that recognition of this need to determine the *value* of the total product (and of the means of production) prior to analysis of distribution only arose *once* a formal attempt to determine the rate of profit was made (see Sraffa, 1951, and Garegnani, 1984). But one of the central findings of this study is that Smith does not seem to have posed the question of the rate of profit in this way – as the ratio of aggregate profits to aggregate capital advanced. It was *this*, rather than the resolution of price into wages, profits and rent, which set the limits to his theory of value and distribution.

Marx's general view was that the idea of resolving price into wages, profit and rent was not constructed by Smith in order to buttress a developed 'adding-up' *theory*, but rather arose from his failure concerning the rate of profit, and was compounded by his observations of business behaviour.[13] The underlying concern in Marx's criticism of Smith's resolution is now clear; he feared that such a resolution, without a theory of the rate of profit, could obscure the central implication that the surplus view of distribution has for the price system – namely, the inverse relation between wages and profits. Smith's error, therefore, was his failure to develop the surplus view into a theory of profit, not an abandonment of that view, nor an adoption of an opposed one.

It remains only to comment briefly on Marx's view that, quite apart from providing no determinate theory of the rate of profit, Smith did, in fact, see price as arrived at by the 'adding together' of wages, profits and rents. It would seem that Marx based this view on two pieces of evidence from the *Wealth of Nations*: first, and very substantially, on a single statement by Smith, that 'wages, profit and rent, are the three original sources of all revenue as well as of all exchangeable value' (*WN*, I.vi.17; see Marx, 1861–63, I, p. 93; II, pp. 217, 347; 1885, p. 377).

Second, Marx's view was based on Smith's argument, in Chapter vii of Book I, that in the gravitation of price to its natural level not only profits, but also wages and rents, play a role (1861–63, II, p. 222).

While this 'adding up' view, as delineated above, contains an element of truth, a number of points should be noted. It was indicated in Section 6.1.3 that in making the first of these statements Smith would seem to have been concerned primarily to distinguish *original* and *derivative* revenues. In addition, he seems to have been somewhat unhappy with the statement that profits and rents were 'sources of value'. Marx's tendency to concentrate his attack on Smith's resolution of price into wages, profits and rent, and on the adding-up of these components, while at the same time being less critical than he might have been of Smith's view that competition lowers profits, may well reflect some general features of his own approach. At all times, Marx stressed the necessity of determining value *prior* to considering distribution; this was the surest guarantee against the 'reversal' into which Smith's resolution of price led him, and against the associated loss of the central implication of the surplus view of distribution. In his own work the labour theory of value provided that prior determination of the value of commodities. Given that Marx considered unequivocally that Smith had all the *other* elements of the surplus approach, he traced Smith's overall failure directly to that loss of the prior determination of value. And, of course, this view of *why* Smith's theory failed would have been greatly re-inforced in Marx's mind, by his belief that Smith did, in fact, have a labour theory of value – initially, and at various points throughout the *Wealth of Nations*. Consequently, Marx focused on the rejection of the labour theory of value and on the resolution of price – especially where statements of that resolution seemed to imply that value was composed by the adding-up of wages, profits and rents. Compared to that fundamental error at the deepest level of analysis – especially having started with the correct theory – Marx would seem to have considered Smith's error concerning competition and profits as secondary – and anyway as an application to the *natural* rate of profit of an argument which has validity, but only for local, temporary or arbitrary profits.

The perspective afforded by Sraffa's theoretical and historical work, when combined with the study of *Smith's* text in Part I of this essay, lead me to a slightly different interpretation of how and why Smith's surplus theory of distribution went no further than it did. It confirms Marx's general point that his explanation of price foundered for the lack of theory of the rate of profit. But it casts doubt on his view that the *cause* of that was Smith's loss of faith in the labour theory of value. To begin with, there is little evidence that Smith ever had a labour theory of value. But, more importantly, he did not consistently relate the rate of profit to the ratio of aggregate profits to aggregate capital (and there is considerable evidence that it was the formulation of the problem in this way which later prompted Ricardo to adopt a labour theory). The implication of these two points is that Smith's views concerning profits and competition may well have had more to do with his not having consistently developed a surplus theory of the rate of profit than Marx thought.

8.5.2 Smith's treatment of net and gross produce

In some of his criticisms of Smith's resolution of price into wages, profit and rent, Marx was concerned with the question of how to define net and gross produce and revenue – definitions which are fundamental in any surplus theory.

This question came up in this context because Marx believed that Smith had resolved price into wages, profit and rent *paid out in the current year*. Recall that Smith said that *just as* that price of any individual commodity resolves itself, 'either immediately or ultimately', into wages, profits and rent '*so* that of all the commodities which compose the whole *annual* produce . . . of every country . . . must resolve itself into the same three parts, and be parcelled out among the different inhabitants of the country' (*WN*, I.vi.17, emphasis added; see also *WN*, II.ii.2 and *WN*, I.xi. p. 7). When he combined this with Smith's famous statement that 'what is annually saved is as regularly consumed as what is annually spent, and nearly in the same time too' (*WN*, II.iii.18), Marx felt sure that, for Smith, the price of the annual produce resolves itself *immediately* (or, at least within the year) into revenues (1861–63, I, p. 99). It was noted in Section 6.1.3 above that this view has been very widely accepted; however, it was also shown that there is really no compelling evidence in favour of this view. Here, however, we can proceed by granting Marx his premise – and, in fact, some of his criticisms of Smith are independent of it.

This resolution had, in Marx's view, several damaging consequences on Smith's work and, through him, on subsequent political economy. First, it rendered virtually impossible a clear analysis of gross and net product and revenue, and consequently hampered rather than helped the development of an analytically clear surplus theory of the economy (1861–63, I, pp. 97–103).[14] In addition, Marx had identified the fact that Smith's definitions of net and gross product were certainly unclear and seem to contain contradictions. Marx was absolutely correct on the first point; we saw in Chapter 3 above that the resolution of price (almost regardless of whether it is conceived as being 'ultimately' or 'immediately' valid), whatever other merits it may have, was a bad starting point for defining the 'necessary inputs' and 'surplus' of the economic system, since it made all value appear as added value. And Marx, who definitely considered that Smith had equated 'the value of the annual *product* to the newly created annual value' (1885, p. 381), explicitly attributed Smith's confused definitions of net and gross produce and revenue to his resolution of price into revenues:

> Adam's twisting and turnings, his contradictions and wanderings from that point, prove that, once he had made wages, profit and rent the constituent component parts of . . . the total price of the product, he had got himself stuck in the mud and had to get stuck. (1861–63, I, p. 103)

It was demonstrated in Chapter 3 that Smith reached a clear definition of surplus when, in Chapter iii of Book II, he *suspended* the resolution of price into wages, profit and rent. Likewise, Marx considered that Smith 'flees from his own theory by means of a play upon words, the distinction between "gross and net revenue"' (1885, p. 367) – a reference to Smith's Chapter ii, of Book II which, it was argued in Chapter 3 of this essay, presented a much less satisfactory account of net and gross produce and revenue.

The second damaging consequences of the resolution of the whole annual produce into current revenues was that it implied, by logical necessity, that all accumulation was 'nothing more than the consumption of the surplus product by productive workers' or, in other words, that all capital was advanced as *wages* (1867, p. 763; 1861–63, II, pp. 463–4; 1995, pp. 231, 376–80). Likewise, it implied that the entire annual product can be consumed (1861–63, I, pp. 103 and 251; 1894, p. 841).

However, in these, as in so many of his criticisms of Smith, Marx later qualified his argument somewhat. In particular, he would seem to have acknowledged that, in the case of Smith, if not of subsequent political economy, these positions may not have resulted from a *firmly held doctrine* but, rather, may have arisen from a combination of careless aggregation and particular beliefs about the actual economy of his day. For example, when dealing with Smith's account of productive labour and accumulation, he said that Smith *'falls into the error* of identifying the size of the productive capital with the size of *that part of it* which is destined to provide *subsistence for productive labour'* and added, significantly, 'But in fact large-scale industry, as he knew it, was as yet only in its beginnings' (1861–63, I, p. 262; see also 1885, p. 203). And recall that Smith did say that 'almost the whole capital of every country is annually distributed among the inferior ranks of people, as the wages of productive labour' (*WN*, V.ii.k.43).

Likewise, he acknowledged that Smith 'opposed the necessary conclusion of his resolution of the . . . social annual product into . . . mere revenue – the conclusion that in this event the entire annual product might be consumed'.[15]

Furthermore, Marx considered that in the course of his unsatisfactory treatment of net and gross revenue Smith had raised, but not solved, an important and difficult question (1861–63, I, p. 98). Limitations of space make a thorough examination of this issue impossible. Marx posed the question as follows: 'How can an annually produced value, which only = wages + profit + rent, buy a product the value of which = (wages + profit + rent) + C?' (1894, p. 835). He struggled at length with this question in Part I of *Theories of Surplus Value* only to defer further consideration of it to Volume II of *Capital*.[16] There, under the heading 'The Reproduction and Circulation of the Aggregate Social Capital', he reviewed 'Former presentations of the subject', devoting greatest attention to Adam Smith, and outlined his own solution in terms of simple reproduction. His own solution depended crucially on the observation that 'the annual product of society consists of two departments; one of them comprises means of production; the other the articles of consumption' (1885, p. 372; see also pp. 355–492). He considered that Smith had, in fact, 'almost hit the nail on the head' (1885, p. 373) but he believed that he was, once again, led astray by the 'absurd dogma . . . that in the final analysis the value of commodities resolves itself completely into income, into wages, profit and rent' (1894, p. 841)

8.5.3 Marx's acceptance of Smith's idea of natural price

In view of the significance attached by Dobb to the relation between price and the elements of production cost in assessing the degree of difference between Smith and subsequent surplus theorists, it was indicated in the previous chapter that Ricardo did not, in fact, reject Smith's view in its entirety (see Section 7.3 above). Likewise, it can be shown that Marx did not fundamentally reject Smith's view of how the elements of production cost relate to natural price.

Notwithstanding the theoretical criticisms reviewed above, Marx made it clear that he did not reject Smith's identification of the component parts of price *per se*. In Marx's view it was wholly incorrect to say that wages, profit or rent are component parts of *value*. Recall that by 'value' Marx meant the labour embodied in a commodity. 'On the other hand, when referring to the *natural price* or *cost price*, Smith can speak of its component parts as given preconditions'. Marx added 'But by confusing natural price with value, he carries over this to the value of the commodity' (1861–63, II, p. 318). This simply confirms that Marx's concern in his criticisms of Smith was with the explanation of distribution. Of course, it is now known that, strictly speaking, Marx was incorrect to say that when referring to natural price one can take its component parts 'as given preconditions' (Sraffa, 1960). Marx's view reflects his belief that, by means of the labour theory of value, the rate of profit could be fully determined prior to calculation of natural prices.

In fact on one occasion Marx went a little further in his acceptance of Smith's component parts of price. In the final chapter of *Theories of Surplus Value*, Part III, entitled 'Revenue and Its Sources: Vulgar Political Economy', he stressed that the 'magnitude of *value* is not determined by the addition or combination of given factors'. On the contrary, 'one and the same *magnitude of value*, a given *amount of value*, is broken down into wages, profit and rent, and according to different circumstances it is distributed between these three categories in very different ways' (Marx, 1861–63, III, p. 517, emphasis in original). However, Marx then cited an hypothetical set of circumstances in which there are no changes in methods of production or, at least, changes in productivity (and consequently in values) are such as to leave unchanged 'the distribution of the value of commodities amongst the different factors of production' (ibid.). 'In that case', said Marx:

> although *it would not be theoretically accurate* to say that the different parts of value *determine* the value or price of the whole (output), it would be *useful and correct* to say that they *constitute* it insofar as one understands by constituting the formation of the whole by adding up the parts. The value would be divided at a steady and constant ratio into (pre-existing) value and surplus-value, and the (newly created) value would be resolved at a constant rate into

wages and profit . . . It can therefore be said that P – the price of the commodity – is divided into wages, profit (interest) and rent, and, on the other hand, wages, profit (interest) and rent are the constituents of the value or rather of the price. (1861–63, III, pp. 517–8, emphasis added)

Of course, Marx added immediately that 'this uniformity or similarity of production . . . does not exist'. Recall, however, that in examining Smith's measure of value I suggested that Smith's system would seem to have been constructed on assumptions somewhat like those hypothesised by Marx.[17] Although this certainly absolves Smith from any accusation that his account of value was fundamentally confused or absurd (see the discussion of Dobb's interpretation in Chapter 10 below) it does not absolve him from Marx's central criticism concerning the rate of profit, nor warrant the conclusion that his adding up was a theoretically adequate approach to value and distribution. The above passage from Marx is cited merely to demonstrate that it was not Smith's whole 'vision' of the price formation process that Marx rejected, but merely his failure to identify the analytical requirements for the formulation of that vision in a theory of value and distribution. The full relevance of my demonstration of this will become clear when Dobb's interpretation of Smith is examined in Chapter 10.

8.6 ASSESSMENT

It has been the contention of this chapter that in all his criticisms of Smith's work Marx was concerned about the surplus theory of distribution and, in particular, with Smith's failure to embed his surplus view of distribution in his treatment of natural price – in other words, his failure to develop a theory of the rate of profit.[18] This line of criticism was, of course, only relevant given Marx's definite identification of Smith as a surplus theorist in the first place. That identification was documented in Section 2 of this chapter, and there seems little that could be disputed in this part of Marx's account.

The idea that Smith held a labour theory of value has been widely attributed to Marx. Marx did, indeed, hold this view but, as was shown in Section 8.3, in a very particular sense. Nevertheless, despite his qualifications, he was incorrect in identifying a labour theory of value in Smith's work. Too much can be made of this inaccuracy, especially as the theoretical point at issue was not the proportionality of prices to labour quantities but the theory of profit. However, having said that, it has to be noted that this inaccuracy has the following important implication for Marx's general account of Smith' work: if he was inaccurate in identifying a labour theory of value in Smith, then it follows that he was also inaccurate in identifying an *abandonment* of the labour theory (or, more pertinently, a *switching* between a labour theory and some other view).

Neither was there much justification for Marx's view that Smith adopted a labour command explanation of value. But, again it is clear that Marx's concern was the implication that Smith's measure of value had for his analysis of the effects of wage (or tax) changes on prices – a concern that was, indeed, warranted.

On several occasions Marx said that in Smith price was 'calculated' or 'discovered' by the 'adding together' of 'independently' determined rates of wages, profits and rents – a procedure which is clearly at variance with the surplus theory of distribution. In view of this, it was judged important to ascertain precisely what Marx meant by this 'adding up' description. A detailed examination of his account reveals that Marx did not consider that Smith had developed independent theories of wages, profits and rents. Rather, in Marx's view the calculation of price by adding up wages, profits and rents was the *outcome* of his abandonment of the labour theory of value and associated failure to determine the rate of profit. Consequently, despite some evidence that Smith was unhappy with his description of profits as a 'source of value', and despite my qualification of Marx's view of *why* Smith failed to determine the rate of profit, his description of Smith's treatment as an 'adding up' would seem to have some validity.

It will be noted that in each of these cases Marx's identification of a sharp dichotomy between two conflicting elements or theories in Smith's work has been questioned – by demonstrating the inaccuracy of some of his interpretations of Smith, and by noting his own qualifications. The result is that Marx's account of Smith has to be modified somewhat.

Marx was quite correct to say that the *Wealth of Nations* contains both a surplus view of distribution and an indeterminate theory of value. But, contrary to his view, the distinction between these two aspects of Smith's work does not *coincide* with the distinction between acceptance and rejection of a labour theory of value. It is not accurate to identify Smith's surplus view with a labour theory of value, and his indeterminate theory of value with a labour command approach. Nor is his surplus approach synonymous with an analysis of labour quantities, and his loss of the implications of that surplus approach synonymous with his analysis of the component parts of price. Rather, the surplus view of distribution and the analytically indeterminate explanation of price would seem to co-exist at almost all points of Smith's work. The defininition and measurement of surplus in a many-good economy was not specified with complete clarity by him and, contrary to what Marx would seem to imply, this did not occur purely as a *result* of his problems with the theory of value. Consequently, when discussing the creation and disposition of surplus Smith frequently fell back on physiocratic conceptions (as, indeed, Marx noted on many occasions). At the same time, Smith's identification of profit as a deduction from the value added by the worker, and profit at a uniform rate as the central form which surplus took in a capitalist economy (central elements of his post-physiocratic surplus view of distribution), arose in the context of his enunciation of the *component parts of price* – notwithstanding the indeterminate nature of his theory of how these prices are determined.

What of Marx's distinction between 'esoteric' (initiated) and 'exoteric' (ordinary) parts of Smith's work? Marx considered that 'one of these conceptions fathoms the inner connection, the physiology, so to speak, of the bourgeois system, whereas the other takes the external phenomena of life . . . and merely describes, catalogues, recounts and arranges them under formal definitions' (1861–63, II, p. 165). Recall that by the 'inner connection' Marx meant the inverse relation between wages and profits (1861–63, III, p. 503). Therefore, the distinction between esoteric and exoteric refers to the presence or absence of the implications of the surplus view of distribution. It is a perfectly valid distinction, since Marx was entitled to classify each chapter, section or, indeed, sentence of Smith's as esoteric or exoteric according to whether it embodied the implications of the surplus view of distribution.

However, the implication of my modification of Marx's account is that the *boundary* between the esoteric and exoteric parts of Smith's work, was *not correctly located* by Marx. The surplus view of distribution was not confined to sections in which value is conceived to be determined by labour time. The idea of profit as an original revenue, and as having nothing to do with the 'labour of super-intendence', would seem to have been born of Smith's analysis of the component parts of price – probably even from his resolution of price into wages, profits and rent (which Marx considered as, in general, exoteric).[19] Marx's concentration on the labour theory of value was such that in his commentary the distinction between esoteric and exoteric come to be *virtually synonymous* with the distinction between labour embodied and labour commanded 'determination' of value. A close study of Smith's text has indicated that the latter distinction fails to provide a useful guide to his work. Adherence to it by writers in the Marxist tradition, as an account of Smith's work, has already led to Marx's more fundamental theoretical distinction being masked or discredited.

It is not a challenge to Marx's distinction between 'esoteric' and 'exoteric', and the theoretical point that this distinction embodied, to say that in Smith's work the line between the two cannot be drawn as sharply as Marx believed it could. The nature and extent of this criticism of Marx's interpretation can be best appreciated by considering the following important passage from Part II of *Theories of Surplus Value*. In summarising Smith's (and Ricardo's) role in the development of political economy he said:

> With Smith both these methods of approach not only merrily run alongside one another, *but also intermingle* and constantly contradict one another. With him this is justifiable . . . since his task was indeed a twofold one. On the other hand he attempted to penetrate the inner physiology of bourgeois society but on the other, he partly tried to describe its externally apparent forms of life for the first time, to show its relations as they appear outwardly and partly he had even to find a nomenclature and corresponding mental concepts for these phenomena, i.e. to reproduce them for the first time in the language and (in the) thought process. The one task interests him as much as the other and since both proceed *independently of one another*, this results in completely contradictory ways of presentation: the one expresses the intrinsic connections more or less correctly, the other, with the same justification – and *without any connection to the first method of approach* – expresses the apparent connections without any internal relation. (1861–63, II, p. 165, emphasis added)

In the light of the evaluation of Marx's account of Smith presented here it would seem that he was more accurate when he said that these two elements of Smith's work 'intermingle' than when he said that they 'proceed independently of one another' – although the latter seems to have been his general view.

Second, this passage confirms once again that Marx did not think of the 'esoteric' and 'exoteric' as two conflicting *theories* developed by Smith. They refer to different *aspects* of Smith's 'twofold task'.

However, it is possible that, in most of his commentary, Marx did not attach enough importance to Smith's job of finding a nomenclature and corresponding mental concepts for economic phenomena. It has been said that in classical political economy the problem of value presented itself as the search for a means of measuring the heterogeneous aggregates of surplus and means of production (Garegnani, 1984, p. 301; Eatwell, 1982, p. 212). But, it can surely be said that, prior to that problem being identified, there is another landmark in the development of the theory of value: that is, the point at which it is seen that the problem of value is the problem of distribution. Now, in much of his criticism of Smith's resolution, and of his exoteric elements, Marx would seem to have taken it for granted (perhaps for the purpose of analytical debate) that the problem of value and distribution, in this more basic sense, *had already been posed*, and he was, quite correctly, critical of Smith's treatment *as a proposed solution*. But we have seen that, in general, Smith did not pose the rate of profit as the ratio of aggregate profits to aggregate capital advanced. Smith's resolution was an important step in identifying that the problem of price was, in fact, the problem of distribution.[20] It is precisely in this sense that Meek described Smith's identification of the tripartite division of produce as a 'paradigm shift' in political economy, and argued that it was this which 'posed the new problem of value' (1973b, pp. viii–x). Now, in the passage quoted above, Marx would seem to have gone some way toward acknowledging that it fell to Smith, as the great post-physiocratic economist, to establish the basic elements of which value and distribution are made.

Strictly speaking, this task would probably be classed as 'exoteric' rather than 'esoteric' in Marx's scheme; but it is clearly an analytical and not just a descriptive one. The enduring part of Marx's insistence on distinguishing 'esoteric' from 'exoteric' aspects, and distinguishing these two 'tasks', relate to his continual insistence that categorisation or *description* of price phenomena cannot, in itself, be taken as theoretical *explanation* (see, for example, 1961–63, III, p. 32). This was a point which needed constant repetition and, if one is to judge from much modern commentary on Adam Smith, still does.

It is now possible to assess Bradley and Howard's assertion that Marx's view of Smith was equivalent to what I have labelled in Chapter 1 the 'two-streams proposition' – namely that Smith would be included as a theorist of 'both distinct and rival traditions in nineteenth century economic thought' – the classical and the neoclassical. The basis of Bradley and Howard's view would seem to be Marx's statement that Smith was 'the source, the starting point, of diametrically opposed conceptions' (1861–63, III, p. 20). These two conceptions were what Marx termed 'classical' and 'vulgar' political economy.

An examination of what Marx meant by 'vulgar political economy' is sufficient to show that Marx's statements cannot be equated to the 'two-stream proposition'. To begin with, Marx was quite emphatic in saying that vulgar political economy was not just a *restatement* of Smith's ideas, but was an *alteration* of them; referring specifically to its relation to *Smith's* work he said that the 'vulgar economist reads into his sources the direct opposite of what they contain' (1861–63, III, p. 504; and see also pp. 25; 32; 495; 499).

Second, add to this what has been demonstrated in Section 5.1 of this chapter, namely, that Marx did *not* consider that Smith had formulated or subscribed to an alternative theory of distribution to the surplus view.

Furthermore, Marx had a very precise idea as to the nature of vulgar political economy. In particular, he considered it as an almost inevitable adjunct to classical political economy. For example, he said that 'the more economic theory is perfected . . . the more it is confronted by its own, increasingly independent, vulgar element, enriched with material which it dreams up in its own way . . .' (1861–63, III, p. 501; see also pp. 500–9). His comments make it clear that to say that Smith or Ricardo 'offered a secure base of operations to the vulgar economists' (1867, p. 679) is not to say that they developed two different theoretical systems of explanation.[21]

It follows that the distinction between classical and vulgar economy as used by Marx was not equivalent in any way to the distinction between classical theory and marginalist theory. It is this latter distinction which features in the proposition that Smith contributed to the development of both streams of theory and, thereby, that he was, in some substantial sense, a forerunner of the neoclassical theory of value and distribution. No support for this view can be derived from Marx's comments on Smith's work.

9 Smith as 'General Equilibrium' Theorist

> Hollander's pathbreaking and critical analysis in large measure tends to confirm Boulding's observation that 'the whole of Walrasian, Marshallian and Hicksian price theory . . . is clearly implicit in Adam Smith's concept of natural price'. (Recktenwald, 1978, p. 62, quoting Boulding, 1971, p. 229)

Professor Hollander's 1973 book *The Economics of Adam Smith* is perhaps the most influential modern interpretation of Smith's work. In that book Hollander successfully challenged the idea, found in the work of Myint (1948) and Hicks (1965), that Smith's system can be adequately represented by a simple 'corn model' of capital accumulation (Hollander, 1973, p. 18).[1] He shows that Smith's concern was with the possibilites of capital accumulation in a many-good economy in which markets are widespread. But there is much more to Hollander's interpretation than this, as is demonstrated by the remarkable statement by Recktenwald, quoted above, in his survey of the bicentenary literature on the *Wealth of Nations*. Indeed, Hollander himself says that 'This work is in essence concerned with the relationship between Smith's analysis of economic development and "general equilibrium" ' (Hollander, 1973, p. 44, and see p. 20). It is this which has attracted great attention to Hollander's book and persuaded many scholars of the view stated by Jaffe that 'it is precisely in Professor Hollander's masterly treatise that we see most clearly the link between the Walrasian and Smithian theoretical systems. To reveal this link was indeed . . . Hollander's purpose, as he tells us explicitly' (1977, p. 20).

In this chapter I identify what it is in Hollander's book that has prompted striking statements of this sort, and I evaluate his interpretation of Smith. Hollander's argument is a complicated one and consequently the first section of this chapter is devoted to an explanation of the structure of the case he builds. Subsequent sections submit that case to detailed scrutiny. (All page references in this chapter are to Hollander's 1973 book *The Economics of Adam Smith*, except where indicated otherwise.)

9.1   HOLLANDER'S ARGUMENT IN OUTLINE

Hollander builds his case in two stages. The first concerns Smith's theory of value and distribution, as presented in Book I of the *Wealth of Nations*; the second concerns the analysis of practical problems found elsewhere in that text. It is argued that in Book I Smith explained value by utility and demand, and attempted to formulate a productivity theory of distribution. However, the analysis of Book I was undertaken on very special assumptions, such that many of the relationships normally associated with a general equilibrium of supply and demand do not appear in this part of Smith's text. The second stage of Hollander's case is that outside Book I Smith was not bound by these restrictive assumptions and, consequently, in his analysis of practical problems concerning agriculture, industry, trade and economic policy, we can see his analysis of the allocation of scarce resources in a general equilibrium of supply and demand. I now spell out these two elements of Hollander's case in a little more detail.

9.1.1 Value based on utility and demand

In a section entitled 'Price Determination' his central proposition is that 'Smith's formal treatment of value theory may best be appreciated if envisaged as an attempt to achieve a conception of long run *general* equilibrium' (p. 114).[2] However, Hollander concentrates on *market* rather than *natural* price. His argument is that the account of the movements of *market* price 'makes it clear that Smith *had in mind* the concept of a negatively sloped demand schedule'; and 'that a positively sloped supply curve *applicable to the market period* was similarly *envisaged* may be also demonstrated' (p. 118, emphasis added). However, in Hollander's view Smith also considered *natural* price to be determined by preferences, scarcity and demand.

On distribution, Hollander considers that there is 'much evidence to support the view that Smith was attempting to formulate a productivity theory of distribution' (p. 170).

9.1.2 Smith's less 'formal' analysis of allocation

It is fundamental to Hollander's case that Smith's 'attempt to achieve a conception of long run *general* equilibrium' can only be appreciated by going beyond the analysis of Chapter vii of Book I. A central element of his interpretation is his argument that 'Despite the overwhelming significance of the mechanism [namely, resource allocation governed by the differential pattern of factor endowments] the reader of the *Wealth of Nations will find no hint thereof in the First Book*' (p. 307, emphasis added). This is because Smith's formal analysis of general equilibrium is constrained in various respects (p. 122).

As a result, the relationships normally associated with such an analysis do not appear. The assumptions which, in Hollander's view, 'constrain' the analysis include: (i) 'constant *aggregate* amounts of each of the three factors' (p. 121), (ii) constant factor prices (p. 122), (iii) constant 'factor proportions' within each productive unit (p. 122), and (iv) 'identical' factor proportions from industry to industry (p. 122–3). The evidence for this view is examined at the start of Section 4.

However, Hollander argues that the proof that Smith's 'formal' analysis of value and distribution was, *nevertheless*, 'an attempt to achieve a conception of long run equilibrium' lies in the fact that *outside of Book I* 'Smith was . . . not bound by the strict assumptions implicit in his formal analysis' (p. 307). He shows that Smith's account of capital accumulation and technical change is replete with instances in which variation in each of the elements mentioned above occur. The inferences which Hollander draws from this 'contrast between the formal analysis and practical applications' (p. 307) are examined in Section 9.4 also.

Ultimately, this part of his case rests on a single aspect of Smith's work, and boils down to a single proposition, namely that Smith's account of the international pattern of production and trade was based on 'resource allocation governed by the differential pattern of factor endowments between economies', thus 'casting a new light upon Smith's contribution to both theoretical and applied economics' (p. 307). This proposition is examined in Section 9.5 below.

9.2   A 'SUPPLY AND DEMAND' EXPLANATION OF VALUE

9.2.1 Smith 'had in mind' demand and supply schedules

Hollander opens his case on Smith's approach to value by taking the case of *market* price. Although supply and demand are 'formally defined' by Smith as specific quantities 'the argument which follows ... makes it clear that Smith *had in mind* the concept of a negatively sloped demand schedule' (p. 118, emphasis added; for a similar view, see Stigler, 1950, p. 69).[3,4] But the argument which follows is no more than that price will rise when 'quantity brought to market' falls short of the 'effectual demand' and *visa versa* (*WN*, I.vii.8–11). This *observation* is *not* equivalent to the supply and demand *theory* of value. As Garegnani, notes, in that *theory* 'we are . . . dealing with a much stricter notion than the immediately plausible one according to which an accidental fall in the quantity supplied below its normal level is likely to be accompanied by a rise in the price' (1983, p. 309). Nor is the *observation* that, at that accidentally high price, less is purchased than at the natural price, evidence of the 'analytical reasoning' (to use Hollander's own criterion) that underlies a demand schedule (for a similar view see Myint, 1948, p. 64).[5]

Hollander proceeds to describe Smith's account of the cases where 'quantity brought to market exceeds effectual demand', and *visa versa*, as 'an attempt to explain the degree of demand [and supply] *elasticity*' (pp. 118–19) and concludes that 'Accordingly, we may say that some justification is provided both for a negatively-sloped demand curve and also for a positively-sloped supply curve – throughout their respective lengths – *relating to the market period*' (p. 120, emphasis added).[6] This is not only implausible history of economics but also implausible economics. Even Marshall, who introduced new concepts relating to the *short* period, rejected any idea of supply and demand curves relating to the *market* period. He insisted on the contrast between 'Market' and 'Normal' price, based on 'the persistence of the influences considered and the time allowed for them to work out their effects', and he stated emphatically that 'the market value as it is often called, is often more influenced by passing events and by causes whose action is fitful and short-lived, than by those which work persistently' (Marshall, 1890, pp. 289–91 and see also pp. 314–15 and Marshall, 1898).

9.2.2 The role of utility and demand

It has long been considered that an explanation of value in terms of
scarcity and utility had been developed by the early scholastic writers,
and that consequently Smith can be seen to have rejected a well-
developed tradition of analysis.[7] Hollander re-examines this literature
seeking, not particular propositions associated with developed
neoclassical theory, but 'the *reasoning* used in support of the
proposition' (p. 35, emphasis added, and see also p. 28). He concludes
that among Smith's predecessors 'the general picture is *not* of such
overwhelming emphasis upon utility and scarcity as has been
suggested' (p. 134), and that there was little 'precise analysis of the
co-ordinating, harmonising and organising function of the price
mechanism' along neoclassical lines (p. 44, see also pp. 27–51). Many
of the claims to have found supply and demand *theory* in early writers
are indeed unconvincing and Hollander's review of this question would
seem to be well founded. Of course, this rejection of the idea that Smith
departed from a well-developed supply and demand theory does
nothing, of itself, to advance Hollander's case that utility and scarcity
played a role in Smith's account of value.[8]

Hollander states the following propositions concerning Smith's use
of utility and demand in explaining value:

(i)   There is 'no convincing evidence to indicate an unconcern with
utility and demand in the *Wealth of Nations* relative to that
reported in the *Lectures*' (p. 135).
(ii) There is no evidence that Smith rejected utility as a *necessary*
condition for a commodity to have exchange value (p. 136).
(iii) Smith did, in fact, account for exchange value 'in terms of utility
and scarcity in the traditional manner' (pp. 136–7).
(iv) 'Smith made extensive use of a theory of choice' by his
'recognition of substitutability in consumption' (pp. 138–9).
(v)   'The tradition that Smith "played down" demand analysis derives
as well from almost exclusive concentration upon [Chapter vii of
Book I] which utilises the assumption that industries are
characterised by constant cost conditions' (p. 140).
(vi) 'The "explanation" of price in terms of "supply and demand" or
"relative scarcity" was not regarded as an "alternative" to that in
terms of costs' (p. 140).

Hollander's argument for these propositions will be examined in turn.

Proposition (i)

This oblique double-negative amounts to the proposition that there is as much concern with utility and demand in the *Wealth of Nations* as in the *Lectures on Jurisprudence*.[9] It is, therefore, subordinate to Hollander's positive proposition that Smith was, in some non-trivial sense, concerned with utility and demand in the *Wealth of Nations* (or the *Lectures*); see proposition (iii) below. Having said that, it should be noted that there *are* differences between Smith's treatment of value in the *Lectures* and the *Wealth of Nations*.[10]

Proposition (ii)

What Hollander has in mind here is an argument by Douglas that Smith went so far as to reject the idea that utility was a 'necessary prerequisite' for a commodity to have value (Douglas, 1928, p. 78). Hollander points out, in reply, that in Smith's statement of the paradox of value (*WN* I.vi.13) – which distinguished use-value and exchange-value – 'the term "value-in-use" must be understood in the narrow sense of biological significance and not in the economists broad sense of desirability' (p. 136).[11] As Hollander says, it follows that 'From his observation in this regard we can learn nothing of his position regarding the relationship between price and utility in the sense of desirability' (p. 136) – except, of course, that he nowhere saw fit to alert his readers to the *difference* between 'value-in-use' (which he often called 'utility') and desirability or preference, (despite using the latter concept extensively in his *explanation* of value – if we accept Hollander's account). Hollander's specific point concerning the meaning of the term 'value-in-use' in the *Wealth of Nations* would seem to be valid.[12] It is clear that judgement must be exercised in reading the modern analytical concept of 'preference' into Smith's work (see proposition (iii) and notes 13 and 14 to this chapter).

Proposition (iii)

This is, of course, the heart of the matter. What evidence does Hollander offer in support of this view? He quotes from three passages from the *Wealth of Nations*; however, none of these offer the least support for the view that Smith conceived of value to be determined by utility and scarcity, *in the sense in which Hollander means those terms*. In order to demonstrate this, there is no alternative to examining these passages, and their contexts, in detail. This is done here for the first of Hollander's quotations, and in footnotes for the remaining two.

Hollander says his proposition 'is clear, for example, from the following extract . . . which is quite unambiguous' (p. 136):

> Unless a capital was employed in manufacturing that part of the rude produce which requires a good deal of preparation before it can be fit for use and consumption, it either would never be produced, because there could be no demand for it; or if it was produced spontaneously, it would be of no value in exchange, and could add nothing to the wealth of the society. (*WN*, II.v.5)

The passage is indeed unambiguous, when placed in its context. It appears early in Book II, Chapter v, 'Of the Different Employment of Capitals'. There, Smith was simply showing that although some lines of industry make a greater contribution to national product than others, still 'Each of these four methods of employing capital is essentially necessary either to the existence or extension of the other three, or to the general conveniency of the society' (*WN*, II.v.3). For the system to function, capital must be employed in producing rude produce (II.v.4), in manufacturing (II.v.5 – the paragraph quoted by Hollander), in transportation (II.v.6), and in distribution (II.v.7). Clearly, these passages refer to the inter-relationship between the sectors of the economy (for a similar view see Campbell and Skinner, 1976, p. 31). If the observation, that if there were no manufacturing then the raw materials for manufacturing would not be produced, or, if they existed in nature, would have no value, is evidence of the explanation of value by utility, scarcity or demand, then clearly every *general* theory of the economic system *must* be a neoclassical theory. Of course, the fact of the matter is that the passage quoted by Hollander quite simply has *nothing whatsoever to do with* utility, scarcity, or demand – in the sense in which these terms are meant in supply and demand theory.

The two other passages quoted by Hollander are also unable to sustain the remarkable inferences drawn by him.[13,14] In summary, therefore, the evidence cited in order to demonstrate Smith's use of utility and scarcity *in a systematic way to determine value*, fail to do this in a convincing manner.

Proposition (iv)

The major piece of evidence cited by Hollander to demonstrate Smith's 'extensive use of a theory of *choice*' is a passage in which Smith stated that 'during the course of the present century' many food items (such as vegetables) have become 'a great deal cheaper', but soap, salt, candles, leather, and fermented liquors, have become dearer because taxes have been laid on them. 'The quantity of these, however, which the labouring poor are under any necessity of consuming is so very small, that the increase in their price does not compensate the diminution in that of so many other things' (*WN*, I.viii.35). To establish a theoretical point Hollander says:

> This observation does not refer to the small weight attached to certain items in an actual basket; it is rather a statement to the effect that consumers are in a position to substitute other goods in place of the relatively expensive items. The implications of this recognition of substitutability in consumption are of considerable importance. (Hollander, 1973, pp. 138–9, emphasis added)

However, the evidence strongly suggests that Smith meant *precisely* the small *weight* of these items in the workers' consumption and *not substitution*.[15]

But quite apart from this problem, Hollander's line of argument is not sufficient to establish the *theoretical* point he wishes to make. If Smith's 'extensive use of a theory of *choice*' is to compensate for the 'absence of a formal notion of marginal utility', then it must be shown to have played an equivalent role in the *determination* of value. The case of a high *market* price of corn in a bad year curtailing consumption (cited by Hollander as a further significant illustration of the role accorded demand by Smith, pp. 139–40) is not capable of bearing the weight of interpretation placed on it by him, since, as was stressed at the outset of this section, there is more to the supply and demand *theory* than recognition that price rises when effectual demand exceeds quantity brought to market.

Propositions (v) and (vi) of Hollander's case on the role of utility and demand are examined in Section 9.4.2 below.

9.2.3 Conclusion on utility and demand

The conclusion is unavoidable that Hollander fails to demonstrate that Smith explained value by utitilty, scarcity and demand. He has, indeed, shown that Smith's treatment may not have marked such a departure from his predecessors as has been hitherto believed. He has shown that there may be less difference between the *Lectures* and the *Wealth of Nations* than has been argued by some. And he has shown that Smith's distinction between 'value in use' and 'value in exchange' may not have been a conscious rejection of 'utility in the sense of desirability'. It is clear that none of these valuable clarifications advance in any way the case that Smith's treatment of value was based on utility and demand. Those propositions which do *positively* attribute a utility and scarcity based theory to Smith must be rejected for two reasons. First, they fail to demonstrate that Smith used utility and scarcity *in analytical roles* even remotely similar to that which they occupy in neoclassical theory. Second, the evidence cited, even for the *existence* of such concepts in Smith's work, is not compelling, when each passage is read in the context in which it occurs in the *Wealth of Nations*.

9.3 DISTRIBUTION

Hollander's approach to distribution in Smith's work is to take the so called 'marginal productivity theory' as a model. Consequently, he perceives his major task to be to demonstrate that Smith considered land and capital, and not just labour, as 'productive' (for a similar approach see Bowley, 1973a, p. 121; 1975, pp. 366–7, and West, 1978, p. 352). He proceeds, with the structure of the marginal productivity theory in mind, to label these discussions of the 'productivity' of land and capital as 'the demand for land services' and 'the demand for capital service' respectively (pp. 149 and 150). These are then combined with factor supplies, and Hollander concludes that 'there is clearly much evidence to support the view that Smith was attempting to formulate a productivity theory of distribution' (p. 170).

9.3.1 The 'productivity' of land and capital

Consider first the question of the 'productiveness' of land and capital. Hollander's view is that because of Smith's statement that 'the value which the workmen add to the materials, therefore, resolves itself in this case into two parts, of which one pays their wages, the other the profits of their employer upon the whole stock of materials and wages which he advanced', it is 'sometimes said that in Smith's view labour was the sole productive factor' (p. 148, and he cites Douglas, 1928, p. 96 as an example of this view). Hollander's aim is to show that 'the statements defining profits as "deductions from the produce of labour" do not seem to bear upon the issue of the productivity of capital' (p. 151). His method is to cite several passages in which Smith described the benefits of using capital in production and the great fertility of the land, and to conclude that 'there is nothing in these statements which denies the contribution to output of real capital goods' (p. 156).

Four comments may be made on this procedure. To begin with, the concept of 'productivity' is nowhere defined by Hollander: the nearest thing to a definition is his statement that 'the return on capital was not regarded as an "exploitation" income, for capital goods *make a net contribution to the national income*'(p. 171, my emphasis). This brings us to the second point; the exercise of showing that Smith did not deny the contribution to output of land and real capital goods would seem to be either trivial or misconceived. Denial or assent of 'the productivity of capital' seems to have little to do with any theory that appears in Smith's work.

Third, Hollander discusses this non-question of 'productivity' under the headings 'The demand for land services' and 'The demand for capital services' respectively. But this arises purely from the relation between marginal productivity and factor demand *in the neoclassical theory* which Hollander uses as his reference point. The actual passages from Smith, cited (to demonstrate his acceptance of the 'productivity' of land and capital), say nothing whatsoever about *demand* for land or capital.

Fourth, Hollander goes beyond the demonstration that Smith considered capital 'productive' and says:

> In a broad sense Smith can be said to have recognised the essence of 'capitalistic' production, namely, the use of methods involving roundabout processes which yield a higher product than more direct methods, but which require a period of waiting and accordingly 'capital' in the form of wage goods (p. 152).

He discusses Smith's account of investment in terms of 'extensions of the time period of production' (p. 155). In the course of this account, he makes the unsupported assertion that 'it would appear that Smith was attempting to formulate a relationship between the productivity of capital goods and the rate of return' (pp. 155–6). It is not clear what theoretical significance Hollander wishes to attribute to Smith's recognition of the essence of capitalistic production; but, no link with neoclassical theory can validly be found there, since it is not the *idea* of 'roundaboutness' or time which was significant in Austrian theory, but the use of it as a *measure of the quantity of capital*.

9.3.2 Wage determination

Hollander opens his account of wages by noting that 'the characteristic features of Smith's analysis is the role accorded to the rate of capital accumulation as an "independent" variable governing the demand for labour' (p. 157) – thus affirming that the natural rate of wages is that which ensures a rate of growth of population in line with the rate of accumulation of capital (see also Eltis, 1975, p. 437).[16]

It will be seen later in this chapter that Hollander does not, in fact, make a strong claim to have found a 'supply and demand' theory of *distribution* in Smith's work. Consistent with that, he notes here that 'as was the case with his successors, Smith failed to account adequately for the allocation of total capital between working and fixed capital', and that 'in Smith's account a change in the wage rate leaves the secular pattern of demand for labour unaffected'. Clearly Smith did not envisage a demand 'function' for labour (pp. 157, 158 and see 59). Likewise, he acknowledges that, even when wages are above subsistence, an increase in corn prices will lead to an increase in money wages – thus confirming the nature of the wage in Smith's analysis (pp. 162–3; for a similar view see Eltis, 1984, p. 335).

Recall that Hollander agrees that in analysing the gravitation to *natural* prices the 'average rates of return are not themselves determined in the adjustment process' (p. 122). But, consistent with his interpretation of *market* prices, he describes Smith's account of the gravitation of wages to their natural level as 'a kind of "Walrasian" competitive process', and concludes that 'it appears that (short-run) labour demand is elastic with respect to price' (pp. 157–9). It must be noted that the term 'Walrasian' here cannot be taken to refer to Walrasian supply and demand *functions*, but simply to the mechanism of price *adjustment* which Walras is believed, incorrectly, to have made his own.[17]

Since publication of *The Economics of Adam Smith*, Hollander has made a stronger assertion concerning Smith's wage theory. In the context of a discussion of Ricardo he said 'Of outstanding significance is the application of market demand-supply analysis to long-run wage determination . . . Ricardo I believe stood four-square in this *Smithian* tradition regarding wage theory' (1977, p. 40, Hollander's emphasis). However, no further evidence from Smith's work was cited there.

9.3.3 The 'supply' of land and capital

Turning to the 'supply' of land services Hollander, in his *Economics of Adam Smith*, notes Smith's use of the typically physiocratic argument that on food-producing land, rent arised because 'land, in almost any situation, produces a greater quantity of food than what is sufficient to maintain all the labour necessary for bringing it to market' (Hollander, 1973, p. 164; *WN*, I.xi.b.2). He argues that 'Smith considered the existence of a physical surplus merely as a *necessary* and not a *sufficient* condition for the appearance of rent', and in his view the additional element was provided by the fact that 'there can be no doubt that he took for granted the scarcity of land services relative to demand which derives in turn from the demand for food' (p. 164). In addition, of course, Hollander notes that the concept of differential rent features in Book I, Chapter xi – but 'differential productivity appears rather as a detail of the analysis than as the characteristic feature' (p. 167).

In Chapter 6 above, it has been argued that there are reasons to doubt this view that Smith attributed rent to absolute land scarcity. As Gee (1981, p. 6) argues, there seems to be abundant evidence that Smith considered the supply of land to be practically unlimited. Smith was unequivocal that 'In all the great countries of Europe, however, much good land still remains uncultivated' (*WN*, II.v.37). And, most important, he considered the real price of corn to be constant over long periods of economic development. Given his idea that in the *Wealth of Nations* rent derived from absolute land scarcity it is significant that Hollander attributes this constant price of corn, not to Smith's assumption of a constant production cost, but to the idea that Smith did not *apply* his general determination of value to *corn* at all (pp. 173–6). This argument by Hollander was examined in detail in my note number 4 to Chapter 5, and shown to be incorrect. In addition, Smith identified as exceptional the cases in which 'the quantity of land which can be fitted for some particular produce, is too small to supply the effectual demand' (*WN*, I.xi.b.29). In pointing out that Hollander's interpretation of Smith's account of rent would appear to be inconsistent with important elements of Smith text, it is not intended to imply that there is an unproblematical alternative interpretation available.

In his account of the 'capital supply conditions' Hollander acknowledges that 'there is little to suggest a conception of interest as a reward for abstinence from present consumption' (pp. 168–9). Indeed, he notes that Smith's account of the propensity of capitalists to accumulate 'represents a position closer to that of Marx than Senior' (p. 169). Finally, Hollander agrees that for Smith, interest represented a 'neat produce' over and above all costs (p. 169).

It is clear, therefore, that the *Wealth of Nations* was not concerned with the supply of factors of production determined by the interaction of factor endowments and preferences.

9.3.4 The productivity theory of distribution

Summarising his examinations of distribution, Hollander says that 'there is clearly much evidence to support the view that Smith was attempting to formulate a productivity theory of distribution' (p. 170: a view put forward by Veblen, 1919, pp. 121–2, and Taylor, 1960. pp. 116–7).[18] I have challenged the relevance of the evidence put forward in defence of this view. The productivity theory of distribution is simply a way of stating the neoclassical theory; it would be remarkable, indeed, if Smith had perceived the relation between productivity and factor demand (and ultimately factor reward) without first having formulated, or even attempted to formulate, the systematic relations between *given* original factors and outputs, via *known* technological possibilities which is vital to that theory. In many respects, Hollander would seem to concede this for he adds:

> This view must certainly be qualified in the light of the fact that Smith lacked any clear conception of a means of isolating the marginal factor products, moreover, the analysis of wages within a wages-fund structure precludes any *direct* connection between the wage rate and productivity. If we ascribe a productivity theory to him, it is therefore as a general conception only. (Hollander, 1973, p. 171)

Even this goes beyond the evidence, for it is said that Smith lacked the *means* of isolating the marginal factor products – implying that in other repects his was a supply and demand theory. In the introduction to his book, Hollander notes the limited significance of certain marginal relations in neoclassical theory (pp. 7–11). This may be valid, but the theoretical proposition, which is indispensible to neoclassical theory, and which margins express analytically, is that endowments are *given* and are *substitutable*. Precisely what Hollander failed to demonstrate, is that Smith treated land and capital as scarce factors in the neoclassical sense.

9.3.5 The theory of value and distribution as a whole

It is of the greatest significance that when he comes to present 'the theory [of value and distribution] as a whole' Hollander does not draw in any substantive way on either the utility and scarcity theory of value, or the productivity theory of distribution which, he has claimed, are to be found in the *Wealth of Nations*. The following statement is central to his account:

> It is clear that Smith's observations relating to value and distribution constitute a more-or-less consistent whole. To summarise briefly, given labour market conditions the money or silver price of corn (governed by the principle of specie distribution) determines the money wage rate and thus labour costs throughout the economy and – taking for granted nominal profits – the silver price of all commodities produced without land. And given the conditions of scarcity and productivity relating to land, the same silver price of corn together with the money wage rate (and profit rate), will govern the rent per acre on corn land and thus the alternative cost that must be met by all other land using products. (Hollander, 1973, p. 179)

Here it is conceded that for the purposes of determining value the real wage and the rate of profit were taken as given by Smith. Prices were determined by methods of production – which were also taken as given. Indeed, Hollander says that the *'formal* analysis of "general equilibrium" in the *Wealth of Nations*, it is true, is given relatively little attention, and is in some respects narrowly constrained' (p. 306). The reason is that 'the analysis suggests' that it was general equilibrium theory carried out on the basis of very special assumptions: constant 'aggregate amounts' of each factor, constant factor prices, and constant and identical, 'technically determined', factor ratios (pp. 121–4 and 306). 'It would not be surprising, therefore', he argues, 'if the formal account was no more than a first approximation' (p. 306). Given Hollander's account of the theory of value and distribution as a whole, it cannot be this part of Hollander's book, or, indeed, this part of Smith's book, to which Recktenwald refers in the statement that 'the whole of Walrasian, Marshallian and Hicksian price theory . . . is clearly implicit in Adam Smith's concept of natural price' (see quotation at the head of this chapter).

9.4 'FORMAL ANALYSIS' AND 'PRACTICAL APPLICATIONS'

Hollander's overall case rests on the distinction between Smith's 'formal analysis of general equilibrium' and his 'practical applications'. His argument is that although the analysis of value in Book I of the *Wealth of Nations* was indeed an 'attempt to achieve a conception of long-run general equilibrium', the reader will find there little trace of the relationships normally associated with such an analysis (and this has been confirmed in the preceding section). The reason was that Smith conducted that general equilibrium analysis on the basis of special assumptions. But, Hollander argues that outside of Book I Smith was not bound by the strict assumptions implicit in his formal analysis and, in his application of his theory to practical problems, we can see that his economics embraced the allocation of factor endowments in a general equilibrium of supply and demand. We have completed our examination of the first part of this argument and must now consider the relation between Smith's 'formal analysis' and 'practical applications'.

9.4.1 Smith's restrictive assumptions: the evidence

The argument that in his 'formal analysis of "general equilibrium" ' Smith assumed (i) 'constant aggregate amounts of each of the three factors' (p. 121), (ii) constant factor prices (p. 122), (iii) constant 'factor proportions' within each productive unit (p. 122), and (iv) 'identical factor proportions from industry to industry' (p. 122–3), is central to Hollander's case that, despite the absence there of the relations normally associated with supply and demand theory, nevertheless 'Smith's formal treatment of value theory may best be appreciated if envisaged as an attempt to achieve a conception of long-run *general* equilibrium' (p. 114).[19] In Hollander's view the 'formal statements of this chapter ['Of Natural and Market Price'] had a well-defined objective – namely the explanation of the broad principles of resource allocation' (p. 307); and, in addition, 'the object of the analysis was precisely to explain how alterations in the particular forms taken by the factors will be brought about' in response to a 'change in the pattern of demand' (p. 121); and 'for this purpose the assumption of constant costs was adequate' (p. 140 and see 306).

This line of argument can be examined in either of two ways. First, we can take Hollander's case at face value and ask what grounds there is for it as history of Adam Smith's economic thought. Second, economic argument shows that Hollander's premise (concerning Smith's restrictive assumptions), even if it were historically verified, is logically incapable of sustaining his conclusion concerning the 'well-defined objective' of Chapter vii

First, let us take Hollander's case at face value. Note that Smith's central statement in Chapter vii, that 'the whole quantity of industry annually employed in order to bring any commodity to market, naturally suits itself in this manner to the effectual demand' is, indeed, *consistent* with neoclassical general equilibrium theory (and with other theories too). As a result it might be argued that Hollander's reading of the chapter will commend itself if there is evidence of Smith having adopted the procedure and assumptions outlined by Hollander.

Here, however, the record is clear. Hollander notes that 'it is, of course, possible that the assumptions of the formal account of the general equilibrium process were introduced as a deliberate first approximation' (p. 124), but he states candidly that Smith *'nowhere* draws attention to the contrast between the formal analysis and practical applications' (p. 307, my emphasis), and concludes that it 'is more likely (that) Smith was simply unaware of all the assumptions implicit in his analysis' (p. 124). Since there is, on Hollanders's own admission, *no* evidence that Smith *consciously* adopted these restrictive assumptions in his 'formal account of the general equilibrium process', we may ask what evidence there is that they are 'implicit in his analysis'. Consider them in turn.

(i) Constant amounts of each factor of production

Hollander says that in Chapter vii Smith was 'enquiring into the equilibration in a state of artificially presumed stationaryness', where stationaryness means 'constant *aggregate* amounts of each of the three factors' (p. 121; see Skinner, 1974, p. 52 for a similar view).[20] Since there is *no* evidence cited for this, it might, at first sight, seem to arise from the now widespread view that the long period method of analysis, the *original source* of which was Smith's Chapter vii, can only be applied to 'stationary' economies (see, for example, Bliss, 1975, p. 55). But, of course, Hollander's view differs from that view, because, by 'stationarity' most theorists do not mean absolutely 'constant' amounts of each factor – but the wider concept of 'steady state' growth. Milgate has shown that no assumption of stationarity, still less of Hollander's absolute 'stationaryness', is involved in specifying natural prices as the object of analysis (Milgate, 1982, pp. 28–30 and pp. 141–2).

(ii) Constant factor prices

Hollander notes that in Smith's analysis of Chapter vii 'the average rates of return are not themselves determined in the adjustment process (p. 122, and recall his account of 'the theory as a whole'). The idea that this feature of his work was the result of a subconsciously adopted *assumption* on Smith's part would seem to arise from the needs of Hollander's case, not from Smith's text. The property noted by Hollander indicates simply that, in examining value, Smith took distribution as given – something which emerged consistently in the detailed examination of Smith's text in Part I of this study.

(iii) Constant factor proportions

Hollander says that 'there is no recognition of variability of factor proportions in any productive unit. It is thus implied that . . . factor proportions in each productive unit are constant' (p. 122). He seeks to enlist Ricardo's support for this proposition, saying that this was 'one of the most serious charges directed . . . against the Smithian analysis of price' (p. 122 n). But this does not withstand examination.[21] The evidence from Smith is quite unconvincing – and, it should be noted, comes from chapters far removed from the 'formal analysis' of Chapter vii (p. 123).[22] But, as will be seen below, that 'formal analysis', with its handy restrictive assumptions, is a very moveable feast indeed.

(iv) Uniform factor proportions

'It is implied . . . that factor proportions are identical from industry to industry' – because 'only then will the average rates of return remain constant following a change in the structure of industry' (p. 122). No evidence, apart from that cited under (iii), above, is given for this.

Again, it is a claim that might be considered to arise from the needs of Hollander's case that, despite what we find in Chapter vii and elsewhere, still 'Smith's formal treatment of value theory may best be appreciated if envisaged as an attempt to achieve a conception of long-run *general* equilibrium' of supply and demand (p. 114).

I say that this latter assumption *might be considered* to arise from the needs of Hollander's case because, in some respects, the assumption of constant factor proportions in each industry, and identical factor proportions across industries, undermines rather than supports his case. On the one hand, Hollander can claim with conviction that Smith explained value by supply and demand – safe in the knowledge that these assumptions, if adopted, exclude the possibility of factor demand functions, remove the relationships between demand and price, and sever any connection between distribution and price. But, on the other hand, these relationships lie at the heart of any supply and demand theory of value. It is, to say the least, hard to see how Smith's analysis of such a restrictive model can, as Hollander suggests, be 'envisaged as an attempt to achieve a conception of long-run *general* equilibrium' of supply and demand (p. 114). All that can happen in such a model is that capital will be moved between industries until, in Smith's words, the 'whole quantity of industry annually employed in order to bring any commodity to market, naturally suits itself . . . to the effectual demand' and a uniform rate of profit emerges (*WN*, I.vii.16). If this were all that Hollander is saying (and he does say this – p. 121) it would be unobjectionable. But such a vision of the operation of competition – which was central to classical economics – is quite a different thing from a general equilibrium of supply and demand.

The properties of Smith's analysis with which Hollander is here struggling, by means of this highly improbable structure of restrictive 'assumptions', are, indeed, real. But, once the attempt to find in Smith the content of the neoclassical theory of value and distribution is abandoned, then these proprties of his analysis lend themselves to a perfectly natural interpretation which involves *no* conjectures of the sort examined above.

9.4.2 Beyond the 'formal analysis': the role of demand

It is the supposed *contrast* between his 'formal analysis' and his 'practical application' that is central to Hollander's reading. It is in this context that I examine the final two propositions in his case that Smith considered value to be determined by utility and scarcity.

(v) The tradition that Smith 'played down' demand analysis derives as well from almost exclusive concentration upon Chapter vii of Book I which utilises the assumption that industries are character-ised by constant cost conditions. (Hollander, 1973, p. 140)

Hollander builds his case on the fact that this 'did not represent Smith's typical position regarding cost conditions' (p. 14). The latter point is, of course, correct. But it has been shown above that there is no basis for the view that, in Chapter vii, Smith assumed constant cost conditions.[23]

We then come to a more serious proposition. Recall that in Book I, Chapter xi (on rent), Smith categorised commodities according to the evolution of their methods of production and values (see Section 5.5 above). Hollander argues that his account of these price *changes* shows that for Smith *natural* prices, as well as market prices, were determined by demand. And, in addition:

(vi) 'illustrates the fact that the "explanation" of price in terms of "supply and demand" or "relative scarcity" was not regarded as an "alternative" to that in terms of costs'. (p. 140, see also p. 137)

Before considering the content of Book I, Chapter xi, it is important to identify the possible meanings of the statement that 'supply and demand' was not an alternative to (or 'not considered in conflict with', p. 137) costs. First, consider a basic analytical point. In Smith, whether the natural price of a commodity rises or falls in the long period it will always equal cost of production, because of the operation of competition. Equally, the 'whole quantity of industry annually employed in order to bring any commodity to market, naturally suits itself in this manner to the effectual demand' (*WN*, I.vii.16). This, too, is a result of competition. As noted in Chapter 2, from the *equality* of natural price and costs of production *per se* we can derive nothing concerning the *theory* of value held by a writer – only his belief in the operation of competition. Unfortunately, many commentators on Smith have used this equality of price and cost of production as evidence in support of one or other interpretation of his explanation of value. This school of interpretation is examined in Chapter 10 below.

Second, what would it mean, in a neoclassical context, to say that 'supply and demand' was not in conflict with cost of production (as, indeed, Wieser and other neoclassicals did say)? In neoclassical theory the equality of price and cost of production has a very specific content:

however high the price of a commodity may go, because of its scarcity relative to demand, this price will be no more than its cost of production, *because* of the mechanism whereby the prices of the given endowments of factors of production are adjusted to reflect the demands for final commodities. It is important, for reasons that will become apparent when we consider Hollander's particular arguments, to note that it is of the essence of the specifically neoclassical approach that this influence of relative factor scarcity applies to *produced* goods and not only to goods that exist in given quantities. (As Wieser said 'where the law of costs obtains, utility remains the source of value', 1888, p. 183.) If Hollander is to apply to Smith the standards he applies to his predecessors (that is, to search for the 'analytical reasoning . . . used in support of the proposition', pp. 28 and 35) he would have to show that Smith explained the relation between scarcity, cost and price, even suggestively, in those terms.

Hollander's argument is that the price changes outlined in Chapter xi, of Book I of the *Wealth of Nations*, show 'Smith's full recognition of the economic role of scarcity' and demand, and the non-conflict between this and cost of production.

In particular he cites Smith's account of: the rise in the price of cattle (and similar commodities); movements in the price of silver; and decline in the price of manufactures (pp. 136–7; 140; 143). But these parts of the *Wealth of Nations* do not, on my reading, support Hollander's interpretation. The evidence suggests that Smith did not consider scarcity to influence the *natural price* of commodities. In several of the passages cited by Hollander, Smith did indeed discuss the influence of scarcity on the *prevailing prices* of rare wines, cattle and precious metals; but he considered these prices to *differ from*, in these cases to *exceed*, cost of production and *natural price*. In his account of the price of rare wines he stressed the exceptional nature of the circumstances, and the fact that price *exceeds* 'the whole rent, wages and profit necessary for raising and bringing it to market *according to their natural rate*' (*WN*, I.xi.b.29).[24] In the case of cattle Smith considered a process during which the prevailing price was less than, greater than, and eventually equal to, cost of production or natural price – as well as noting that the natural price itself changes during this process.[25] Smith viewed the natural price of silver as a *lowest* price, and did *not* consider increases in its price, due to intermittent scarcity, to be increases in its *natural* price. Hollander bases his case on the role of scarcity in Smith's analysis, and its congruence with cost of production, largely on three incidental uses, by Smith, of the word 'scarcity' when discussing the high and rising natural price of silver.[26]

Quite apart from the clear *distinction*, in Smith's work, between prices reflecting scarcity and natural prices, even those scarcity prices cannot be said to have been explained in the manner of supply and demand theory.[27] Adherence to sound economic theory shows that it is mistaken to contrast 'demand' and 'cost' explanations of value; any real differences on the role of cost boil down to differences on the relation of *value* to *distribution*. The essence of the supply and demand theory is that the prices of produced goods are determined by the relation of preferences to the ultimate scarcities of given endowments, whose prices are simultaneously determined in this process. In short, the essence of the theory is a particular view of the relation of *value* to *distribution*. Adam Smith related the natural price of goods to their cost of production – where this cost arose not only from physical inputs but also from the prevailing rates of wages, profits and rent. The additional analytical relations which would make this price-cost equality a supply and demand theory are simply not to be found, even in embryo, in Smith's work.

Finally, consider what Hollander infers from the evolution of the price of manufactures. He draws attention to Smith's statement that 'an increase in demand, besides, though in the beginning it may sometimes raise the price of goods, never fails to lower it in the long run' because production and competition lead to the adoption of 'new improvements in art, which might never otherwise have been thought of' (*WN*, V.i.e.26). Hollander infers from this that Chapter vii (which, he asserts, was 'strictly limited to the case of constant long-run costs') 'is not representative of Smith's general position according to which demand plays a fundamental role in the long run as well as in the short run' (p. 143). But it is quite inappropriate to read Smith's account of the *secular* movement of price, caused by division of labour and extension of the market, as evidence of a relation between quantity and price analogous to that expressed by a demand function in neoclassical theory.[28]

9.4.3 Beyond the 'formal analysis': technical change

In order to present this reading, Hollander contrasts the highly restricted case of Chapter vii (*sic*) with Smith's 'treatment of actual problems'. It is worth noting exactly what inferences such a contrast allows him to make. Hollander points out that: 'differential factor ratios, for example, between broad categories of products play a vital role in Chapter II.v' (p. 124); 'the strict conditions of constant proportions is in practice relaxed' (p. 307); 'the possibility of alteration in the machinery-labour ratio is admitted' (p. 306); 'variation in the intensity of operating given land areas was allowed for'; and 'finally, the implicit assumption of identical technical proportions between sectors, which is characteristic of the formal analysis of general equilibrium is also not consistently maintained' (p. 307).

Since there is a world of difference between 'allowing for' such changes and the supply and demand *analysis* of them, Hollander concedes that between wages and technical change 'no causal relationship is defined'. The new methods of production 'are still technically defined', such that even here, well away from the restricted analysis of Chapter vii, *'there is no generalised recognition of factor substitutability'* (pp. 306–7, and see pp. 219–21, and 124, my emphasis). It would seem that not only did Smith 'nowhere draw attention to the contrast between the formal analysis and practical applications', but he let elements of his formal analysis escape from Chapter vii to menace other parts of his text.

Hollander considers that the falling price of manufactures is evidence of the 'fundamental role' of demand, and this view has been questioned above. He adheres to it despite what he calls a 'conceptual difficulty': namely, that little purpose is served 'by strict conceptualisation' of Smith's account of the cheapening of manufactured commodities in terms of the modern distinction between a change in the production function and a movement along a given production function (p. 142). 'It would appear' he argues 'that Smith had in mind a combination of the two notions' (pp. 142–3).[29] But this observation has potentially serious implications for Hollander's case. It is not that one demands to find a production function *per se* in Smith's work; but, the ultimate analytical role of production functions in 'supply and demand' explanations of value is as an expression of *given* and *substitutable* endowments. It is the presence of this feature in Smith's work that Hollander must demonstrate.

Since, even outside of Chapter vii, in his analysis of the changing relative price of commodities, Smith 'did not formally introduce the substitution relation into his analysis as a general phenomenon' (p. 124), it is clear that we have to look elsewhere in Hollander's book to find what Recktenwald may have had in mind in the statement quoted at the head of this chapter.

9.5 A THEORIST OF RESOURCE ALLOCATION DETERMINED BY FACTOR ENDOWMENTS

It transpires that Hollander's case that Smith should be seen as a general equilibrium theorist rests on one particular aspect of his work – the international allocation of economic activity. He argues that:

> It is in the course of Smith's treatment of the historical sequence of investment priorities according to the principle of profit rate equalisation, that the fundamental equilibrating mechanism is utilised, namely, resource allocation governed by the differential pattern of factor endowments between economies. Despite the overwhelming significance of this mechanism, the reader of the *Wealth of Nations* will find no hint thereof in the First Book. (Hollander, 1973, p. 307)

What he refers to here is Smith's idea that 'in the natural progress of opulence' agricultural development precedes the growth of towns (*WN*, III.i.3), and his view that in the new colonies, 'where uncultivated land is still to be had upon easy terms', farming yields high profits while 'no manufactures for distant sale have even yet been established in any of their towns' (*WN*, III.i.5).

Clearly, Smith envisaged that these natural conditions would influence the methods and patterns of production, and in places this is all that Hollander infers. For example, on Smith's observation that 'Every colonist gets more land than he can possibly cultivate. He has no rent and scarce any taxes to pay' (*WN*, IV.vii.b.2) he says; 'here we see that the price of land *certainly comes into the picture*' (p. 281n, emphasis added). And, elsewhere he says: the 'fact is that Smith *did not lose sight of* factor endowments and relative prices in dealing with economic development' (p. 288 – though, see the comments below on factor endowments). In particular, Hollander makes clear that Smith's account of development could not be adequately conveyed by means of a corn model of accumulation.

But on occasion, and very definitely in the 'Conclusion' of his book, he goes beyond this and attributes to Smith a fully neoclassical theory of allocation: 'In effect, his analysis defined each country's "advantages" in terms of its relative factor endowments' (pp. 283–4; see also pp. 274n, 278, 281–302) and, as quoted above, Hollander considers that 'a fundamental equilibrating mechanism is utilised namely resource allocation governed by the differential pattern of factor endowments' (p. 307). There are a number of reasons why this strong conclusion seems unwarranted.

It has been argued throughout this chapter that Hollander has not succeeded in demonstrating Smith's use, in even a rudimentary manner, of essentially 'supply and demand' theorising concerning value and distribution. In particular, it has been indicated that the passages cited by Hollander do not show that, in explaining natural price and the relation of value to distribution, Smith made use of systematic price-quantity relationships, and still less do they show that he *derived* such relationships using the *logic* of neoclassical theory. These arguments apply here equally. Smith's statement of the efficiency gain from trade (*WN*, IV.ii.12), and his statement that 'Agriculture is the proper business of new colonies; a business which the cheapness of land renders more advantageous than any other' (*WN*, IV.vii.c.51), though *consistent* with the conclusions of modern factor proportions theory of trade, are not, in themselves, evidence of a 'supply and demand' theory of value and distribution (for a similar view see Myint, 1977, pp. 236–9).

In addition to that, there are several other reasons why Hollander's interpretation of Smith's treatment of international trade, as neoclassical general equilibrium theory, should be treated with severe caution. Such a reading would seem to limit the scope of Smith's account of international trade in several ways.

To begin with, right from the 'Introduction and plan of the work' Smith *played down* the influence of 'the soil climate or extent of territory of any particular nation' as a determinant of the 'abundance or scantiness' of its supply of goods. In direct contrast, he stressed two other factors – first, 'the skill, dexterity, and judgement with which its labour is generally applied' and, second, the proportion of productive to unproductive labour (*WN*, I.3). This emphasis on the causes and consequences of the division of labour runs right throughout the *Wealth of Nations* and is clearly visible in his account of the international pattern of production and trade. For example, he attributed the prosperity of the new colonies first and foremost to what the colonists 'carry out with them', namely 'a knowledge of agriculture and other useful arts . . . the habit of subordination [and] some notion of regular government' (*WN*, IV.ix.22, and *WN*, IV.vii.b.2; and see Hollander p. 281n). More specifically, rather than assuming that the technical conditions of production were identical between trading economies, and *attributing* the pattern of trade to relative quantitative endowments, Smith would simply seem to have visualised natural conditions and resources *influencing* the methods of production in each country. Myint, in developing this argument, draws attention to Smith's treatment of transport costs as 'an integral part of the process of long-run economic development' (Myint, 1977, p. 237; Hollander acknowledges the importance of *qualitative* differences between countries in Smith's account, p. 274n).

Furthermore, not only did methods of production differ between countries but, as Myint points out, Smith did not treat the 'factor endowments' of a country as given exogenously (Myint, 1977, p. 235). The central feature of Smith's analysis was that the *static* gains from trade were much less significant than the *dynamic* effects on economic development (for a similar view see Myint, 1948, p. 61, 1977, p. 234; Bloomfield, 1975, p. 469 and, indeed, Hollander).[30] This perspective derived from his fundamental proposition that 'the division of labour is limited by the extent of the market' and the conception of *increasing returns to scale* that was embodied in it (Myint, 1977, p. 237; Bloomfield, 1975, p. 457). For all these reasons Myint contrasts his own reading of Smith's study of international trade with attempts to fit 'Smith's theory into the procrustean bed of the conventional theory in which the production possibilities of a country are fully determined once the resources and technology are given, irrespective of the internal state of the development of its domestic economic organisation' (Myint, 1977, p. 245).

Finally, and most fundamentally, Smith's recognition of the influence of natural conditions and resources on methods of production, and consequently on prices and the pattern of production and trade, is not incompatible with the surplus approach to value and distribution – in either its developed or rudimentary forms.

9.5.1 Conclusion

In many respects Hollander's view of the *Wealth of Nations* is similar to that presented in Part I of this study. He says that 'the object of the work was ultimately to define the necessary conditions for rapid economic development in contemporary circumstances and Smith's treatment of the price mechanism must accordingly . . . be considered with this end in view' (p. 307). His view is that, given that object, Smith's conclusion was that the 'maximisation in each period of national income . . . guaranteed the greatest achievable surplus – income over subsistence – available for taxation, for capital accumulation and for current consumption' (p. 308).

One of the central aims of Hollander's book was to question the accuracy of representing Smith's theory by a corn model of accumulation – and to challenge the assumption implicit in that approach – that Smith was concerned with growth *to the exclusion* of allocation. There can be no doubt that he has succeeded in demonstrating that a corn model neglects many aspects of Smith's work. But it does follow from this that Smith's was a theory of the allocation of *given endowments* – still less that his theory was that given endowments are allocated in a process of substitution and price adjustment which brings unco-ordinated individual consumption and production choices to consistency (for a similar view see Walsh and Gram, 1980, pp. 62–3). In evaluating this influential book every passage from the *Wealth of Nations* cited by Hollander has been examined and it has been found that none of these offers support for the radical new interpretation of Smith as a general equilibrium theorist.

10 Smith as 'Cost of Production' Theorist

For a developed industrial society . . . Adam Smith advanced an expenses-of-production, or 'components', theory of value . . . As for these components revenues themselves, these were determined by conditions of supply and demand prevailing respectively in the market or labour, for capital, and for land. (Dobb, 1975, pp. 327–8)

As I see it, the really central element in that work was Smith's new division of society into landlords, wage-earners, and capitalists, which was implicitly accepted as a datum throughout . . . This threw up a number of crucial problems for solution. The most basic problem – as it was bound to appear if one assumed as Smith did that the economy was ruled by the price mechanism – was that of *value*. (Meek, 1973b, pp. viii–x)

10.1 'COST OF PRODUCTION' INTERPRETATIONS

In a great many commentaries it has been said that Smith had a 'cost of production theory of value'. What inferences are drawn from this concerning Smith's position in the development of theories of value and distribution clearly depends on what is meant by 'cost of production theory'. Statements on the nature of the 'cost of production theory' in Smith's work can be classed into three categories.

First, it is pointed out by some writers that a 'cost of production theory' of value is no theory at all unless a determinate theory of costs is presented also.[1]

The second class of statement concerning cost of production in Smith's work is the view that the determination of price by cost of production reflected a conscious or unconscious asssumption of constant costs.[2,3] Explicit or implicit in the statement that Smith assumed constant costs is the view that his approach to value was essentially that of supply and demand theory – whatever the limitations of his treatment of utility, demand, or other details of analysis.[4,5]

We may identify a third class of statement concerning cost of production in Smith. Very frequently the term 'cost of production theory' has been used as a counter distinction to 'labour theory'. Thus, if Smith explained relative price by relative labour embodied this would be a labour theory of value; if, in contrast, he recognised that in a capitalist economy relative prices would not be proportional to relative labour embodied, then this would be called a 'cost of production theory' (see, for example, Cannan, 1929, pp. 164–77; Schumpeter, 1954, pp. 594 and 600; Stigler, 1958; Gordon, 1965; and West, 1976, p. 201). Discussions along these lines have a highly unsatisfactory element. Clearly the question – did Smith consider prices determined by relative labour embodied? – is an important one. If the term 'cost of production theory of value', was simply a synonym for 'no labour theory of value', then no confusion need result. But this has not been the case; the term 'cost of production' has denoted not only non-labour theory but, in addition, supply and demand theory – since the rejection of the labour theory was seen as a move towards a supply and demand approach to distribution. For example, the debate on whether Ricardo had a surplus theory or a supply and demand theory was conducted, for some time, in terms of whether he had a labour theory or a 'cost of production theory' (Marshall, 1890; Schumpeter, 1954, Stigler, 1952, 1954, 1958; Viner, 1954).

While the question of the labour theory is historically important, it can be seen now that conducting this debate in terms of labour theory versus 'cost of production theory', was fundamentally misconceived. In particular, while the connection between the labour theory and the surplus theory could be defined fairly clearly, the connection between 'cost of production theory' and neoclassical theory could not. That connection was frequently implicit rather than explicit.

But if conducting debates on Ricardo in these terms was misconceived, Smith's work was placed in an even more invidious position. In many commentaries of Smith, the statement that he held a 'cost of production theory of value' would seem to *implicitly* contain the statement that he was a supply and demand theorist, *because*, in *the debate on Ricardo*, the term *'cost of production'* had come to mean 'supply and demand theory', as opposed to the labour theory of value.

One possible reason for the anomalous position of Smith's work in debate on the notion of a dual development in economic thought may be traced to Schumpeter – a major protagonist in that debate. While he argued that in Smith's work, and not just in Ricardo's, the 'factor-value aspect of distributive shares is brushed aside in favour of quite another' (1954, p. 558) he also, paradoxically, accepted Marshall's view of Smith, 'at least as to the facts of the case'. Thus, he said that Smith had a 'cost of production' explanation of value – a view which was, he said, 'the opinion of many students' (1954, pp. 189 and 309). But he explicitly rejected Marshall's *interpretation* of these facts (op. cit., pp. 307–8n). Nevertheless, the result was that when Stigler, Viner and Robbins opposed Schumpeter's view of classical economics, they challenged in detail his interpretation of Ricardo and defended Marshall's position; they took issue with Schumpeter's *low opinion* of Smith's work; but did *not*, because they did not need to, dispute his *account* of Smith's treatment of value and distribution (Stigler, 1954; Viner, 1954; Robbins, 1955).

Having identified three categories of the idea that Smith determined value by cost of production we can now state their significance. Both the second and third class of statement concerning cost of production in Smith involve the view that Smith was essentially a supply and demand theorist. But in both cases (the idea of constant cost, and the idea of cost of production as a rejection of the labour theory of value – views which are found together in many accounts of Smith) the connection with supply and demand theory is *implicit* rather than explicit. Thus, though belief that Smith's work was essentially supply and demand theory would seem to be very widespread, *explicit* statments of this, or attempts to demonstrate it, were remarkably rare. This is the background against which the later work of Maurice Dobb and Ronald Meek should be examined.

10.2   DOBB'S 'TWO STREAMS' PROPOSITION

The most recent major statment of a cost of production interpretation of Smith was that by Dobb (1973, 1975) and Meek (1977). They argued that Smith must be considered the source of both the classical and neoclassical 'lines of tradition' (Dobb, 1973, pp. 112–15, 1975, p. 329; Meek, 1977, p. 154, and, for what seems like a similar view see Groenewegen, 1974, p. 193, 1975, p. 142). It is of great significance that both writers accepted the view of Sraffa (1951) and Schumpeter (1954) that Ricardo's approach to distribution was fundamentally different from that which was found in the subsequent neoclassical theory.[6] Sraffa's work demonstrated that is was wrong to describe Ricardo as a 'cost of production' theorist. Acceptance of this new view had the important consequence that the idea of Smith as essentially a supply and demand theorist, could no longer be maintained as an *implicit corollary* of the view that Ricardo (and Smith) had a 'cost of production', as opposed to a labour, theory of value. Consequently, in order to maintain that Smith was the source of the supply and demand line of tradition they had to argue *explicitly* that some key elements of supply and demand theory can be found in his work.

This they did. Dobb said:

> Thus we have in Smith a theory of price that can be characterised (in Mr Sraffa's description of it) as an Adding-up Theory – a summation (merely) of three primary components of price. It has alternatively been described as a simple Cost of Production Theory; in which guise it has been handed down through the nineteenth century and became known in textbooks of the subject. (Dobb, 1975, p. 46)

To this was added the crucial proposition on distribution:

> As for these component revenues themselves, these were determined by conditions of supply and demand prevailing respectively in the market for labour, for capital, and for land. Such was the fountainhead of the cost of production, or expenses of production, theory as this was to prevail as orthodoxy throughout most of the nineteenth century and to be defended by Marshall. (Dobb, 1975, p. 328; see also 1973, pp. 50, 72, 76, 97, 112–13, 119 and Meek, 1974, p. 153)

Although this argument was much more *explicit* than that usually associated with the 'cost of production' interpretation of Smith, there was little *evidence* from Smith's work presented in support of it. Instead, the evidence was very largely circumstantial. The proposition that Smith was the 'fountainhead' of the neoclassical theory emerged from Dobb's account of two aspects of the history of economic thought since Smith's time: first, Ricardo and Marx's surplus theory, and second, the development of supply and demand theory from the 1820s through the marginal revolution to Marshall. Therefore, to assess his interpretation of Smith's work we have to consider his account of these episodes in the history of economics.

10.3   RICARDO'S CRITICISM OF SMITH'S THEORY

Smith's role as the source of supply and demand theory emerges from four aspects of Dobb's account of Ricardo: (i) the contrast between Ricardo's price theory and Smith's Adding-up Theory, (ii) Ricardo's rejection of 'pure exchange' theory, (iii) Ricardo's rejection of supply and demand theory, and (iv) Ricardo's introduction of the concept of a given real wage. Dobb's account of these topics, and the inferences which he drew from them concerning Smith's role, are examined in turn.

(i) The contrast between Ricardo and Smith's price theory

As is well known, Ricardo was critical of Smith's treatment of value, and his new theory of the rate of profit led him to different conclusions about the relation of wages (and taxes) to prices. Dobb's account of Smith's analysis and Ricardo's criticism of it lead to the conclusion that the two writers differed – *to the extent* of belonging to two different 'traditions' of value and distribution theory.

This conclusion was reached as follows. Dobb portrayed Smith's component parts of price, and his account of the relation between wages and prices, as parts of a single, coherent and consistently held adding-up *theory* of value. Thus he said that it was this *theory* which *led* Smith to the 'absurd conclusion' that 'the money-price of corn regulates that of all home-made commodities' (Dobb, 1975, pp. 47–7 and 75–6). This conclusion formed an obstacle to Ricardo's presentation of his new theory of profits (ibid.). A *theory* which generated such a result would, indeed, be incompatible with Ricardo's theory of profits – and could, therefore, be said to belong to a different tradition of value and distribution theory (Dobb, 1975, pp. 112–15; 1975, p. 328).

All the elements necessary for an assessment of this argument have been put in place in previous chapters of this essay. Indeed, it was precisely with this argument in mind that certain aspects of Smith's work, and Ricardo's criticisms of it, were explored in such detail.

My examination of Smith's treatment of value in Chapters 5 and 6 above shows that Dobb misrepresented Smith's position. He did that by conflating into one proposition Smith's account of two different things: the case of a tax on wages and the case of the corn export bounty (see Sections 6.4 and 6.5). It was shown that Dobb was not correct to view Smith's adding-up approach to value as the sole theoretical source of the idea that the money price of corn regulates that of all home-made commodities (*WN*, IV.v.a.11). Dobb was quite correct, however, to say that the idea (which, incidentally, remained a common place in political economy well after Smith's particular assumptions were abandoned) did, indeed, form an impediment to Ricardo's clarification and defence of his new theory of profit (Sraffa, 1951, p. xxxiv). But it did not do so as an idea generated by an opposing *theory* of distribution.

Furthermore, it has been shown in Chapter 7 that by not distinguishing sufficiently between the new theory of profits itself, and particular wage-price results derived from a particular set of assumptions ('some of which' in Sraffa's words 'have come to be regarded as the most characteristic of Ricardo's theory' 1951, p. xxxiv), Dobb exaggerated the extent of the difference between Ricardo's and Smith's theories of value and distribution (see Section 7.1 and 7.2 above).

(ii) Ricardo's rejection of 'pure exchange' theory

Dobb's view of the nature of Smith's treatment of value, and hence of his place in the development of theories of value and distribution, emerges also from his account of the debates between Ricardo and Malthus. He says that *in choosing a labour theory of value* Ricardo:

> rejected the Adding-up-components Theory, and by implication rejected the possibility of treating the sphere of exchange-relations as an 'isolated system', and anchored the explanation of these exchange-relations firmly in conditions and circumstances of production. (Dobb, 1973, p. 115)

Here Dobb implied that Smith treated the sphere of exchange relations as an isolated system. In this he was surely mistaken. It is very widely accepted, by writers who differ diametrically on the interpretation of Smith, that relative to most of his predecessors he emphasised the connection between *production* and *price* – although views differ on the exact extent and nature of his shift of emphasis.[7] Furthermore, there is no evidence that Ricardo thought that Smith 'treated the sphere of exchange-relations as an isolated system'.

(iii) Ricardo's rejection of supply and demand theory

A third aspect of Dobb's account of *Ricardo*, which served as indirect evidence that Smith was the source of the neoclassical stream of theory, was his argument that in opposing supply and demand:

> What Ricardo had in mind was the use of the notion of supply-demand relations by Smith in his system as a whole - as a vehicle and framework of determination. Ricardo was using it, in other words, as a label for the rival theory of value and distribution that he was combatting. (1973, p. 119. See also 1975, p. 334)

This claim has been investigated in my chapter on Ricardo, Chapter 7, and shown to be without any foundation. There is no evidence that Ricardo considered Smith to have explained price by supply and demand, indeed, *all* his references to Smith's use of the idea of demand were approving.

(iv) Ricardo's introduction of the given real wage

Finally, in explaining Ricardo's role in the development of classical theory Dobb said:

> So far as distribution is concerned Ricardo could be regarded as extending and developing the brief section on the subject in the *Wealth of Nations*. But the *extension contained a crucial additional element. This was the introduction, implicitly if not explicitly, of a social or institutional datum in the shape of the socio-economic conditions* defining the level of real-wages. (1973, p. 116, emphasis added)

This implies that it was Riacrdo who introduced not only the new determinate theory of the rate of profit, but also the basic element of the surplus theory in its entirety. It flies in the face of much evidence from the physiocrats, Smith and Marx, (see Sections 3.4, 6.2, and 8.2). Furthermore, it contradicts Dobb's overall interpretation that *both* 'lines of tradition' on value and distribution *derived from Smith* (1975, p. 329). For, it quite undermines his case that Smith made any contribution to the development of the surplus theory *at all* (see 1973, pp. 45–6). We will have cause to examine, in further detail, Dobb's view as to *how* Smith did contribute to this 'stream of theory'.

In conclusion, the indirect evidence that Smith was the source of supply and demand theory must be discounted. It derives from an account of Ricardo's work which is questionable in all relevant aspects.

10.4   THE 'COST OF PRODUCTION TRADITION'

We have seen that Dobb's idea, that Smith was the source of what ultimately became neoclassical theory, was backed up with little evidence from Smith's work, but received indirect support from two sources: his account of Ricardo, and his account of the development of supply and demand theory. That account of Ricardo's development of the *surplus* theory conveyed the idea that Smith's view of distribution, and its relation to value, was fundamentally different to Ricardo's – Smith's being labelled a 'cost of production' theory. It was Dobb's account of the development of *supply and demand* theory that linked this 'cost of production' theory of Smith's with neoclassical theory. It did that by identifying a theoretical continuity from Smith, through Malthus, and Mill to Marshall. It is, therefore, to this account that we must look to find the final element in the circumstantial evidence for the view that Smith was the source of supply and demand economics.

In his 1975 paper, 'Ricardo and Adam Smith', Dobb outlined his interpretation as follows:

> A fairly common view of textbooks on the history of economic thought is (or used to be) that as regards the theory of value there is a fairly direct and unbroken tradition running through Smith to Ricardo . . . and hence through J S Mill to Marshall; this tradition emphasising cost of production and conditions of supply as determinants of what Smith called 'natural value' . . . This 'classical' type of theory was depicted as standing in contrast with the search for basic determinants on the demand side, namely in utility, *ophelimité*, or consumers preferences, which had been anticipated by J B Say, and then explicitly championed and developed by Jevons and the Austrians. The reality is, however, less simple than this, and, I believe, in some important respects quite different from what is implied in the usual view, (Dobb, 1975, p. 327)

It might seem that Dobb intended to challenge the theoretical foundation of this 'text book view'. In fact, his objection was simply that the name of *Ricardo* should be *removed* from the list of cost of production theorists. In all other respects he fully accepted that textbook view.

Indeed, one of the textbooks which Dobb may have had in mind, but he did not name, was his own *Political Economy and Capitalism*. In his essay 'the Requirements of a Theory of Value', of 1937, he outlined the major theories of value – each of which adopts a 'value constant'. These were the classical or *cost* theory, and the utility/demand theory. He argued, however, that the *value constant* which underlay the cost theory changed from labour embodied (in Ricardo and Marx) to 'subjective real costs' (in Marshall).

All of this was retained in his later book. There he defined what he called the 'supply-demand-cum-component-parts-of price line of tradition' (p. 113), which started with Smith and ran through Malthus, Senior, and Mill to Marshall (pp. 47–8, 80, 97,112–15, 119, 122). An important element in the notion of a theoretically meaningful continuity running from Smith through Mill to Marshall, is the idea of a contrast between *cost* and *demand* based theories. Dobb consistently contrasted these. For example, he said:

> What Marshall was really defending against Jevons was that line of tradition from Smith's 'components of price' to Mill's 'expenses of production' theory of natural value rather than the Ricardian theory in its proper interpretation. (Dobb, 1973, p. 185; see also pp. 31, 112–4, 122, 167, 170 and 1975, p. 332)

Dobb's interest would seem to have been confined to the latter part of this statment (the Ricardian theory in its proper interpretation). My concern is to question, as well, the validity of the first part (that what Marshall was defending against Jevons was *Smith's* theory).[8] Dobb described the 'Jevonian revolution' as the development of 'more sophisticated versions of the supply-demand-cum-component-part-of-price line of tradition', in which 'increasing emphasis is inevitably thrown up upon conditions of demand (and its subjective determinants) compared with which the Cost of Production Theory inevitably fades into the background' (1973, pp. 113–14). Dobb viewed Adam Smith as the founder of this 'supply-demand-cum-component-parts-of-price line of tradition'.

Meek, drawing on Dobb's argument, said that 'there are *three* different kinds of "explanatory principle" in the history of economics'

(1974, p. 153). The first of these was that 'which explains prices in terms of man's activities and relations *as a producer*'.

> Second, there are various kinds of 'demand and supply' explana-
> tions, the most significant of which (historically speaking) is that
> which treats the price of a commodity as being determined by
> 'adding up' the different expenses or costs incurred in producing it,
> each of these component parts of price being determined by (in some
> sense) 'demand and supply'.

The third was that which 'explains prices in terms of man's activities *as a consumer*' (ibid.). Citing Dobb, he grouped the latter two together, leaving *two* rival traditions, *both* of which, in his view, 'derive from the same source – Adam Smith' (Meek, 1974, p. 154)
 . Thus, in the view of both Dobb and Meek it is this 'supply-demand-cum-component-parts-of-price line of tradition', in its *cost version*, that derived from Adam Smith (Dobb, 1973, p. 112). However, as will be seen below, Meek qualified this proposition considerably.

There are two aspects to this proposition that must be considered: its theoretical coherence and its historical accuracy. There are problems with the definition of the 'two rival traditions' of theory around which this historical proposition is built. These are outlined by Bharadwaj (1978a and 1980). We may state the central problem in the terms which Dobb adopted. Once Ricardo's role as a surplus theorist is accepted, the idea of contrasting 'cost' and 'demand' based theories cannot be carried over from what Dobb called the 'textbook view'. It is not only the *historical accuracy* (concerning Ricardo), but also *theoretical meaning*, of the idea of a cost of production tradition that is challenged by Sraffa's historical and theoretical work (see Section 2.3.2 above). Indeed, ever since Marshall's time a series of neoclassical theorists have been at pains to show that (contrary to what so many textbooks say) Marshall's 'real costs' theory was identical, in all essential respects, to utility-based neoclassical theory (Wieser, 1888; Whitaker, 1904; Schumpeter, 1954).

Rejection of the idea of a cost-of-production theory does not dispose of the historical proposition. It is still possible that Smith was the 'fountainhead' of neoclassical economics, and that there was a development of this theory through the nineteenth century (excluding Ricardo and Marx) to modern general equilibrium. (But for criticism of several aspects of Dobb's account of nineteenth-century economics see O'Brien, 1974, pp. 193–4). The difference that the theoretical clarification makes is that the relation of price to cost of production *per se* (or the contrast between this and labour embodied) can no longer be cited as evidence for such a view. If it is to be asserted that Smith was a supply and demand theorist then some *theoretically relevant* similarity between his work and neoclassical theory must be demonstrated.

To this end, Dobb cited Smith's account of the influence of accumulation on wages, and the tendency of profits to fall, as examples of the 'supply-and-demand explanations upon which Smith . . . so largely relied' (Dobb, 1973, pp. 50–2). It has been argued in Section 6.3, and throughout Chapter 9, that Smith's approach to distribution (in which he included the effect of accumulation on wages) and then, taking distribution as given, his determination of natural price, should not be seen as supply and demand theory (for a similar view see Garegnani, 1984, p. 297; Bharadwaj, 1978a, pp. 167–8 and 1980).[9]

Meek, although he would seem to have accepted Dobb's view that Smith's component parts of price were determined by supply and demand (see especially 1977, pp. 12–13), considerably qualified the proposition that Smith was a forerunner of neoclassical theory (Meek, 1974, p. 153). In his view, although Smith's 'generalised picture of the interdependence of the elements in the economic system ... was such as to give a certain impetus to the development of explanatory principles oriented towards "supply and demand", nevertheless Schumpeter had *exaggerated* the similarity between this and modern theory (Meek, 1974, pp. 156–8). In particular, Smith's 'main emphasis is not on the reciprocal interdependence of factor prices and commodity prices' (ibid.). This reservation is hardly surprising given that only two years earlier Meek had stated a very different view of the nature and significance of Smith's natural prices – a view which is embodied in the quotation placed at the head of this chapter, and which restated an idea found throughout his extensive writings on physiocratic and classical economics (see 1954, 1956, 1962, 1977, p. 8).

10.5 SMITH'S CONTRIBUTION TO SURPLUS THEORY

If Smith explained the natural rates of wages and profits by supply and demand (Dobb 1973, pp. 50, 72, 76, 97, 112–13, 119 and 1975, p. 328), and if it was Ricardo who added the 'curcial additional element' of a given real wage (1973, p. 116), what was Smith's contribution to the development of the surplus theory?

Dobb's answer to this question is clear from his statement that:

Thus there were essentially *two* lines of tradition, or separate branches of classical theory, so far as value and distribution were concerned; both of them deriving from Adam Smith, but one of them *limited by him to an outmoded socio-historical context*, and accordingly left undeveloped and unutilised by him. (Dobb, 1975, p. 329, my emphasis)

What was 'limited by Smith to an outmoded socio-historical context' was, of course, the labour theory of value (see Dobb, 1973, p. 45). In Dobb's view Smith's contribution to the surplus theory consisted in his occasional use of a labour theory of value (see also 1973, p. 115). A corollary of this view is, of course, the idea that Smith's *general* treatment of value, his 'component parts of price', was entirely a contribution to a different, opposed, theory. And this is precisely Dobb's case, as examined above.

This concentration on Smith's occasional labour theory of value (or, more accurately, his occasional explanation of relative prices in terms of labour quantities) clearly derives from Marx. In Chapter 8 I have examined Marx's reading of Smith and, while the reason for his concentration on the labour theory was clear and rational, the accuracy of his account of Smith's work was questioned. In particular, the usefulness of dividing Smith's work into theoretically distinct parts, *on the basis of the labour theory*, was shown to be limited. In addition to that, Dobb's view that Smith's contribution to the surplus theory was the labour theory of value, is rendered even less convincing by the following contrast between his view and Marx's. Marx concentrated on Smith's (rejected) labour theory – having unequivocally classified him as a surplus theorist on the basis of his treatment of the wage, and his description of profits (see Section 8.2 above). Now, Dobb would seem not to have accepted these latter views on Smith; but in that case, no amount of evidence that Smith held a labour theory of value would be sufficient to identify his work as belonging, even to the least extent, to the surplus 'stream of theory'.[10]

On this question of Smith's contribution to the surplus theory, Meek again differed somewhat from Dobb. He cited Smith's 'class stratification', his 'emphasis on the role of production', and the 'new concept of surplus (in value terms) which Smith developed as a substitute for the Physiocrats' concept', in addition to his treatment of labour embodied/labour commanded (1974, p. 156). This echoed his earlier work where, although he followed closely Marx's interpretation of Smith's labour command measure (1973a, pp. 60–81), he implicitly contradicted, or at least qualified, Marx's criticism of Smith's component parts of price. His work on the physiocrats led him to the view that Smith's identification of profit (at a uniform rate) as part of natural price, and his division of produce into the incomes of three classes, was a remarkably important achievement (see the quotation at the head of this chapter, and Meek, 1954, 1962, 1977, p. 6).

10.6   DOBB AND SCHUMPETER: A CLARIFICATION

On the question of Smith's position as the source of a cost of production stream of theory a confusion would seem to have crept into the literature in recent years. in a critical review of Dobb's work Bharadwaj said:

> A somewhat debatable attribution of the supply and demand approach to Adam Smith in *Theories of Value and Distribution since Adam Smith* (along lines suggested by Schumpeter) appears to reflect a vestigial continuance of such [Marshallian] reasoning. (1978a, p. 155, see also p. 167)

Roncaglia also connects Dobb's case with Schumpeter (Roncaglia 1978, p. 18, n.16). Schumpeter's general antipathy to Marshallian reasoning on this question prompts one to investigate this connection between Dobb and Schumpeter further. Schumpeter specifically rejected Marshall's idea of a continuous development of economic theory in the nineteenth century, and refuted his idea that there is a theoretically meaningful distinction between cost and demand theories (1954, pp. 921–3). When we combine this with his opinion that Smith rejected utility and scarcity, and explained distribution in a way that led straight to the theories of Ricardo and Marx, it confirms the hunch that Dobb's attribution of a supply and demand approach to Adam Smith, cannot possibly have been 'along lines suggested by Schumpeter' (Schumpeter, 1954, pp. 189n, 190, 301, 309, 558, and 1054).

This incorrect identifaction of Dobb's interpetation with that of Schumpeter would seem to have crept into the literature as a result of a highly misleading quotation by Dobb. Remarkably, Dobb *cited*

Schumpeter in defence of the view that there was a cost of production stream of value theory from Smith to Marshall. Discussing John Stuart Mill, he said:

> We shall see that he ended-up, at any rate, with a Cost of Production Theory which was essentially the Adding-up-of-Components Theory of Smith, borrowing something from Senior and even Say, on the one hand, and trying to reconcile the result with some Ricardian propositions, on the other. Schumpeter speaks of the 'Smith-Mill-Marshall line', and refuses to include J. S. Mill in Ricardo's school . . . (Dobb, 1973, p. 122)

It is this statement of Dobb's which is cited by both Bharadwaj (1978, p. 167) and Roncaglia (1978, p. 118) when linking Dobb's interpretation of Smith with Schumpeter's. But the passage in which Schumpeter said 'The Smith-Mill-Marshall line is clear enough' (p. 530) was not a discussion of the theory of value and distribution at all. Rather, it was an aside in which he compares the position and influence of the three great treatises, Smith's *Wealth of Nations*, Mill's *Principles*, and Marshall's *Principles*. In Schumpeter's view all three were summaries of theory as it stood in their day, rather than theoretical innovations; all three were encyclopaedic in their coverage; and all three became the dominant textbook of their age (p. 530).[11] Dobb's selective quotation from this passage is seriously misleading and, consequently, there is no basis for the idea that Schumpeter shared Dobb's interpretation of Smith.

11 Conclusion

> The problem facing Adam Smith was not an easy one, and it is therefore not surprising that his solution of it was far from complete ... Above all, we find in Adam Smith a correct formulation of the problem to be solved which is undoubtedly very important for its correct solution. (Dmitriev, 1889, p. 41)

It is clear from the literature that has been surveyed in Part II of this study that debate on the theory of value and distribution in Adam Smith's *Wealth of Nations* has been very lively for almost two centuries, and is likely to continue. It is entirely appropriate that the work of one of the greatest ever economists should be re-read and actively debated as economic theory develops and our understanding of its history changes. The central purpose of this study has been to examine the partly conflicting and partly complementary interpretations advanced by Dobb and Hollander by means of a detailed study of the *Wealth of Nations*. Both Dobb and Hollander advance interpretations which stress Smith's role in the development of value and distribution theory. Consequently, the secondary aim of this study has been to demonstrate the importance of adopting analytically correct definitions of the theories of value and distribution when considering Smith's work in relation to them or assessing his role in their development.[1]

11.1 SMITH AND THE SURPLUS THEORY

11.1.1 Summary of findings

In this section the main findings concerning Smith's work and the classical or surplus approach to value and distribution are first set out. Then the implications of these findings for the major modern interpretation of Smith's role in the development of classical theory are considered. It will transpire that the findings of this study all tend to undermine the conventional view, as expressed in the work of Dobb and Meek. In the third part the contrasts between the interpretation developed in this study and a number of other modern interpretations are outlined.

211

First, it has proven possible to identify Smith's definition of surplus in his discussion of the accumulation of capital in Book II, Chapter iii of the *Wealth of Nations*. This has hitherto been obscured by confusions about the meaning of his term 'annual produce', and by complications arising from his distinction between net and gross revenue (see Chapter 3 above). As a result it was shown that, contrary to the view of Spengler, Dobb and many others, Smith did not differ from the physiocrats, Ricardo and Marx, by including wages in his concept of economic surplus. In addition, it has been shown that in analysing accumulation Smith took total *produce* and the *capital* requirements of production as given magnitudes (explained by his theories of output, technology and the real wage), leaving the surplus – profits plus rents – as a residual. A number of other surplus relationships were identified in the *Wealth of Nations*, indicating that Smith had a rudimentary surplus theory of explanation of aggregate profits plus rents (see Section 3.4.2).

However, what is striking about these surplus relationships is that they dealt with accumulation rather than distribution. In particular, Smith did not use his surplus explanation of aggregate profits and rents to develop a theory of the *rate of profit*, his concern being, almost exclusively, the *amount* of surplus and its implications for accumulation. Finally, it was found that this proposition that Smith had a surplus theory of the non-wage share, is subject to a number of qualifications arising from ambiguous statements concerning the surplus nature of non-agricultural profits.

A detailed study of Smith's *measure* of value has revealed two things of significance. First, that the labour command measure was devised in order to measure changes in value due to changes in method of production. Second, that the measure was predicated not only on the assumption of a constant corn wage, but also on the assumption of a constant production cost of corn. The rational foundation which this gives to the famously difficult fifth chapter of Book I of the *Wealth of Nations*, and the consistency with which he adhered to the assumption of a constant price of corn, have not been appreciated to date. In addition, the investigation of the details of Smith's measure has raised serious doubts about the validity of the most widely accepted modern interpretation – that Smith's measure was not a measure of *value* at all, but a measure of welfare (see Section 5.4.4).

Turning to Smith's approach to price it was found that he made a major advance in the analysis of the relationship between price and costs of production. His resolution of price into wages, profits and rents *only*, was logically correct and was, indeed, formally similar to the reduction of price to dated or weighted labour of Dmitriev and Sraffa (see Section 6.1.1). However, it constituted a *theory* of value only in so far as there was a prior, or even a simultaneous determination of the rates of wages, profits and rents. But Smith provided no clear theory of the rate of profit. Despite his surplus *view* of aggregate profits he did not consistently relate the *rate* of profit to the *ratio of aggregate profits to aggregate capital* advanced – although hints at such an explanation can be seen (Sections 3.4 and 6.2). As a result we can only divine his theory of profit from his account of *movements* of the rate of profit in the face of various economic events. But his account of the eventual fall in the rate of profit was also unclear – occasionally relating the falling profit rate to the rising ratio of capital to output, more often ascribing it to increased competition. As a result of this failure to provide a theory of the rate of profit Smith's overall theory of value and distribution was judged to be indeterminate. In assessing his approach I identified the following dichotomy in the *Wealth of Nations*: Smith kept his surplus explanation of *aggregate* profits plus rents, when considering accumulation, quite separate from the theory in which he related the price of *individual* commodities to the *rates* of wages, profits and rents. Precisely what was needed to give explanatory value to this component parts of price was a *combination* of these two approaches (Section 6.3).

As a consequence of this indeterminacy Smith's approach to value provided an insufficient basis for the analysis of how *changes* in the rates of wages, profits or taxes, influence prices and distribution. In Sections 6.3, 6.4 and 6.5 it was shown that Smith's analysis of taxes and export subsidies were the least satisfactory parts of the *Wealth of Nations*. More importantly, it was shown precisely why this was so. The problems in Smith's analysis arose from the indeterminacy of his theory of profit, and from his continued adherence to his assumption of a constant price of corn – in situations where that assumption could not be valid. It should come as no surprise that his theory of distribution and his specification and use of a measure of value were related to one another, and this is precisely what has been found.

However, despite the formal indeterminacy of Smith's theory of price, due to the lack of a clear theory of the *rate* of profit, it would be quite wrong to conclude that Smith's *view* of the relation between price and its component parts was completely circular. His account of price and, in particular, price changes, make clear the direction of causation he envisaged in price determination. In explaining price he consistently took the rates of wages and profits as given, and focused on changes in price due to changes in methods of production. He considered that the rates of wages and profits change more slowly and less frequently than methods of production (Section 6.1.4).

Such was the dominance of Ricardo in nineteenth century economics that much of what is commonly believed about Adam Smith's ideas derives not from study of the *Wealth of Nations*, but from Ricardo's criticism of it in his *Principles*. This seems to be nowhere more true than in Dobb's interpretation of Smith's role in the development of economic theory – which placed great emphasis on Ricardo's supposed rejection of Smith's theoretical approach.

It was shown in Chapter 7 that once we have paid meticulous attention to Smith's text much of Ricardo's criticism of Smith appears in a subtly different light. But this subtle difference is crucial in accepting or rejecting Dobb's view of the way in which, and the extent to which, the theoretical approaches of Ricardo and Smith differed. In general, it emerged that Ricardo's rejection of Smith's assumption of a constant price of corn, in favour of the assumption of diminishing returns, played an important role in bringing him to different conclusions than Smith. In particular, it turns out that Ricardo did *not* consider Smith to have confused labour embodied and labour commanded. In addition, Ricardo did not consider, as Dobb says he did, 'that the Adam Smith theory leads to an absurd conclusion that the value of everything can rise simultaneously whenever one of the "components" rises for any reason' (Dobb, 1973, p. 76). Concentration on Ricardo's particular results concerning the relation between wages and prices, rather than on Ricardo's main substantive propositions, as for example by Dobb, has not only obscured the true theoretical innovation in Ricardo's work, but has also led to *exaggeration of the differences* between the theories of Smith and Ricardo.

Finally, Marx's extensive commentary on Smith was examined in detail in Chapter 8. It was confirmed that Marx viewed Smith as a surplus theorist. His many criticisms of Smith were studied and shown to boil down to one central point: Smith's failure to provide a theory of the rate of profit. For Marx, this meant that Smith had not developed his surplus *view* of distribution into a logically sound *theory* of value and distribution. This point was, of course, correct. As a result of it Marx said that in the *Wealth of Nations* prices were 'calculated' or 'discovered' by adding-up wages, profits and rents. In Chapter 8 I have explored in great detail what Marx did, and did not, mean by this description. In particular, it is shown that he did not consider Smith to have developed, or even attempted to develop, *independent* theories of wages, profits and rents. The adding-up was not a *theory* of value and distribution but the *outcome* of Smith's failure to close his theory of price with a clear theory of profit. Marx put it well when he said that rather than determine the *natural level* of the rate of profit, 'Adam Smith seeks refuge in a subsidiary investigation into the level of interest in different periods' (1861–63, II, p. 228).

Nevertheless, despite the validity of this criticism, Marx's account of Smith's work contained several inaccuracies. There arose from his idea that Smith alternated between a labour embodied and labour commanded explanation of value, and from his own strong belief that the labour theory of value was the *only* way to turn the surplus *view* of distributon, which he considered that Smith and he shared, into a *theory* of value and distribution. Although these inaccuracies might be considered to have been relatively slight, they do have significant *implications* for the validity of Marx's general account of Smith's work and, given Marx's influence, for the validity of the prevailing interpretation of Smith's role in the development of classical political economy. Marx was quite correct to say that the *Wealth of Nations* contained both a surplus view of distribution and an indeterminate theory of value. But, contrary to his view, the distinction between these two aspects of Smith's work does not *coincide* with the distinction between acceptance and rejection of a labour theory of value. It is not accurate to identify Smith's surplus view with a labour theory of value, and his indeterminate theory of value with a labour command approach.

11.1.2 Implications of these findings

We can now state the implications of these findings for our understanding of Smith's place in the development of classical political economy. They all serve to undermine the conventional view of Smith's role, as expressed in the later work of Maurice Dobb and, to a lesser extent, Ronald Meek.

The demonstration that Smith's concept of economic surplus consisted of profits and rents, but not wages, undermined the idea of Spengler, Dobb and others, that Smith's approach differed, in a very basic way, from that of the physiocrats, Ricardo and Marx. It also confirms that in seeking Smith's contribution to a classical or surplus tradition we must examine his idea of surplus, and the conceptual framework which underlies it, rather than seeking all sorts of incidental similarities between his work and that of Ricardo and Marx – such as his occasional relation of value to labour embodied, or hints at an 'exploitation' view of distribution (see Dobb, 1975).

Given his definition and use of profits plus rents as a surplus we can dispense with any idea that Smith's connection with a surplus approach was tenuous, or must be sought in incidental features of his work. At the same time one of the most important findings of this study was that Smith frequently considered changes in the *amount* of profits, but rarely related changes in the *rate* of profit to these. Furthermore, he did not consistently relate the natural rate of profit to the ratio of aggregate profits to aggregate capital advanced. But this means that his failure to determine the rate of profit, and through that, the indeterminacy of his theory of value, cannot be traced to the *problem of measuring* aggregate profits and aggregate capital advanced (see Bharadwaj, 1980; Kurz, 1980).

But this has immediate further implications for Dobb's interpretation of Smith's role in development of classical economics – since that interpretation derives from Marx's account of Smith and a particular reading of Ricardo's criticism. In the work of both Ricardo and Marx the labour theory of value was used precisely in order to measure aggregate profits and aggregate capital advanced (Sraffa, 1951; Garegnani, 1984). It follows that the adoption of the labour theory of value could suggest itself only *after* a formal attempt to determine the rate of profit was made. But since Smith did not relate the natural rate of profit to the ratio of aggregate profits to aggregate capital advanced he could not have seen the need to use the labour theory of value. It follows that Smith's failure to solve the problem of value and distribution should not be traced to his 'abandonment' of the labour theory of value. This tends to undermine Dobb's view that Smith's contribution to the development of classical political economy was his occasional relation of relative value to relative labour quantities (Dobb, 1973, 1975).

These points are independently confirmed by my clarification of the fact the Smith's measure of value was designed to measure changes in value due to changes in methods of production. In addition, the identification of the assumptions which Smith adopted in using his labour command measure show that it is not correct to say that he confused labour embodied and labour commanded. Nor did he vacillate between a labour embodied and labour commanded *explanation* of value – a fact which is confirmed by the argument that he was not aware of the device of reducing means of production to past labour (see Appendix to Chapter 6).

This new study of Smith's approach to value in the *Wealth of Nations* (Chapter 6) and the re-examination of Ricardo's and Marx's commentaries on Smith (Chapters 7 and 8 respectively) seriously undermine what remains of Dobb's interpretation of Smith's place in the development of classical political economy. Dobb's case was that Smith's contribution to classical economics was his analysis of a pre-capitalist economy – the labour theory of value. An important corollary of this view was that Smith's analysis of price in a *capitalist* economy – the 'component parts of price' – was inherently a contribution to an opposed stream of theory. A vital part of this argument was that Smith's component parts of price, and his account of the relation between wages and prices, were part of a single, coherent and consistently held *adding-up theory* of value. In Dobb's view it was this theory which led to the 'absurd conclusion that the value of everything can rise simultaneously whenever one of the "components" rise for any reason' (Dobb, 1973, p. 76).

It was this theory that Ricardo was said to reject in his criticism of Smith's determination of value by 'supply and demand reasoning'. Finally, the term 'adding-up' clearly derived from Marx's commentary on Smith, as did the idea that Smith's essential contribution to classical theory was the labour theory of value, and that his essential error was the abandonment of that theory.

But the reading of Smith's component parts of price inherent in this interpretation has been shown in Chapter 6 to be quite mistaken. The idea that Smith had a single, coherent and consistently held adding-up theory is untenable. Dobb derived it by conflating Smith's analysis of two different things: a *tax on wages* and the *corn export bounty*. From this he attributed to Smith the view that a tax on wages would raise all prices.

The clarification of Smith's analysis of taxes and the corn export bounty confirms that the analysis was unsatisfactory, but shows that, contrary to what Dobb says, Smith did not hold that a rise in any component of cost would raise all prices. Furthermore, Smith's proposition that the 'money price of corn regulates that of all home-made commodities' was confined to the case of the corn export bounty and, more importantly, was not a corollary of a developed and consistently held adding-up *theory* of value and distribution. That view ignores completely the role of Smith's assumption of a constant price of corn in generating these results.

Likewise, the clarification of Smith's account of value and of Ricardo's criticism of it show that Dobb's interpretation involved a great exaggeration of the differences between Smith and Ricardo.

Finally, the study of Smith himself, of Ricardo and of Marx allow us to clarify in what sense we may say that in the *Wealth of Nations* price is arrived at by 'adding-up' wages, profit and rents. It can be said that for Smith prices were determined by methods of production and the state of distribution. But this state of distribution was not successfully analysed by Smith; his failure to determine the rate of profit meant that no clear analytical relationships between wages, profits and rents were specified. The result was that in his account, in which value was related to methods of production and distribution, prices were, in effect, arrived at by adding up wages, profit and rent.

But this was emphatically *not* a *theory* of value in the sense that Smith had coherent and *independent* theories of the rates of wages, profits and rents. Rather it was the *result* of an *absence*, or failure, of his theory of distribution (see Chapter 6.1). Indeed, it was indicated in Chapter 8 that this was how Marx viewed it when he invented the 'adding up' description (see Section 8.5.1 above). This view of the precise sense in which Smith's approach to natural price can be described by the term 'adding up' would seem to be confirmed by the words which Marx chose in making this observation. Rather than say that Smith's *theory determined* prices by adding up, he said that in Smith's work prices are 'calculated', 'compounded', or 'discovered' by adding up – a description which was echoed by Sraffa, who said that prices were 'arrived at by a process of *adding up* the wages, profit and rent' (Sraffa, 1951, p. xxxv).

This view that 'adding-up' was not a *theory* of value and distribution is confirmed when Smith's various statements concerning the relation between wages, profits, rents and taxes are studied in detail. Smith's results derived from his theory of distribution (such as it was) and his measure of value. By ignoring the role of Smith's measure of value Dobb saw all his results as a 'corollary' of what he calls Smith's 'Adding-up Theory' (Dobb 1973, pp. 46–7 and 76; and see Section 10.2 above). In doing this he went beyond what the adding-up description validly implies – and, most significantly, went well beyond what Marx meant by it.

11.1.3 Contrast with other modern interpretations

In recent years a number of authors have presented interpretations of where Smith fits into the development of the classical or surplus approach to value and distribution. The analysis undertaken in this study provides the means to critically evaluate these interpretations and to point to an older one which was more satisfactory. Christensen has argued that because Smith's approach to price determination is consistent with a modern version of the classical system, 'Smith is the solution to the set of Sraffian equations!' (Christensen, 1979, pp. 107–8). However, he comments that:

> Unfortunately (Smith's production prices) are not set out in terms of the valuation of the matter (raw materials and intermediate goods) and labour required in production (along the lines indicated by Cantillon) ... but as the wages and profits to which they reduce ... *Consequently* the decomposition of prices into wages, rents, and profit *did not readily indicate the direction for the later development of production prices.* (Christensen, 1979, pp. 107 and 102, emphasis added)

The findings of this study imply that this is an unsatisfactory statement of the exact relation of Smith to the surplus theory of value and distribution.

First, Smith was, in all probability, unaware of the possibility of reducing means of production to past labour (see the Appendix to Chapter 6). This provides an explanation of *why* he set out production cost as he did. Second, strictly speaking, from the point of view of *price*, it makes no difference whether the equations refer to the 'valuation of matter' or to the wages and profits to which they reduce.[2] Consequently, it is hard to see this as a *reason* why Smith's treatment 'did not readily indicate the direction for the later development of production price'.

Another discussion of how Smith's work relates to the surplus theory in its logically coherent form is to be found in Kurz (1980). He argues, in criticism of Christensen, that any comparison between Smith and Sraffa must focus on their respective explanations of profits, 'since in this seems to be the key to a proper understanding of both the unifying and separating elements in the two theories' (Kurz, 1980, p. 271). Because of the limitations of Smith's explanation of value and profits he concludes that Christensen's assertion that 'Smith is the solution to the set of Sraffian equations' is 'vastly exaggerated' (Kurz, 1980, p. 275). On the other hand what similarity there is between the two theories arises 'precisely . . . because Smith's explanation of profits is based on the *surplus approach*' (ibid., p. 271). It is hard to find fault with these conclusions, as they stand. However, the position from within which Kurz launches this criticism is one which has been the subject of detailed investigation in this study and found wanting in several important respects. Kurz embraces a number of traditional views on Smith, which mostly derive from Marx, and which they were re-stated in the later work of Dobb (1973 and 1975) and Meek (1974 and 1977).

He suggests that Smith had a labour commanded explanation of value – and this is certainly very doubtful (Kurz, 1980, pp. 272–3; see Sections 5.6 and 6.2). Related to this, it is argued that Smith's measure of value did not succeed in expressing a given social surplus and a given social capital in value terms, in order to arrive at a determination of the uniform rate of profit (ibid., p. 273). But it has been shown in this study that Smith's measure of value was not *designed* for that purpose.

Indeed, Kurz's view of what Smith aimed for, but failed to achieve, in proposing his measure of value, is inconsistent with his next, and central, point: namely, that the *evidence* that 'Smith's explanation of profits is based on the surplus approach' lies in the fact that he described profits as a 'deduction from the produce of labour', and that he considered that profits would be high when wages were low and *vice versa*. 'Thus', concludes Kurz, 'he advocated an embryonic "exploitation" theory' (Kurz, 1980, p. 273; a conclusion with which Christensen agrees, op. cit., p. 94). But it would surely be remarkable indeed for Smith, with only this *embryonic* surplus theory of profits, to have sought a measure of value in order to solve the ratio of aggregate profits to aggregate capital advanced. It would seem that one or other proposition must be abandoned.

Kurz argues that a 'further illustration' of the 'esoteric' side of Smith is that, 'although he rejected a labour embodied approach to value theory, he nevertheless used it in comparison to labour commanded and suggested that a difference between the two is indicative of the existence of profits' (Kurz, 1980, p. 274). But it was pointed out in Section 5.4 that there is only *one* passage in which Smith cited the *difference* between the labour embodied in, and labour commanded by, the annual produce as a measure of potential accumulation (*WN*, I.vi.24). The passage refers to the *sum* of profits and rents and is concerned with accumulation and not distribution. Although Smith's argument contains an interesting insight it is significant that it was nowhere developed by him. In particular, these aggregates were *not* referred to when considering the determination of the *rate* of profit.

Kurz seems to accept Marx's view that Smith's study of the component parts of price was entirely 'exoteric' or shallow. He says, quite correctly, that Smith's resolution of prices 'misled him to the proposition that the same holds true for the *whole* price of exchangeable value of the annual produce', but he *infers*, incorrectly, from this that 'he *thus* confused net and gross product' (Kurz, 1980, p. 274, emphasis added). It has been shown in Chapter 3 that Smith did not confuse net and gross produce – and that *when considering accumulation* he made telling use of the concepts of produce, capital and revenue. What is true is that, *when dealing with value and its relation to distribution*, he had recourse to the idea that the whole annual produce resolves into aggregate wages, profits and rents – an idea which was of little help, and may have been a hindrance. What this suggests is that, contrary to what Kurz argues, the limits of Smith's surplus theory of distribution were not those posed by the simultaneity of prices and the rate of profit (and for which the labour theory of value or a certain measure of value would be an appropriate solution) but were those which arise at a more rudimentary level.

A second implication of the resolution of natural price into wages, profits and rents was Smith's idea that natural price varies with variations in the natural rates of its component parts. 'The spurious impression is close at hand', Kurz argues, 'that the real wage rate and the rate of profit could be determined *independently*'. It follows that 'therefore, Smith's failure to offer a consistent theory of value not only *prevented him from a correct determination of the rate of profit* but also led him to develop a *harmonious* view of capitalism' (Kurz, 1980, p. 274, first emphasis added). My study indicates that the limitations of Smith's treatment of value and distribution would be more accurately described the other way around; in other words, that his failure to determine or even pose the problem of the rate of profit *was the cause* of his failure to provide a complete theory of value. And, furthermore, that his failure concerning profits arose because of his not having gone much beyond a rudimentary surplus view of the *amount* of profits plus rent, combined with his partial adherence to a vaguely specified traditional theory that the rate of profit was influenced by the intensity of competition. Finally, it was shown in Section 6.1 that Smith's statement that natural price varies with the natural rates of wages and profits must be read in its context.

Kurz's conclusion is that 'Adam Smith was a most important progenitor of Sraffa's surplus-equations approach to the explanation of the rate of profit' (Kurz, 1980, p. 279). The only evidence cited in defence of this is Smith's *description* of profits as a 'deduction', his belief that wages and profits were inversely related, and his single comparison of aggregate labour embodied and labour commanded (ibid., pp. 273–4). My findings suggest a number of important qualifications to Kurz's conclusion. Smith's most striking achievement, where value was concerned, was his simplification of the relation between price and production cost. To this extent he might be more properly considered a progenitor of what Garegnani calls the 'price-equations method' rather than the 'surplus-equations' approach (Garegnani, 1984, p. 309). For, although definite surplus relationships are to be found in his work, he did not explicitly or consistently explain the *rate* of profit in that fashion. The most that can be said is that running through his explanation of the rate of profit in different countries and stages of development, there was, among others, an argument which related it to the relative magnitudes of produce and capital (see Section 6.2 above).

In considering Smith's role in the development of the classical theory both Christensen and Kurz have, following Dobb, elevated the particular work of Ricardo and Marx into a yardstick against which to measure Smith's performance. The major feature of such an approach is, of course, to attach unwarranted significance to the labour theory of value; but, in addition, insufficient attention is given to the *concept* of surplus and the conceptual framework which underlies it. This results in them posing irrelevant questions and stating inconsistent conclusions, such as those that have been noted above. In this study an attempt has been made to identify in more detail the exact nature of any surplus theory in Smith, and then to take account of the implications which that theory would have for his treatment of value and distribution. This constitutes an attempt to escape from the tendency to ascribe a very rudimentary 'deduction' or exploitation' theory to him, while at the same time critically evaluating his treatment of value as if he were in a position similar to that of Ricardo sometime between the *Essay on Profits* and the *Principles*.

A much more satisfactory account of the relation of Smith's work to the surplus theory of value and distribution was presented by Dmitriev as early as 1898. Having identified the correct solution to the analytical problem posed by the surplus approach to value and distribution, Dmitriev credited Smith with having made a major contribution to that theory. In considering the determination of price Smith was faced with the long list of production costs as presented in Steuart's *Principles* (1767):

> Naturally, at this stage of development the theory of production costs fully merits the reproach so often levelled at the theory of production costs *in general* . . . that it defines price from prices, that it defines one unknown from other unknowns. (Dmitriev, 1898, p. 41)

Dmitriev's view, as conveyed in the statement which has been placed at the head of this chapter, was that faced with this difficult problem Smith made a number of modifications to the theory of production costs, and thereby formulated it as the problem of value and distribution.

To begin with, Smith pointed out that the value of tools and materials 'could invariably be broken down, in its turn into *wages, profit* and *rent* . . . so that all production costs may be reduced to (these) three elements' (Dmitriev, 1898, p. 42). Second, he further simplified the equation of production cost by showing that the *amount* of profits was determined by the *rate* of profit, the value of goods advanced as capital, and the time for which goods were advanced (Dmitriev, 1898, pp. 46–7). The importance of thus relating price to the *rate* of profit 'is only revealed', in Dmitriev's view, when we introduce the uniform rate of profit – 'another hypothesis of prime importance established by Adam Smith' (Dmitriev, 1898, p. 48). With each price related to production costs in this manner the relative price of goods will be determined once the rate of profit is given – but Smith did not succeed in providing a convincing theory of that rate (ibid., pp. 49–50).

Dmitriev's account of Smith's contribution, and of the basic continuity of production cost theory from Smith to Ricardo, accords with the findings of this study. Recall that we considered Smith closer to the 'price-equations approach' than the 'surplus equation approach'. But, by stressing the formal identity of Smith's price equation with that found in the complete solution it is important not to conceal the *process* by which Ricardo reached his new theory of the rate of profit (ibid., p. 59). The process by which Ricardo reached that new theory – or at least, the process whereby he, and Marx, found a means of presenting it – involved a *retreat* from Smith's equation of *price* to money costs of production to the *physical* data of inputs and outputs.

General conclusion on Smith and the classical tradition

The conclusion of this study is that Smith can be seen to have been at once both further from, and nearer to, the surplus theory of value and distribution, than has hitherto been thought. Further from it, in that his analysis of surplus concentrated almost completely on the question of accumulation and very little on distribution – and, in particular, he was a long way from a surplus theory of the rate of profit. Yet, he can be seen as *nearer* to the surplus theory in that the element of surplus theory in his work was more *certain* than one would gather from those accounts which, focussing on the labour theory of value, have to explain his vacillation and ultimate rejection of the surplus approach (*sic*). Ironically, a realistic recognition of the limited state of the surplus theory of *value and distribution* in Smith's work, and in his time, leads to much more positive assessment of his contribution overall. For, in that case, he is not seen to have switched incomprehensibly between two conflicting and relatively complete theories.

11.2 SMITH AND THE NEOCLASSICAL THEORY

In assessing Hollander's claim that Smith was attempting to formulate a general equilibrium of supply and demand it is vital to make reference to a clear definition of general equilibrium. There were several implications of adopting an analytically correct definition of neoclassical theory. The first was that a neoclassical explanation of value and distribution relies, at even the simplest level, on the specification of particular price-quantity relationships which are, to borrow Marshall's term, 'normal'. Those relationships describe the activity of substitution by consumers and producers. The second implication, going somewhat deeper, was the importance of *utility* as the indispensible foundation for an analytically sound derivation of supply and demand. Recall Wieser's criterion: 'as forerunners of the theory, we may name generally all those who have derived value from utility' (Wieser, 1888, p. xxxii). The third implication was recognition of the importance of *given endowments*, both in the supply and demand 'vision' of the economic process, and in the rigorous derivation of supply and demand relations. And the final implication was a distinction between two quite different concepts of 'self-adjustment'.

11.2.1 Findings

In Chapter 9 the structure of Hollander's case in his *Economics of Adam Smith* was identified and each of the arguements assessed. It was concluded that, despite its many valuable contributions to our understanding of Smith, the book fails to demonstrate that Smith attempted to formulate a general equilibrium of supply and demand.

The *Wealth of Nations* contains many statements relating quantity and price. Hollander has argued that these are evidence that Smith 'had in mind' demand and supply schedules, both 'applicable to the market period' and operating in the long run. The evidence cited to demonstrate these propositions has been examined in detail and shown to be unable to support them. Smith's account of the fluctuations of *market* price and quantity supplied around their natural levels, on the one hand, and of the *secular* movements of price and quantity made possible by division of labour and extension of the market, on the other, cannot validly be portrayed as examples of a 'supply and demand' explanation of value. And other isolated statements relating price to quantity were not developed in any systematic way by Smith (see Sections 9.2.1 and 9.4.2 above).

Hollander's case is unusual in that, unlike almost all other scholars, he does not accept that Smith did little to develop a utility and demand based explanation of value. Because of this striking departure, and because of the importance of utility in a supply and demand explanation of value, this part of his case deserved particular attention. Study of the passages which, in his view, demonstrate Smith's explanation of value in terms of utility and scarcity, in my judgement, shows no use of these concepts in a systematic way to determine value (see Section 9.2).

Perhaps the most ubiquitous argument for a theoretical continuity from Smith to modern economics is that based on the idea that he explained value by cost of production. Frequently this was seen as significant because it indicated Smith's rejection of the labour theory of value, and consequently of the sort of theories associated with Ricardo and Marx (see the references cited in Section 10.1 above). Such a reading is understandable given the importance of Ricardo's work, and the way his labour theory was interpreted by both supporters and opponents in the mid-nineteenth century. However, recent historical and theoretical work allows a different perspective on the labour theory of value, and this in turn allows a different view of Smith's rejection of the labour theory.

The idea that Smith and other writers of the classical era had a cost of production theory was seen by Marshall as evidence that neoclassical theory was not 'a new doctrine of value which is in sharp contrast to the old' (Marshall, 1890, p. 676). This view of Smith's, so-called, cost of production theory, *as a version of supply and demand theory*, has always required, and received, the support of some additional argument to the effect that he assumed constant returns to scale (see the works cited in Section 10.1). However, the logic of this interpretation breaks down once it is moved outside of partial equilibrium (see Bladen, 1938, pp. 41–2). The assumption of constant returns to scale is not sufficient to remove the effect of demand on prices. Alterations in the pattern of demand will cause changes in factor prices and hence in product prices. What was revealed when attention was given to the properties of a *general* supply and demand theory, and to the properties of the surplus theory, was that the relation between price and cost of production has, fundamentally, much less to do with the contrast between *demand* and *cost*, than with the relation between *value* and *distribution*.

Consequently, Hollander was the first to undertake a detailed study of Smith with a view to demonstrating that he formulated 'the *general* theory of economic equilibrium by way of price mechanism' (Hollander, 1973, p. 15). However, as has been revealed in Chapter 9, this does not consist of an extension to Smith's account of *distribution*, of the argument that Smith considered value to be determined by supply and demand, and the presentation of compelling textual evidence for this view. Instead, it consists, very largely, of an extension to distribution of the traditional argument that Smith's account of value was *confined to a restricted special case*. Thus, in moving from a partial equilibrium to general equilibrium interpretation, Hollander has added to the traditional argument, that Smith assumed constant returns to scale, the additional proposition that he also assumed constant quantities of each factor, *constant* factor proportions within each industry, and *identical* factor proportions across industries (Hollander, 1973, pp. 140, 121–3). It can be seen how Smith's adoption of these assumptions (*sic*) might explain why in his work, as Hollander explains, 'the average rates of return remain constant following a change in the structure of industry', how 'there is no generalised recognition of factor substitutability' and how 'a change in the pattern of demand would lead to a reallocation of factors' (Hollander, 1973, pp. 122–3, 306–7 and see also 219–21 and 124). But it is not clear how such an analysis can be a demonstration of Hollander's central proposition, that 'Smith's formal treatment of value theory may best be appreciated if envisaged as an attempt to achieve a conception of long-run general equilibrium' (ibid., p. 114, see also pp. 121 and 307). This is because with those restrictive assumptions there can be no factor demand functions, and consumer demand can play no role in the determination of price.

Hollander has successfully challenged the view that Smith was concerned with accumulation and growth to the exclusion of allocation. However, he has not demonstrated that the question of allocation which concerned Smith was similar to the question of allocation which is central to supply and demand theory. This is because he has emphatically not shown that Smith considered labour, capital and land to exist in given endowments. This is the crucial requirement and at several places it undermines Hollander's interpretation (see Sections 9.4.3 and 9.5).

Another argument which has been used to identify Smith as an important forerunner of neoclassical theory is that based on his analysis of natural prices as a 'centre of repose and continuance' (see for example, Blaug, 1978, pp. 41–2; Kaushil, 1973, pp. 67–8, and Jaffe, 1977, p. 21). Adherence to clear definitions indicates that a distinction can, and should, be drawn between the gravitation towards natural price created by the action of competition (as analysed by Smith in his famous Chapter vii), and the movement towards equality of supply and demand of goods and factors of production by *substitution* in reponse to prices. In addition to this *analytical* distinction between these two, the examination of the evidence cited by Hollander has shown that no systematic development of the concept of substitution has been demonstrated in the *Wealth of Nations* (indeed Hollander agrees with this conclusion – see his statements on pp. 124 and 306–7 of the *Economics of Adam Smith*).

However, there would seem to be a further element in the argument that Smith's analysis of Chapter vii of Book I of the *Wealth of Nations* marks him as essentially a supply and demand theorist. Implicit in the case seems to be the view that, theoretically, the gravitation in question, if it were fully understood, would *necessarily imply the determination of value by supply and demand* in both the long run and the short run. Where this view is simply asserted it is quite unsatisfactory – for the explanation of the *process* of gravitation to an equilibrium of supply and demand is acknowledged to be a difficult and unresolved question. As a speculative proposition, it is open to considerable doubt.[3] Pending further exploration of this question we must note the historical fact that theorists with quite different *explanations* of value and distribution have shared the single long period *method* of analysis. In this situation we have no alternative but to base our conclusion on Smith's *text*. Examination of his account of gravitation to a uniform rate of profit shows no systematic explanation of prices by supply and demand, in the sense which these terms have in neoclassical theory.

Dobb's case that Smith was the 'source' of supply and demand theory had two elements. The first was to contrast Smith's approach to value and distribution with that of Ricardo and Marx – identifying Smith's theory as a cost of production theory in which distribution was determined by supply and demand. The second was to link Smith's 'cost of production' theory with neoclassical theory by identifying a theoretical continuity from Smith, through Malthus and Mill to Marshall. Both these elements have been questioned in this study.

In Chapters 7 and 10 it was shown that Dobb greatly exaggerated the differences between Ricardo and Smith, by presenting a very questionable reading of Ricardo's criticism of the *Wealth of Nations*. In Chapter 8 it was shown that Dobb used the term 'adding-up theory' to describe Smith's work in a way which differed considerably from Marx's usage. Finally, Dobb drew so strong a contrast between Smith, on the one hand, and Ricardo and Marx, on the other, that he ultimately questioned whether Smith made *any* contribution *at all* to the development of the classical or surplus approach to value and distribution (see Section 10.5). The idea of a continuity of cost of production theory from Smith to Marshall was also challenged (see Section 10.4). It is argued that from the perspective of either neoclassical or surplus theory the contrast between *demand* and *cost* is not significant – what matters is the relation between *value* and *distribution*. In fact Dobb did not undertake a fresh investigation of the factors which link the work of the mid-nineteenth-century theorists (Malthus, Senior and Mill) with Smith, on the one hand, and with neoclassical theory, on the other. The research reported in this study makes no claim to be such an investigation. But the clarification of a number of aspects of Smith's own work does provide the basis for a more detailed study of some of their claims to Smithian orthodoxy.

The way in which that two streams interpretation was stated by Dobb and Meek tends to create the impression of *symmetry* between propositions linking Smith with classical theory and those linking him with neoclassical economics. This appearance of symmetry is strengthened by the fact that both writers said, not only that Smith *contributed* to both 'streams of theory', but that he was a *source* of both streams (Dobb, 1975, p. 329; 1973, pp. 112, 118; Meek, 1975, p. 154). However, this study shows that, as presented to date, these two propositions are not at all symmetrical. Smith was a *part* of the development of classical theory. This proposition, as re-fashioned in this study, does not require the attribution of any later theories to Smith. Nor does it require any speculation concerning what Smith may have 'had in mind', as opposed to what he said. Nor does it require any explanation as to why Smith's anticipation of sophisticated theories was so completely misunderstood by his successors. Finally, the case presented here does not require that where Smith was confused, unclear or contradictory he must be said to have been moving in the direction of surplus theory. Indeed, what has emerged is that a surplus approach to value and distribution was only a very small part of a work which contained many elements. These elements may, in fact, be parts of systematic lines of thought inherited from various predecessors. It has not been possible, in this study, to trace the *origin* of many of Smith's ideas. Ultimately, the case made rests on what has been cited from his work.

Notes and References

2 THEORIES OF VALUE AND DISTRIBUTION

1. The term 'classical economics' has been used in two other senses also. It is used in many modern commentaries to denote the major British writings in the period from Adam Smith to John Stuart Mill (see, for example, O'Brien, 1975). Secondly, the term was used by Keynes to describe economics from Ricardo up to and including Marshall, Edgeworth and Pigou (Keynes, 1936, p. 3). My usage is that proposed by Marx (1859, p. 52).

2. The analytical problem of determining the rate of profit and relative prices was solved, prior to Sraffa, by Dmitriev (1898) and Bortkiewicz (1906). Recent presentations of the analytical structure can be found in Pasinetti (1977) and Garegnani (1984) and more general discussion, and further references, in Bradley and Howard (1982).

3. See Malthus, 1820, pp. 36–43. There is disagreement among historians of economic thought on the extent to which the critics of Ricardo anticipated neoclassical theory. Ekelund *et al.* (1972) survey these developments and suggest, following Schumpeter (1954, p. 602), that Malthus may have been an exception to what they describe as the 'hopeless confusion in classical writings on demand' (Ekelund *et al.*, 1972, p. 8; see also Walras, 1874, p. 202; Stigler, 1954). Bowley considers that 'Longfield and Malthus did not realise there was any clear connection between utility and demand', and concludes that the writers of this period cannot be considered to have anticipated Jevons (Bowley, 1972, p. 26; and see also Moss, 1976, p. 39 and 1974).

4. This definition of equilibrium has been changed in modern formulations. In these the equilibrium condition is that the price of each good be equal to *or less than* its cost of production. If cost exceeds price then the optimal output of the good is zero – it is not produced (see Intrilligator, 1971, p. 336). This change has important consequences for neoclassical theory, which have been brought to light by Garegnani (1976). However, these are not directly relevant to the subject matter of this book – though see note 3 to Chapter 11.

5. In his earlier work Marshall had explicitly denied the symmetry of demand and supply, which he was later to describe as 'fundamental' (see Marshall, 1879a, p. 2).

6. Thus, for example, Stigler identified his own cost of production interpretation with that of Marshall and Viner, and contrasted this with the view of Schumpeter, Cannan and Whitaker, who considered that Ricardo held a labour theory of value (Stigler, 1958, p. 332;

Marshall, 1890, pp. 416–17 and pp. 671–2; Viner, 1930, pp. 78–80; and see also Gordon, 1959; Schumpeter, 1954, pp. 590–95; Cannan, 1929, p. 172; and Whitaker, 1904, p. 130).

7. It involved a confusion between what Smith and what Ricardo said on the labour theory of value. Smith confined the labour theory to a pre-capitalist economy; when he added capital, he added profit to his definition of price (*WN*, I.vi.7). Ricardo, on the other hand, made it absolutely clear, in his reply to Malthus, that even where the labour theory holds the value of a commodity equals its cost of production *including profits* (Ricardo, *Works*, II, p. 42, see also pp. 34, 46, 101, and 47).

3 SURPLUS

1. Black gives an account of the changing perception of Smith's work and notes that 'the striking point which emerges here is how very recently the position from which we are not accustomed to judge Smith's contribution has been reached'. He says that it was really only after the appearance of Myint (1943) and (1948) that economists generally began to see Adam Smith in this light (Black, 1976, p. 61). O'Brien considers that Myint's 'important message, well-formulated though it was, might have fallen on much less receptive ears but for the change of focus which the subject itself had experienced' (O'Brien, 1976b, p. 64).

2. References to Smith's work are to the Glasgow Edition of the *Works and Correspondence of Adam Smith* commissioned by the University of Glasgow to celebrate the bicentenary of the *Wealth of Nations*. The abbreviations and method of reference used in the Glasgow Edition are adopted in this volume. Thus the *Wealth of Nations* is abbreviated to *WN*, *Lectures on Jurisprudence*: Report of 1762–63 is abbreviated to *LJ*(A), and *Lectures on Jurisprudence*: Report dated 1766 is denoted *LJ*(B). References to the *Wealth of Nations* are given according to the original divisions, together with the paragraph numbers added in the margin of the Glasgow Edition. For example, *WN*, I.x.b.1 refers to *Wealth of Nations*, Book I, Chapter x, section b, paragraph 1.

3. Cannan considered it a 'mere chimaera' because 'It is impossible to form any conception of the aggregate of products, intermediate and ultimate, all jumbled together. We cannot think of a country's annual produce as consisting of x qrs. of wheat and y sacks of flour and z lbs. of bread' (Cannan, 1898, p. 60; but see *WN*, IV.ix.32). This comment was written before the development of input-output theory (indeed, before Keynes' definition of 'total sales' in Chapter 6 of the General Theory) and reflects the enthusiasm of its era with Marshall's definition of 'Social Income' as including everything which yields utility (see Keynes, 1936, p. 62; Marshall, 1879b, p. 53; and Kendrick, 1968, p. 21).

4. The question of whether Smith considered all capital to consist of workers' subsistence, or at least of circulating capital, is one that has been much discussed. There seems little doubt that Smith was aware of

the importance of fixed capital; yet, his analytical system would frequently seem to be unable to deal with this (for a similar view see Hollander, 1973, pp. 154–6 and pp. 188–92).

5. There has been much discussion of Smith's 'debt' to the Physiocrats which, of course, raises also the question of the influence of his British predecessors (see Cannan, 1896, 1898, 1937; Meek, 1951, 1954; Groenewegen, 1969; Hollander, 1973; and Skinner, 1976).

6. This resolution of the annual produce has been the subject of much criticism. We are not concerned in this chapter with its validity or usefulness as a way of analysing the determination of value or distribution (see Section 6.1 below).

7. Smith introduced his distinction between 'gross' and 'neat' revenue, a measure of social *consumption* as follows:

> *The gross revenue of all the inhabitants of a great country, comprehends the whole annual produce of their land and labour; the neat revenue,* what remains free to them after deducting the expense of maintaining; first, their fixed; and secondly, their circulating capital; *or what, without encroaching upon their capital, they can place in their stock reserved for immediate consumption, or spend upon their subsistence, conveniences, and amusements. Their real wealth too is in proportion, not to their gross, but to their net, revenue.* (*WN*, II.ii.5, italics added)

In my view the italicised words contain Smith's meaning, and the remainder is the cause of the mistaken view that Smith was here attempting to define net produce or surplus. To see this, note exactly what elements of fixed and circulating Smith did actually deduct from gross revenue to get net revenue (see text below, and Notes 8 and 9).

8. Smith's procedure here was perfectly rational and was, indeed, virtually identical to modern national income accounting. The materials and tools used up in maintaining fixed capital are part of gross revenue (annual produce) but are not part of net revenue (*WN*, II.ii.6). But the wages of workers employed in maintaining fixed capital are part of net revenue because they are 'placed in the stock reserved for immediate consumption'.

He compared this production devoted to fixed capital maintenance with other lines of production, where 'both the price [of the labour] and the produce go to this stock [reserved for consumption], the price to that of the workmen, the produce to that of other people, whose subsistence, conveniences, and amusements, are augmented by the labour of the workmen' (*WN*, II.ii.6). This reflects his view that, as Eltis puts it, 'so long as investment in fixed capital... is ignored, the entire National Income is consumed in each period' (1975, p. 435).

9. When including *money* in circulating capital, and the cost of maintaining it among the deductions from gross revenue, Smith had commodity money (gold and silver) in mind (see *WN*, II.i.27 and *WN*, II.ii.13).

When explaining the detailed calculation of 'neat' revenue Smith spelt out clearly that, *for the purpose of measuring social consumption*, there is a difference between the circulating capital of an individual undertaker and the circulating capital of society as a whole:

> The circulating capital of a society is in this respect different from that of an individual. That of an individual is totally excluded from making any part of his neat revenue, which must consist altogether of his profits. But though the circulating capital of every individual makes a part of that of the society to which he belongs, *it is not upon that account totally excluded from making a part likewise of their neat revenue.* (*WN*, II.ii.10)

This explains why Smith's *initial statement* of the distinction between 'gross' and 'neat' revenue (quoted in Note 7 above) was misleading.

10. In the previous chapter (II.i) Smith would seem to have allowed that some elements of *circulating* capital also might be turned over in *longer* than a year (*WN*, II.1.23). But thereafter he seems to have ignored this possibility.

11. See, for example, Malthus, 1820, p. 51; Böhm-Bawerk, 1884, p. 242; Douglas, 1928, pp. 95 *et seq.*; Hutt, 1954, p. 44; Knight, 1956, p. 13; Dobb, 1973, pp. 45–6; Reisman, 1976, pp. 167–9; Bowley, 1937, p. 58 – but for a rejection of her earlier view, see Bowley, 1973a, pp. 120–1.

12. While I question the validity of making inferences about Smith's *theory* purely from his use of the term 'deduction' I cannot share Hollander's view that 'the statements referring to profits as deductions from the produce of labour do not refer to the non-productivity of capital but reflect rather the "injustice" of profits as a separate class income' (Hollander, 1973, p. 152). We can find no evidence that Smith considered profits to be ethically wrong (see his statement at *WN*, V.ii.f.2 and our discussion of it below). Hollander's views on the 'non-productivity' of capital are discussed in Section 9.3.1.

13. Smith said that interest seems '*at first sight*' a good subject for taxation because he saw two problems with implementing such a tax. First, it is difficult to ascertain how much capital each person owns and, second, capital is highly mobile (*WN*, V.ii.f.5 and 6). However, he did consider that several taxes on profits, which were in operation in Europe, did in fact 'fall upon the interest of money' (*WN*, V.ii.g.13, and see *WN*, V.ii.f.7–14).

14. See, for example, Myint, 1948, p. 78; Spengler, 1959b, p. 2n; Hollander, 1973, ch. 10, and Campbell and Skinner, 1976, pp. 32–4, who cite an early objection by Governer Pownall.

15. There were further *changes* or *differences* considered by Smith in the analysis of which he made explicit or implicit reference to his *theory of what determines output*. See, for example, his argument that the operations of banking cannot augment the capital of the country and his identification of the limit of the quantity of paper money which can remain in the country (*WN*, II.ii.86, and 48). See also his refutation of what he saw as the opinion of Locke, Law and Montesquieu – that an

increase in the quantity of specie lowers the rate of interest. Against this Smith insisted that the interest always keeps pace with profits of stock (*WN*, II.iv.9–11).

In explaining the 'Discouragement of Agriculture' in Book III, Chapter ii, Smith restated Quesnay's view that the French *taille* removes the surplus and inhibits the accumulation of capital by farmers (*WN*, III.ii.19). Likewise, once market relations were established the great estates of Europe were reorganised: 'By the removal of unnecessary mouths, and by extracting from the farmer the full value of the farm, a greater surplus, or what is the same thing, the price of a greater surplus, was obtained for the proprietor...' (*WN*, III.iv.13).

16. For example, he was surely correct to argue that given that the physiocrats acknowledged that the class of artificers, manufacturers, and merchants 'reproduces annually the value of its own annual consumption, and continues, at least, the existence of the stock or capital which maintains and employs it... it seems, upon this account, altogether improper to consider artificers, manufacturers and merchants, in the same light as menial servants' (*WN*, IV.ix.30 and 31).

17. In the same vein, we would not doubt that Marx considered accumulation to arise from surplus, just because he said 'there develops in the breast of the capitalist a Faustian conflict between the passion for accumulation and the desire for enjoyment' (1867, p. 741).

18. Hollander says that in Book II, Chapter v, and Book IV, Chapter ix (on physiocracy) 'Smith consistently classifies employers... as productive labourers and their profits as the return to labour' (Hollander, 1973, p. 194n). While the former point is correct, it is clear that the latter did not represent Smith's general position (see, for example, *WN*, I.x.b.34).

4 COMPETITION

1. To see that by 'rudimentary equilibrium theory' Schumpeter meant Smith's analysis of the relation between natural price and market price, and not Smith's *explanation* of price, consider first the two places in which he made this observation. Immediately preceding his reference to the 'rudimentary equilibrium theory of Chapter 7' we find Schumpeter's account of the component parts of price of Chapter vi of the *Wealth of Nations*. In criticising this, he made clear the distinction in question: 'This is no doubt very unsatisfactory as an explanation of value but serves well as an avenue both to a theory of equilibrium price and to the theory of distribution' (Schumpeter 1954, p. 189). Second, on repeating the point Schumpeter referred to Smith's 'concept of equilibrium or "natural" price' which, he said, gives us 'a glimpse of Marshall's distinction between short-run and long-run phenomena, A. Smith's market price being essentially a short-run phenomenon, his "natural" price a long-run phenomenon – Marshall's long-run normal' (ibid., p. 308).

Furthermore, Schumpeter explicitly identified this equilibrium theory or natural price with that 'conceptual construct or *tool of analysis* that serves to isolate, for the purposes of a preliminary study, the group of economic phenomena that would be observable in an unchanging economic process' (Schumpeter, 1954, p. 562, emphasis added). And 'statics as thus defined pivots on the concept... of equilibrium that appears in Mill and in the "classic" literature generally, for example, in the garb of such constructs as the "natural" or "necessary" prices' (ibid., p. 563; and see p. 963). It is not surprising, therefore, that Schumpeter identified a continuity of *this* 'equilibrium theory' from Smith to Walras. Indeed, when confronted with Walras' analogy of market equilibrium to a lake agitated by the wind his first comment was, quite justifiably, that 'These views do not differ essentially from those of A. Smith' (ibid., p. 1000n).

Finally, further confirmation of the view stated in my text can be found if we note the contrast between Schumpeter's description of 'equilibrium theory' as a '*method*' of analysis, and his definition of a *theory* of value as a set of relations capable of 'determining' value and a set of propositions that 'explain' the laws to which values are subject (see 1954, pp. 590, 968, 309, 562, and 601).

5   THE MEASURE OF VALUE

1.   Blaug (1978, p. 52), Hollander (1973a, p. 128), Skinner (1974, p. 50), Rogin (1956, p. 79), Meek (1973, p. 62), Napoleoni (1975, p. 40) and Whitaker (1904, p. 16).
2.   Several authors have noted this switch in perspective, see Whitaker (1904, p. 26), Myint (1948, pp. 19–21), Roll (1973, p. 160) and O'Brien (1975, p. 83) – but none has interpreted it in this way.
3.   This view of Smith's measure of value differs from that of most other commentators in acknowledging his conscious switch of perspective and in identifying the assumptions which make the two approaches to 'real price' consistent. Sowell, for example, says 'At a given time, under given technology, an index of the amount of "other men's labour" is the same as an index of "the *produce* of other men's labour", and from this Smith *drifted into* using the terms synonymously over time and without regard to changing technology' (1974, p. 99). Myint noted the existence of two different meanings of the term 'value' in Smith but considered that the second approach, in which real price is defined in terms of the subsistence bundle of a worker, *totally superceded* the first approach, in which real price is defined in terms of labour time expended (Myint, 1948, pp. 19–21). O'Brien notes the different meanings of 'real price' but does not identify the assumptions which link them to each other (O'Brien, 1975, p. 83).
4.   The evidence that Smith considered the value of corn and silver to be determined in the same manner as the value of other commodities is overwhelming (*WN*, I.v.7; *WN*, I.v.16; *WN*, I.xi.c.31; *WN*, I.xi.g.21; *WN*,

IV.vii.a.19; see also Cassel, 1932, p. 478; Vickers, 1975, p. 494; Green, 1982, p. 73; Hegeland, 1951, p. 47; Laidler, 1981, p. 187). Yet Hollander (1973, p. 172), following Rosenbluth (1969, p. 310), insists that in the *Wealth of Nations* 'the price of corn is not determined by production costs in the manner of all other commodities' (p. 173; and see Hunt, 1979, p. 48 for a similar view). To justify this view, Hollander ignores the fact that Smith explicitly based his choice of corn as a measure of value on its constant production cost; Hollander dismisses this by saying that 'this argument is difficult to appreciate' (1973, p. 130n). In addition, he cites Buchanan and Ricardo in support of the view that in Smith the price of corn was unrelated to its production cost (p. 172n). But Buchanan had substantially departed from Smith when he developed his *new theory* that any good that yielded rent was a monopoly commodity (1814, 1817). It is not clear whether or not Hollander wishes to adopt Buchanan's view that corn is a monopoly commodity. His selective quote from Ricardo, when read in its context, far from supporting his view actually undermines it. In that passage Ricardo rebuked Smith for *excluding corn*, not from the cost theory, but from the *rise* in price which Smith considered would occur in the case of other 'rude produce' (*Works* I, p. 374).

Finally, in the face of Smith's unequivocal statement that 'The proportion between the value of gold and silver and that of goods of any kind, depends in all cases... upon the proportion between the quantity of labour which is necessary in order to bring a certain quantity of gold and silver to market, and that which is necessary in order to bring hither a certain quantity of any sort of goods' (*WN*, II.ii.105), Hollander says that 'a specific reference to corn is conspicuously absent' and arranges his quotation from Smith in such a way as to convey the impression that when Smith said 'goods of any other kind' he meant 'goods *other than* corn' (1973, p. 174n).

5. Despite its central role in Smith's treatment of value this assumption of a constant price of corn is not noted in most commentaries – and is denied in some. Bowley, for example, goes as far as to say 'What [Smith] claimed, and what Ricardo could not accept of course, was that it was not the variability of the price paid for labour as such, nor the cost of producing labour as such that influenced the suitability of labour as a measure of value' (Bowley, 1973a, p. 116). The assumption on corn is, however, given prominence by Lowe (1954, p. 141; and 1975, p. 417), Sylos-Labini (1976, p. 209), Eltis (1975, p. 431), Gee (1981, p. 7), and noted by Stigler (1965, p. 197).

6. Smith frequently referred to a decrease (or increase) in the quantity of *labour* required to produce a particular commodity when he would seem to have had in mind a proportionate decrease in the quantity of labour and other inputs together (see, for example, *WN*, I.xi.o.13 and *WN*, II.ii.105).

7. This numerical example does not convey the full sense of Smith's approach because the value of silver has been held constant and hence the change in *money* price also gives an unambiguous signal of the change in the difficulty of production (see Section 5 of this chapter). See

Deane (1978, p. 26), Dobb (1973, p. 49n) and Sylos-Labini (1976, p. 209) for somewhat similar numerical examples. The latter two use an example in which the price of *corn* changes and this, in my view, is at variance with Smith's usage.

8. This is the way Sylos-Labini expresses the 'proportionality' property of Smith's measure (1976, p. 207). In my view his use of Smith's 'resolution' of the price of inputs into wages, profits and rents, when explaining these properties conceals the full importance of the assumption of a constant price of corn. For this reason I have included material inputs in my numerical examples.

9. Caravale and Tosato (1980) argue that a 'logical inconsistence arises' if we attribute to Smith the three *independent* propositions: (a) choice of the wage as *numéraire* ($w = 1$), (b) assumption of a given corn wage ($w = P_c \bar{x}$, where P_c is the corn price and $\bar{x}$ is the corn wage), and (c) the assumption of a constant price of corn – since the third of these follows from the other two (p. 25). But even this did not require the precise assumptions about corn production adopted by Smith. More importantly, it is questionable whether Smith's idea that labour is the 'real measure of value' is validly, or usefully, represented by the idea that the wage is a *numéraire* (see Section 5 of this chapter where Smith's practical *use* of his labour command measure is examined). The assumption of a given corn wage, $w = P_c \bar{x}$, alone implies a constant labour command value of corn. It is not clear that the additional idea, $w = 1$, really adds anything to this. For once the wage is defined as the *numéraire* then P_c no longer denotes the money (silver) price of corn; it denotes its labour command price. But the general point raised by Caravale and Tosato is interesting in that one is, in fact, unlikely to argue that the labour measure of value, the constant corn wage, and the constant cost of corn, were adopted by Smith as *independent* propositions. The difficulty arises in deciding which proposition represented Smith's primary *intention*.

10. Recent study of production price systems akin to Smith's reveals that the assumptions which he adopted are, strictly speaking, not sufficient to ensure that the labour embodied and labour commanded value of a good move in line with one another. A change in the value of a manufactured commodity (due to a change in methods of production) will, in general, cause a change in the rate of profit, which will in turn change the value of many other commodities in an unpredictable way – including, of course, the price of corn (Sraffa, 1960). This will destroy the proportionality between the labour embodied and labour commanded measures of changes in value. Smith's result will only be *guaranteed* if corn is the only 'basic' commodity; then changes in the value of other commodities will not affect the rate of profit and price of corn will be unaffected. Alternatively, if there was a uniform ratio of labour to means of production then the prices of commodities (including corn) would be unaffected by changes in wages and the rate of profit.

11. Whitaker noted the close link between the labour command measure of value which Smith actually used and labour embodied but, not identifying Smith's particular assumptions, he considered that the labour command measure depended on a labour *theory of value* (1904,

p. 40; and see also Cannan, 1929, pp. 165–6). Given the additional conditions which are necessary for Smith's relation between labour embodied and labour commanded to be exactly established, there is a sense in which Whitaker was correct about the labour theory of value.

12. Smith said 'the annual produce of its labour will always be sufficient to purchase or command a much greater quantity of labour than was employed in raising, preparing, and bringing that produce to market. If the society was annually to employ all the labour which it can annually purchase, as the quantity of labour would increase greatly every year, so the produce of every succeeding year would be of vastly greater value than that of the foregoing'.

13. It has been widely but incorrectly believed that these allegations were made by Ricardo and Marx (On Ricardo, see Schumpeter, 1954, p. 310; Dobb, 1973, p. 77; Douglas, 1928, p. 91; Bladen, 1975, p. 513; and especially Kaushil, 1973, p. 70; on Marx see Douglas, 1928, p. 91; Blaug, 1978, p. 53 and my Chapter 8). In fact the strongest and most influential statement of both allegations of confusion was made by Douglas (1929) – and taken up by Robbins (1958, p. 67), Dobb (1973, p. 49, 1975, p. 324) and Meek (1973, p.99) among others. The *significance* of these allegations is confused because they relate to the labour *theory* of value – and the role of that theory in classical economics has been the subject of much dispute.

14. In rejecting the idea that Smith confused labour embodied and labour commanded I am in good company. Schumpeter disputed the accuracy of both allegations against Smith – although he considered that Smith 'flounders so badly in conveying' his measure of value that he 'undoubtedly argued in several places as if his use of labour as *numeraire* did imply a theory of value', he 'confuses it with philosophies concerning the nature of value and real price', and 'he repeatedly *seems* to confuse the quantity of labour a commodity will exchange for with the quantity of labour this commodity costs to produce – which is what Ricardo criticised' (1954, p. 188, emphasis added; see also Rogin, 1956, p. 79). But he insisted, correctly in my view, that 'this indictment fails', and he considered this important, because 'taking what a commodity exchanges for . . . as an *explanation* of its value would be one of the worst slips in the history of theory' (1954, p. 310; this view is echoed by Kaushil, 1973, p. 63; Blaug, 1978, p. 53; O'Brien, 1975, p. 83; Hollander, 1973, p. 128 and Raphael, 1985, p. 64).

15. See also Barber (1967, p. 33), Deane (1978, p. 27), Stigler (1965, p. 193) Jaffe (1977, p. 24).

16. See also Hollander (1973, p. 127) Campbell and Skinner (1976, p. 24) Skinner (1974, p. 50) Sowell (1974, p. 99) Robertson and Taylor (1957, p. 197), Raphael (1985, p. 64) West (1976, p. 200) and Gordon (1959, p. 467).

17. Barber, faced with productivity changes, in effect adopts the same 'solution' as Hollander but reveals the implausibility of this position by making the astonishing statement that 'Smith appeared to have thought that the effects of this gain in productivity would be fairly uniformly distributed throughout all productive branches' (1967, p. 35). Kaushil

deals with productivity changes by saying that 'having no statistics of
GNP, and, more important, no index numbers, Smith would seem to
have resorted to productivity per man-hour as the index of economic
progress' (1973, p. 36n, n. 2). Kaushil does not suggest the productivity
of which industry Smith might have resorted to as an index of progress. In
fact, Smith stated clearly, and in great detail, his index of economic
progress in Book I Chapter xi (see Section 5 of this chapter).

18. It is ironic that these writers, who recoil from any suggestion that Smith
confused labour embodied and labour commanded, should so blithely
attribute to him the heroic assumption that productivity changes would
not alter relative prices, and are prepared to say that he settled for a
welfare measure in which an increase in welfare could show as either a
rise or a *fall* in the index. Schumpeter, and others, would have done
better to pay more attention to the close links between labour
commanded and labour embodied and between the *measure* and *theory*
of value, which they sensed in Smith's work – rather than to dismiss them
as mere difficulties of Smith's presentation of a price index. For, if the
arguments of this essay are valid, it has now been shown that it is in these
links (and the assumptions which underlie them) that the meaning of
Smith's measure of value is to be found.

19. A similar view on the significance of some of Smith's statements
concerning labour would seem to have been held by Viner, who
described him as 'decorating his exposition (in a manner common then
and not unknown now) with traditional maxims exalting the role of
labour – maxims whose familiarity alone made them seem to carry
logical or empirical weight' (Viner, 1968, p. 327).

20. In his account of Chapter v, Meek also distinguished between those
passages which refer to a capitalist economy and those which refer to a
pre-capitalist exchange economy. And he made the important point that
there are certain *connections* between the arguments found in the two sets
of passages, and that the task of interpretation is to identify them. In his
view Smith attempted to *apply* his labour command measure (as designed
for analysis of a *capitalist* economy) to all forms of exchange economy.
Indeed he said: 'Smith's theory of value, I believe, cannot be properly
understood unless it is appreciated that his argument concerning the
"real measure" consisted essentially of an attempt to generalise the basic
concept in this way' (1973a, p. 67). The 'basic concept', in Meek's view,
was command over live labour as a measure (essentially) of *accumulation*
under capitalism; and the 'attempt to generalise' was found in the early
paragraphs of Chapter v, where Smith defined 'value', 'real price', 'real
worth' and 'real measure' in terms of labour expended and/or
commanded (*WN*, I.v.1–3).

My interpretation of Smith's measure of value suggests that the links
between Smith's account of the capitalist economy and of the pre-
capitalist economy run in the *opposite direction* to that identified by
Meek. In other words, Smith attempted to generalise from his account of
pre-capitalist exchange to capitalism, from the early paragraphs of
Chapter v to the later, and not *visa versa*. The main reason for this is the

fact that the most important property which is found in Smith's measure of value in *both* pre-capitalist and capitalist exchange is the *proportionality of labour commanded and labour embodied.*

21. For the same reason he considered that wool and hides *tend* to rise in price, but may not, because they are joint products with mutton and beef (*WN*, I.xi.m.1).

6 VALUE AND DISTRIBUTION

1. Indeed, it can be said that no single theme emerges more strongly from Meek's extensive work on Physiocracy and English classical economics than the importance of Adam Smith's identification of profits at a uniform rate as a part of natural price and related adoption of a tripartite division of economic and social classes (1954, 1962, 1973b, p. vii).

2. It will be shown in Chapter 8 that Marx considered this a considerable achievement on Smith's part: in particular, he attached great significance to Smith's view that 'the interest of money is always a derivative revenue' (*WN*, I.vi.18), despite his severe and continual criticism of Smith's resolution of prices into wages, profits and rent.

3. Although I have disputed Cannan's view that Smith used the term 'annual produce' first in a 'British' and then in a 'physiocratic' sense (see Section 3.2.3 above) the research undertaken for this study does not permit me to take a strong view, one way or the other, on Cannan's wider interpretation of the development of Smith's thought and the influence in it of the physiocrats.

4. Sraffa linked the idea of a maximum rate of profits with Marx's emphatic rejection of Smith's claim that the price of every commodity resolves itself entirely into wages, profits and rent, on the grounds that such a claim presupposed the existence of 'ultimate' commodities produced by labour alone and which was, therefore, incompatible with a fixed upper limit to the rate of profits (Sraffa, 1960, p. 94). While Smith certainly did claim that prices resolve themselves in this way he cannot be said to have eschewed the idea of a maximum rate of profit. Of course, the maximum rate which Sraffa examines, and which was suggested by Marx, corresponds to a *zero* wage not, as Smith's 'highest ordinary rate' did, to the biological subsistence wage.

5. In the case of a 'new manufacture' or new process the 'extraordinary profits' were considered to be purely temporary (see *WN*, I.x.b.43).

6. Smith's belief in the inevitability of decline and decay, when combined with his advocacy of rapid accumulation, has been described as a *paradox* by Heilbroner (1975).

7. In explaining the *rising* share of rent Smith based this on the assumption that although the *price* of various agricultural commodities would rise in the 'progress of improvement' the *labour required* to collect or produce the goods in question would *not increase.* Consequently, a smaller proportion of the value of the output would be sufficient to replace the capital, with the ordinary profit; a 'greater proportion of it must,

consequently, belong to the landlord' (*WN*, I.xi.p.3). Quite apart from any other aspects of this argument the *assumption* which underlay it, that the increased *price* of rude produce in the progress of improvement was *not* the result of *increased* labour and material *inputs*, was flatly contradicted in the course of Smith's detailed account of the evolution of the price of various types of 'rude produce' (see, for example, *WN*, I.xi.1.13). In explaining the *falling* share of rent, Smith based this on the contrary assumption that the proportion of output 'destined for replacing the capital' of the farmer had increased enormously, leaving a smaller proportion for the landlord (see *WN*, II.iii.9). The identification of the different assumptions underlying Smith's contradictory predictions provides a basis for a more detailed study of his theory of rent – but that cannot be undertaken in this study.

8. It was shown in Section 5.5 that Smith went to great lengths in his 'Digression on the value of silver' in I.xi to challenge the prevailing view that the value of silver was still falling.

9. Viner considered that Smith 'made no reference' in the *Wealth of Nations* to the self-regulating specie-flow mechanism, and referred to this as 'one of the mysteries of the history of economic thought' (1937, p. 87). This view has been persuasively disputed by Eagly (1970) and Bloomfield (1975, p. 479). See also Hollander (1973, p. 205).

10. Viner pointed out that these specie points were clearly identified in the late seventeenth century by Locke and others (1937, p. 78n). Indeed, Smith's account was very similar to Locke's (Vaughn, 1980, p. 71).

11. In the first edition Smith had said that corn had a 'real value which no human institution can alter'. This was criticised by both Pownall and Anderson. In a letter to Andreas Holt, Smith referred to Anderson and commented: 'I happened to say that the nature of things had stamped a real value upon corn which no human institution can alter. The expression was certainly too strong, and had escaped me in the heat of the writing. I ought to have said that the nature of things had stamped upon corn a real value which could not be altered simply by altering its money price. This was all that the argument required, and all that I really meant' (*WN*, IV.v.a.23.n.28).

12. Smith did not believe that the money wage would change with *every* change of the corn price. The 'temporary and occasional price of corn' can rise or fall without necessarily changing money wages (*WN*, I.v.16) – indeed, the relationship between this temporary price of corn and the money wage can be quite complex (*WN*, I.viii.46).

13. See, in addition to the passage quoted, *WN*, I.v.16; *WN*,I.xi.c.11; *WN*, I.xi.g.28; *WN*, I.xi.m.13; and *WN*, II.ii.105.

14. Smith's statement that a commodity, or the price of a commodity, can 'put into motion a quantity of labour *equal* to that which had originally produced it' is somewhat puzzling in view of his earlier recognition that in a capitalist economy the labour commanded value of a good *exceeds* the labour used in its production (*WN*, I.vi.7), and that the whole annual produce can 'purchase or command a *much greater quantity* of labour than what was employed in raising, preparing, and bringing that produce to market' (*WN*, I.vi.24). Too much significance should not be attached

to what is probably a slip; Smith can be read to say that the price of a commodity can put into motion a quantity of labour *at least* equal to that which produced it (for a similar view, see Myint, 1948, p. 74). The purpose of the passage was not to deal with the *quantitative* relation between labour embodied and labour commanded, but to establish the *distinction* between *productive* and *unproductive* labour, by showing that unproductive labour consumes revenue while productive labour does not – 'he, in reality, costs [his master] no expense, the value of those wages being generally restored, together with a profit, in the improved value of the subject upon which his labour is bestowed' (*WN*, II.iii.1).

15. Indeed, Meek noted that the pamphlet 'is not entirely free from the confusion...between the reward of labour and the labour itself as determinants of value, but on the whole it represents a considerable achievement' (1973a, p. 42).

16. Cannan continued by saying that Smith, 'without argument, or even warning, simply substitutes the remuneration of labourers, capitalist and landlords for labour, capital, and land' (ibid.). This is incorrect, since Smith's replacement of capital and land by wages, profits and rents was based on his resolution of prices – which has been vindicated by modern theorists. Cannan's comment may be the source of the widespread belief that Smith's resolution of prices into wages, profits and rents, involved the determination of price by the distributive variables alone; in fact, the *quantities of means of production* used are the most important part of these price equations.

7 RICARDO'S DEVELOPMENT OF SMITH'S THEORY

1. Tucker points out that, with accumulation, wages would always be above the 'natural price of labour', as defined by Ricardo, and considers that 'it would, therefore, have been more efficient if he had considered the various levels of the commodity-wage, corresponding to different rates of accumulation' (1960, p. 113) – which was, of course, exactly Smith's procedure (see Section 3.4.1). But Tucker adds that 'there can be little doubt that he had this idea in mind, however, imperfectly'.

2. Contrary to my interpretation, Tucker considers that the view which Ricardo took of the determination of value in the *Essay* was a *new* view, and should be considered to be associated with the new theory of profits presented there (Tucker, 1960, p. 99).

3. See MacDonald, 1912, pp. 555–6; Schumpeter, 1954, pp. 188, 310; Douglas, 1928, p. 91; Blaug, 1978, p. 54; Meek, 1973a, p. 99; Dobb, 1973, and 1975; Kaushil, 1973; Sylos-Labini, 1976, p. 207; Bladen, 1975, p. 513.

4. See Cannan, 1929, pp. 326–42; Marshall, 1890, p. 672; Viner, 1930, 1954, p. 358; Stigler, 1952, 1954; Robbins, 1955, p. 62; Robertson and Taylor, 1957, p. 188; Hunt, 1979, p. 50; Meek, 1973a, p.64.

5. Consider also the following passage: 'If it be agreed, that by taxing the profits of one manufacturer only, the price of his goods would rise, to put him on an equality with all other manufacturers; and that by taxing

the profits of two manufacturers, the prices of two descriptions of goods would rise, I do not see how it can be disputed, that by taxing the profits of all manufacturers, the prices of all goods would rise, provided the mine which supplied us with money, were in this country, and continued untaxed' (*Works*, I, p. 213).

6. Of course, the price of *no* commodity will rise in the case where the labour theory of value has general validity – but Ricardo was aware that this was not the case (*Works*, I, p. 30; Groenewegen, 1972, p. 96). In one place Ricardo did insert the word 'all' to the third edition, when he said 'if the prices of all commodities could be raised, still the effect on profits would be the same' (*Works*, p. 127; and see Section 7.3.5 below).

7. Modern developments of the surplus approach to value and distribution have shown that the relation between wages and prices depends on the *numeraire*, while the 'rate of profits, as a ratio, has a significance which is independent of any prices' (Sraffa, 1960, p. 33; see also Broome, 1983, p. 49).

8. However, this is done without departing from the view that even if this supposition concerning the basis of Ricardo's criticism of Smith were correct, and even if Smith's '*theory*' had 'led to' the 'absurd conclusion' which Dobb said it did, *these would still not be sufficient grounds* to classify them as belonging to two different streams of theory. But Dobb's theoretical definitions differ from those adopted in this study; and it will be shown in Chapter 10 how he used these two suppositions to classify Smith as having contributed to what was to become the neoclassical theory.

9. Except that, as noted in Section 7.2.3 above, he did not notice that an assumption of constant labour cost of production underlay Smith's assumption of a constant *value* of corn.

10. In one place Ricardo did accuse Smith of having used arguments which lead to 'absurd conclusions' (*Works*, I, p. 225) – and this may well have been the source of Dobb's usage of the term (1973, p. 76). However, the 'absurd conclusion' which Ricardo referred to was not that 'the money-price of corn regulates that of all other home-made commodities' – and, in a sense, it was the direct opposite of that. Rather, it was Smith's idea that a tax on wages would raise the price of manufactured commodities and reduce rent (since the price of corn could not rise), *and if* manufactures 'are real necessaries of life' then their increased price 'must be compensated to the poor by a farther advancement of their wages' (*WN*, V.ii.k.9). The argument certainly lacks plausibility, and can be seen to have been forced on Smith by his attempting to analyse a tax on wage goods while holding the price of corn rigidly fixed (recall the discussion of this issue in Section 7.2.6 as above). But Ricardo's criticism that the inflationary spiral was 'without any assignable limit' hardly seems accurate (see also Hollander, 1973, p. 182, n. 118).

Although Ricardo, in these passages, clearly recognised that Smith did *not* consider that a tax on wages or necessaries would raise *all* prices (but would raise all prices relative to corn), later in the same chapter, when he discussed 'the opinion' that 'taxes on necessaries and on wages would raise all prices', he added to his third edition that this opinion was 'given by Adam Smith' (p. 232). Despite the deficiencies of Smith's analysis this was clearly misleading.

11. He allowed for a similar effect in analysing taxes on raw produce: a 'tax which should have the effect of raising the price of all home productions, would not discourage exportation except during a very limited time' (*Works* I, p. 169). See also the case of taxes on profits, p. 214, and taxes on wages, where he said '...when the price of commodities are raised, either by taxation, or by the influx of the precious metals...' (p. 229; and see also p. 232).

12. In his *Reply to Bosanquet* (*Works*, III, pp. 242–3) of 1811 Ricardo held that all prices would rise without an increase in the quantity of money. He denied this possibility in the first edition of his *Principles* but, as noted above, reverted to his earlier view in the third edition (see Sraffa's account, and Ricardo's 'Note on Prices and Taxation', *Works*, IV, pp. 320–2; and the letter to McCulloch of February 1822, *Works*, IX, pp. 158–9).

13. Ricardo considered that corn (as labour) 'is itself subject to fluctuations in value', and insisted that 'That commodity is alone invariable, which at all times requires the same sacrifice of toil and labour to produce it'. Allowing that he did not share Smith's assumptions about corn it is clear that he saw the true nature of Smith's measure: 'supposing either of these to be a correct standard of value, still it would not be a standard of riches, for riches do not depend on value' (*Works*, I, p. 275).

14. Lauderdale argued that if water became scarce then riches will be increased, because water will then attain a value.

15. Ricardo considered that Say's view, that value equals utility, was a direct consequence of his abandonment of Smith's distinction between value and riches (e.g. p. 286, n).

16. On this 'note' Dobb said 'Does not this comment of Ricardo place it beyond doubt that he was thinking of both wages and profit as being determined independently of and prior to market-price or even natural value? (1973, p. 120).

8 MARX ON SMITH

1. Marx considered that Smith had, in fact, two different definitions of productive labour, one correct, and one in which he 'abandons his own view of surplus-value and accepts that of the Physiocrats' (1861–63, I, p. 163). Too much can be made of this duality in Smith's definition and, indeed, Marx considered that there was, in fact, a 'concealed association of ideas that exists between Smith's first distinction... and his second' (ibid., p. 186 and see 1857–58, p. 273).

2. Although it is clear that Marx considered Smith to have been a pioneer in this particular endeavour, in his *Contribution* he described Sir James Steuart as 'the first Briton to expound a general system of bourgeois economy' (1894, p. 57).

3. Of course Marx also cited Smith's view that in a *pre-capitalist* economy commodities exchange in proportion to labour embodied; but our interest here is in the view that, having abandoned the labour theory of value, Smith *returned* to it even for a *capitalist economy*. Little can be inferred from his view that in a pre-capitalist economy goods exchange in proportion to labour quantities (Schumpeter, 1954, p. 310). In fact, Marx was quite critical of Smith's idea of an 'early and rude state of society which precedes both the accumulation of stock and the appropriation of land' (*WN*, I.vi.1). He described it as the 'paradise lost of the bourgeoisie' (1859, p. 59) and considered that the very thing that is true of capitalist society 'Adam Smith, in the true eighteenth-century manner, puts in the prehistoric period, the period preceding history...' (1857–8, p. 156).

4. It is interesting that, although Marx attributed to Smith the determination of value by labour-time, the way in which Smith was considered to have adopted the labour theory of value (by resolving surplus value into surplus labour) did not require that Marx attribute to him the resolution of tools and materials to 'indirect labour'. Nowhere in his published writings did Marx attribute awareness of this calculating procedure to Smith (see my Appendix to Chapter 6).

5. Not surprisingly, Marx approved of Smith's description of the work process: that the labourer 'must lay down . . . his ease, his liberty, and his happiness' (*WN*, I.v.7; 1857–58, p. 611). But Marx did not consider this a universal feature of labour (ibid.; and see pp. 831–2).

6. Rosdolsky, in his account of the development of Marx's thought, was of the opinion that Smith's measure of value was based *solely* on his idea that 'equal quantities of labour, at all times and places, may be said to be of equal value to the labourer' (*WN*, I.v.7; Rosdolsky, 1977, pp. 535–6).

7. Before considering Marx's theoretical criticism it is necessary, first, to cite a purely analytical objection which Marx raised against Smith's resolution of prices into wages, profits and rent. Steedman implies that Marx was wholly in error in his objections to the analytical possibility of such a resolution (1982, p. 128). But this would seem to ignore the fact that Marx, at one point in Volume II of *Capital*, argued that the resolution would be a 'hollow subterfuge' unless goods were ultimately produced by unassisted labour (1885, p. 378). This was surely valid despite the fact that subsequent mathematical knowledge shows that the commodity residual can be made vanishingly small. Steedman does make a valid point when he notes the 'irony involved in Marx's polemics against the resolution of prices into wages and profits'. For, the same point could be made against the calculation of the labour embodied in commodities (1982, p. 155, n. 10).

8. See, for example, 1861–63, I, p. 95; II, pp. 217, 246; III, pp. 504 and 514.

9. This point, which is fundamental to an understanding of Marx's commentary on Smith, receives indirect confirmation. Marx considered that the adding up of revenues was, in Smith's work, 'a confusion', but one 'which Malthus *elevates into a law*'. But even when so elevated by Malthus and the 'vulgar' economists, Marx saw it as a 'mere triviality expressed in high-flown language' and not as a *theory* of price (1861–63, III, p. 32). Still less, then, could he have considered it a theoretically formulated position of Smith's.

10. Marx said that 'For Adam Smith, the accumulation of capital is identical with growing demand for labour, continual rise of wages *and consequently* with a fall of profits' and added, in exoneration of Smith, that 'In his time, the demand for labour did in fact grow at least in the same proportion in which capital was accumulated because manufacture still predominated at that time and large-scale industry was only in its infancy' (1861–63, III, p. 335).

11. Later, in volume II of *Capital*, when discussing Smith's problem of determining the revenues (wages, profits and rents) in order to 'compose' the total value 'by addition', Marx was to take a different tack, saying that 'in the case of wages it *can* be done'. He meant, of course, that the value of labour power 'is determinable by the labour required for the reproduction of this commodity' (1885, p. 387). Recall that he had said that in investigating the natural price of wages, Smith 'in fact falls back – at least in certain passages – on the correct determination of the value of commodities' (1861–63, I, p. 96). And, as I have pointed out above, he used this to defend his view that a labour theory of value could be found in Smith's work.

12. It is clear from the passage cited here that Marx was of the opinion that Smith had resolved price into the revenues *paid out in the current year* – so ignoring the existence of durable capital equipment. Marx's comments on this aspect of the 'resolution' is the subject of Section 8.5.2 below.

13. Marx said that 'Adam Smith also tells us the *source* of the whole notion, that the price of the commodity or its value, is made up out of the value of wages and profits – namely the *amis du commerce*' (1861–63, II, p. 230; see also I, p. 97) – a speculation which has received some confirmation in subsequent research. Dugald Stewart, in his *Lectures on Political Economy*, said that the idea of resolving price entirely into wages, profit and rents, had been suggested to Smith by the businessman James Oswald of Dunnikier (Stewart, 1856, ix. p. 6; see also Scott, 1937, p. 117; Meek, 1954, p. 150, and 1973a, p. 55n).

14. In Chapter 49 of Volume III of *Capital*, Marx set out his own definition of 'gross output', 'net output', 'gross income' and 'net income',

15. Marx continued 'It is never the original thinkers that draw the absurd conclusions. They leave that to the Says and McCullochs' (1885, p. 394).

16. See Marx, 1861–63, I, Chapter III, Section 10, entitled 'Inquiry into how it is possible for the Annual Profit and Wages to buy the Annual Commodities, which besides Profit and Wages also contain Constant Capital'.

17. Smith's system can be said to have been constructed on assumptions somewhat like those hypothesised by Marx, because he normally treated changes in the value of commodities (due to changed methods of production) as having no effect on distribution, and he made several assumptions (a constant corn wage and a constant cost of production of corn) which went some way towards ensuring that result. But this does not provide a basis for saying that his approach to value was correct. The logical reason why not is that his assumptions are not sufficient to exclude the effects of price changes on the rate of profit, and are, therefore, not sufficient to preserve the proportionality of labour embodied and labour commanded. The real reason why not, is that his *theory* of profit was not such as to bring to light the effects of prices on the rate of profit.

18. In addition to the criticisms surveyed above Marx undertook, in Chapter x of Volume II of *Capital*, a detailed criticism of Smith's treatment of fixed and circulating capital. Although the issues raised there are of considerable interest, limitation of space makes it impossible to discuss them in any detail here. However, from the point of view of ascertaining Marx's view of Smith's role in the development of political economy, we may state that, despite the severity of his criticisms of Smith's treatment of fixed and circulating capital, Marx did *not* see Smith as having departed from the surplus theory.

19. At one place Marx did confront the fact that the sentence to which he objected most in the *Wealth of Nations* ('wages, profit, and rent, are the three original sources of all revenues as well as of all exchangeable value') had a meaning in addition to the one he always stressed, and was followed by the statement that 'all other revenue is ultimately derived from some one or other of these' (*WN*, I.vi.17). Marx's comment was that 'the circumstance that they are at the same time different sources of revenue for different classes engaged in production has nothing to do with the determination of the magnitude of each of these component parts and of the sum of their values' (1885, p. 376). This once again reflects Marx's conviction that the only way to solve the problem of distribution was to find some way to determine value prior to, and independently of, the analysis of distribution. If we put aside the limitations of the labour theory of value we can agree that Marx had a point, but in this comment he surely underestimated the importance of Smith having identified what variables a theory of distribution would have to explain, and also that the problem of value consisted essentially of determining these distributive variables.

20. The fact that a similar recognition would be required in the development of neoclassical theory (although the distributive categories need not be wages, profits and rents) has misled some modern commentators, for example Kaushil (1973), into the belief that Smith had developed the particular neoclassical theory of how value and distribution are related (see Chapter 10 below).

21. For Marx's view on the relation of Ricardo's work to 'vulgar' political economy see 1861–63, II, p. 191, p. 217, pp. 396–8, and 1867, p. 679.

9 SMITH AS 'GENERAL EQUILIBRIUM' THEORIST

1. For the duration of this chapter, all page references are to Hollander, 1973, unless it is stated otherwise.
2. Somewhat surprisingly Recktenwald also says that Kurz (1976) has formalised Smith's 'labour value theory'. He does not reconcile this with the statement about Hollander's book which has been placed at the head of this chapter (Recktenwald, 1978, p. 229).
3. As was pointed out in Chapter 1, it is more common to see Smith's treatment of value as a forerunner of Marshallian *partial* equilibrium analysis (see, for example, Blaug, 1978; Kaushil, 1973; and Bladen, 1938).
4. There are many parallels between the case Hollander makes concerning Smith and that in his *Economics of David Ricardo* (1979). One of these is to argue that, despite what they may have written or omitted to write, the writer '*had in mind*' certain concepts. Indeed, in his book on Ricardo, he has mounted a defence of this method of 'personal exegesis' (see 1979, p. 643; further similarities between the two books are reported in note 19 below).
5. Hollander's argument here stands in stark contrast to the rigorous method he himself adopts in investigating the claim (of Schumpeter and others) that Smith's predecessors had a well-developed utility based theory of value (see pp. 27–51, and pp. 133–5).
6. In his subsequent book on Ricardo, he has argued that Ricardo also must be considered as one of the originators of the elasticity concept (1979, p. 277n).
7. The most famous example of this view was Kauder's statement that by rejecting utility and scarcity Smith 'made waste and rubbish out of the thinking of two thousand years' (1953, p. 650). See also Douglas, 1928; Schumpeter, 1954, p. 301; and Robertson and Taylor, 1957. O'Brien (1975, pp. 78–80 and Hutchison (1978, pp. 13–15) restate the view that Smith consciously rejected a subjective explanation of value. Viner (1954) was an early critic of Schumpeter's view that the seventeenth century writers had a well-developed supply and demand theory.
8. Of course, there remains significant differences between Smith and his predecessors which should not go unnoted. The most remarkable of these is noted by Groenewegen: that while writers such as Cantillon and Turgot devoted considerable attention to the process whereby market price is determined 'This type of analysis, with its greater emphasis on subjective considerations in the determination of value has no real counterpart in the writings of Smith' (Groenewegan, 1983, p. 46).
9. It will be noted in the course of the following examination that a remarkable proportion of Hollander's key propositions are presented as negative statements – frequently double negatives. Such statements are often virtually irrefutable, and this makes critical appraisal of his work difficult. This is a method of argument which he has also adopted in his subsequent work (see 1979, p. 282).

10. These differences are, first, the extent of explanation of the determination of market price (Smith, 1763, LJ (B) paragraphs 227–8; *WN*, I.vii.9–10) and, second, the *content* of natural price. Douglas (1928) and Robertson and Taylor (1957) cited the first of these differences as evidence that between the *Lectures* and the *Wealth of Nations* Smith had *moved away* from the explanation of value by means of scarcity and demand. What is worthy of note is that Robertson and Taylor claimed only that there was a 'presence' and 'linking together' of utility, scarcity and demand in the *Lectures*. Yet Hollander, in claiming that in the *Wealth of Nations* Smith *explained* value by utility and scarcity, nowhere cites direct evidence even as strong as that cited by Robertson and Taylor from the *Lectures* (see my examination of Hollander's evidence below).

11. Although the substance of Hollander's point is correct, it would seem more appropriate to label biological significance as the 'broad' sense of 'value in use', and the economist's sense of desirability as the more 'narrow' meaning – given the very particular way in which the concept of 'preference' must be specified if it is to be used in an explanation of value.

12. But O'Brien (1975, p. 80) and Hutchison (1978, pp. 13–15), who accept this point, see in Smith's terminology itself an even greater rejection of the subjective explanation of value found in the work of some of Smith's predecessors.

13. Hollander argues that Smith's account of certain price variations over time was based on his perception that goods possess 'a high "value-in-use" (in a biological sense), yet whose "usefulness" (per unit) in the sense of desirability varies with quantity' – thus revealing his grasp of the role of utility in demand and price determination.

   The passage quoted by Hollander to demonstrate this comes from Book I, Chapter xi (on rent) and in it Smith was explaining the evolution of the price of 'the materials of clothing and lodging'. Recall Smith's view on the price of goods 'which human industry can multiply in proportion to demand' – as reported in Section 5.5 above. The materials of clothing and lodging were initially available in great abundance as 'spontaneous productions of nature', but with the cultivation of land, the destruction of the forests, and the increase of population, this availability was reduced, at the same time as demand was increased. Their prices rose until they were sufficient to repay their production yielding normal profits, and, in general, a rent roughly equal to that available from corn land (*WN*, I.xi.c.3). But infertile or distant lands may not yield this rent and so can only be worked by their owners (*WN*, I.xi.c.9–15). Further details of Smith's argument can be found in my detailed discussion of his account of the evolution of the price of *cattle* in note 25 to Chapter 9; Smith explicitly related the case of clothing and lodging to the case of cattle (*WN*, I.xi.c.16).

   Turning to Hollander's use of this passage we must state the following. The passage has nothing to do with relative subjective evaluation as a determinant of value. It does have to do with the role of scarcity in driving up price; but this is not surprising since Smith was attempting to explain the existence of differential *rent* in the price of these commodities. But in quoting the paragraph *WN*, I.xi.c.3 Hollander removes all Smith's references to rent, and makes no allusion to the fact that Smith's *stated topic* was the circumstances in which the production of wood, hides, coal, stone and metals will or will not yield a rent!

Second, he argues that the passage, so arranged, demonstrates Smith's usage of the concept of utility, because the goods in question possess 'a high "value-in-use" (in a biological sense), yet those "usefulness" (per unit) in the sense of *desirability varies with quantity*' (p. 136, emphasis added). This is both implausible and inaccurate. It is implausible because, the transition from an economy with unused natural forests and low population (in which much wood is useless), to an economy with commercial forestry and a high population (in which wood has great usefulness),is simply not comparable to the concept that for each individual at any given time the marginal utility yielded by a good is inversely related to the quantity of it consumed.

It is inaccurate because, just a few pages later, Smith said 'the desire of food is limited in every man by the narrow capacity of the human stomach; but the *desire of the conveniences and ornaments of building, dress, equipage, and household furniture, seems to have no limit or certain boundary*' (*WN*, I.xi.c.7, my emphasis).

14. Hollander introduces his third piece of evidence saying that the 'role actually accorded utility in the broad sense is equally clear in the following discussion of the demand for precious metals' (p. 137). Recall that by 'utility in the broad sense' Hollander means utility in the neoclassical sense; that is, *preference* (p. 136). Hollander's argument is that Smith considered that the demand for precious metals 'is based on a wide variety of desirable characteristics, which happens to include their "value-in-use", (p. 137). Thus, he cites Smith's statement that their demand arises from the industrial uses, but perhaps principally from their beauty – which is in turn enhanced by their scarcity, since that allows their owner to 'parade' not only beauty but riches also (*WN*, I.xi.c.31). 'To these determinants of general desirability', says Hollander, 'Smith adds finally the *utilitarian* demand for the metals arising from their monetary function' (p. 137).

In assessing this, the following points should be borne in mind. First, Smith considered silver and gold to have natural prices like other produced goods (*WN*, I.xi.g.21 and see Smith, 1763, *LJ* (A).vi.106). Their principal peculiarity lay in the fact that in producing them 'the efficacy of human industry seems not to be limited but uncertain' (*WN*, I.xi.m.17). This gives rise to *long* departures from natural price and to movements of natural price itself (*WN*, I.xi.g.37 and see my detailed discussion of this in note 26 to Chapter 9).

Second, the passage in question cannot bear the weight of interpretation placed on it by Hollander. In examining the evolution of the production of hides, wood, coal, wool, etc., Smith traced the growth in demand to the growth of population and wealth, since their roles as necessaries and luxuries are obvious (*WN*, I.xi.c.1–21). Clearly the precious metals are somewhat different; but recognition of the role of beauty and ostentation, as well as industrial and monetary uses, does not imply that he used preference or desirability in the way in which these are used in the supply and demand theory. It is significant that having cited the passage in question Hollander does not explain 'the role actually accorded utility in the broad sense' but simply asserts that it is '*clear* in the...discussion of the demand for precious metals'.

15. This is clear when, later in the *Wealth of Nations*, he reiterated the point, explaining that 'the *quantity* [of salt] annually consumed by an individual is so small', and said of salt, soap, leather and candles: 'all of those four commodities are real necessaries of life, such heavy taxes upon them must increase somewhat the expense of the sober and industrious poor, and must consequently raise more or less the wages of their labour' (*WN*, V.ii.k.11 and see also *WN*, IV.ii.33). Smith did consider spirits a luxury, a tax upon which will tend to diminish consumption (*WN*, V.ii.k.3 and see also 6 and 50).

16. Hollander points out that the population mechanism invoked by Smith was unconvincing in a number of respects (pp. 162–3).

17. Hollander's use of the terms '*Walrasian* competitive process' and '*Walrasian* market prices' in this context would seem to refer to the *tâtonnement* process of price *adjustment* rather than to Walrasian *theory* itself. In using the term 'Walrasian' to describe this he may be supposing that the adjustment process utilised by Walras and Marshall differed. This has been shown to be incorrect by Newman, 1965, p. 106–8; Davies, 1963; and Takayama, 1974, pp. 295–301.

18. A second conclusion reached by Hollander is that the distinction between the reward of the entrepreneur and of the capitalist 'is apparent in the *Wealth of Nations*'. 'But', he adds, interestingly, 'it is the case that the "source" of the return to the entrepreneur as such is formally traced (together with the return to the capitalist proper) to the use of capital goods in production, a practice which camouflages "entrepreneurship" as a separate factor' (p. 170) – and confirms the classical nature of Smith's view of profits.

19. There is a remarkable similarity between the case constructed here and that presented in Hollander's book on Ricardo (1979); First, in both cases, he employs the same general method of argument: he denotes certain important statements by Smith and Ricardo as 'formal' and argues that, as such, they do not convey (or contain) the authors' *real* or *general* meaning and consequently can be accorded less weight (see, for example, 1979, pp. 124, 134, pp. 281–2).

Second, the *content* of these 'formal' statements by Smith and Ricardo is said to be consistent with supply and demand analysis because they are statements derived on the basis of particular restrictive assumptions' and, both Smith and Ricardo are said by Hollander to have at least one highly restrictive assumption in common – namely, 'uniform factor proportions throughout all sectors' (1979, pp. 202, 270). It is scarcely an accident that this is the very assumption which, if adopted, removes the relationships between demand and price, and between distribution and price, which lie at the heart of the 'supply and demand' theory.

20. Since Hollander says that 'it is also evident that the amounts of the *particular kinds* of each factor were *not* given' (p. 121) I take him to mean here a given aggregate *value* of capital. Hollander refers to the

debates in capital theory associated with this assumption by quoting Robinson's statement that 'in a market economy, either there may be a tendency towards uniformity of wages and the rate of profit . . . or prices may be governed by supply and demand, but not both' (1961, p. 57). He dismisses this observation because it is 'based (apparently) on the supposition that, among the *data* of the system, are included the quantities of each and every specific kind of labour, capital good, and land' – which does not accord with Smith's given '*aggregate* amounts of each factor'. He says that 'the existence of a tendency towards a uniform level of wages, of profits and of rents does not seem to be ruled out in such a system which is intended to apply to a 'long-run situation' (p. 121). This is correct, but the existence of certain important *supply and demand relations* can be ruled out in such a system, so undermining the account of the 'process of equilibration' which the system of Chapter vii was designed, in Hollander's view to illustrate (see Garegnani, 1970, 1976).

21. Hollander refers to Ricardo's disagreement with Smith's idea that as soon as stock has accumulated then the quantity of labour no longer determines exchange value (*WN*, I.vi.7). But Ricardo's point was *not* that Smith had, as Hollander says 'failed to recognise differences between the capital structure of various industries' but that Smith had, to use Ricardo's own words, 'no where analysed the *effects* of the accumulation of capital... on relative value' (Ricardo, *Works I*, p. 23n, my emphasis). This point concerns Smith's failure to identify clearly the relation between wages and profits, not any accusation by Ricardo that Smith had assumed identical ratios of labour to means of production. If anything, the opposite was the case; it was *Ricardo* who, in order to make a theoretical point, insisted on examining the case of uniform durability of capital. Consequently, the source cited by Hollander lends no support to his assertion.

22. Hollander asserts that the 'formal analysis of the effects of changing wage rates in manufacturing also implies strongly that factor proportions were taken to be constant and identical across the board' (p. 123). In evidence he cites two statements in which Smith describes the effect of wage changes on prices (*WN*, I.viii.57 and *WN*, V.ii.k.39). The reader can confirm that these statements do not say, and do not imply, that factor proportions are 'identical across the board'. More important, however, for forming a judgement on the strength of Hollander's case, is the fact that these passages, which are supposed to demonstrate the 'formal' assumption of identical factor proportions, come not from Smith's 'formal analysis' of Chapter vii, but from diverse chapters in the *Wealth of Nations*. But, Hollander has elsewhere told us that in these chapters we can find Smith's *less restrictive* analysis of general equilibrium

Smith's assumption of *given* proportions between labour and means of production in a given industry at a given time is another matter altogether, and lends no support to Hollander's case (see, for example, *WN*, I.x.c.44).

23. Indeed, it is ironic that Hollander should end up *asserting* that Smith
     assumed constant costs in the production of many goods, where there is
     no evidence whatsoever for that view, and *denying* that Smith assumed
     constant cost in the one case where there is abundant evidence – the case
     of corn (see note 4 to Chapter 5 above).
24. The fundamental proposition of Chapter xi is that 'the rent and profit of
     corn, or whatever else is the common vegetable food of the people, must
     naturally regulate . . . the rent and profit of all other cultivated land'
     (*WN*, I.xi.b.14,23). One exception to this arises because 'it sometimes
     happens' that the quantity of land available for making a particular
     product 'is too small to supply the effectual demand' (*WN*, I.xi.b.29).
     Such cases bring to light the first relation between price and cost that is
     worthy of note. Smith said that the price of these goods *exceeds* the
     'whole rent, wages and profit necessary for raising and bringing it to
     market, *according to their natural rates*' (ibid., emphasis added). In other
     words, in this case, 'and in this case only', price *exceeds* natural price, or
     cost of production (*WN*, I.xi.b.32).
25. Consider those agricultural commodities which are reproducible but
     which, Smith argued, nevertheless 'naturally grow dearer as the society
     advances in wealth and improvement' (*WN*, I.xi.l.1). The dominant
     example was cattle. Hollander bases his case for the role of demand in
     determining natural price, and the non-conflict between this and cost of
     production, largely on this part of Smith's account (p. 140, and see
     pp. 136–7). The reason why these commodities rise in price is that they
     were originally available free (in the wild) but, as more and more land is
     cultivated and the society becomes richer, their availability is diminished
     at the same time as the demand is enhanced. Their price rises 'gradually'
     over 'a long period in the progress of improvement' until 'it gets so high
     as to render them ... profitable' to produce commercially (*WN*, I.xi.l.1).
     We wish to draw attention to the relation between price and cost in
     Smith's account. During the period of rising prices, although cattle are
     scarce, their price is clearly *below* their cost of production, that is, below
     their natural price (*WN*, I.xi.l.6). However, immediately prior to 'the
     general practice of cultivating land for the sake of raising it' cattle are at
     their dearest, and it is clear that Smith considered them *above* their cost
     of production or natural price (*WN*, I.xi.l.8). Finally, once they are
     generally produced they sell *at* their natural price.
          Smith distinguished between 'spontaneous productions of nature', and
     commodities which are the 'production of human industry' – the central
     difference being that 'the average product of every sort of industry is
     always suited, more or less exactly, to the average consumption' (*WN*,
     I.xi.e.27). It is clear that his account included both types of goods.
     Furthermore, it is clear that his analysis of cattle (and other agricultural
     goods with similar properties) – an analysis which included the effect of
     demand and scarcity on prevailing price (and upon which Hollander
     places great emphasis) – was a theory of a commodity in *transition* from
     being a 'spontaneous production of nature' to being a 'product of human
     industry'. Although *during* this period of transition (rising price) the
     price is *below* its natural level, when the process is viewed from first to

last, that *natural* price itself can also be seen to have risen: 'As it costs a great quantity of labour and subsistence to bring them to the market, so when they are brought thither, they represent or are equivalent to a greater quantity' (*WN*, I.xi.1.13).

26. The case of silver allows a further clarification of the relation between price and cost in the *Wealth of Nations*. Smith counted silver among that class of goods 'in which the efficacy of human industry in augmenting the quantity, is either limited or uncertain' (*WN*, I.xi.m.1). The price of such goods *tends* to rise in the course of economic development, but the presence of a random element makes this uncertain (ibid.). Nevertheless, Smith definitely considered silver (and other precious metals) to have a natural price, which he defined in terms of the method of production and the distributive rates (*WN*, I.xi.g.21). In addition, he said that the *relative* value of silver and any other good depended on the relative quantities of labour necessary to bring each to market (*WN*, II.ii.105).

Because the fertility or barrenness of the mines 'is a circumstance which ... may have no connection with the state of industry in a particular country' (*WN*, I.xi.m.21), the price of silver may go above its lowest level (which is determined by the physical cost of production plus profits on these), to a 'highest' level which is determined only by the 'actual scarcity or plenty of those metals themselves' (*WN*, I.xi.c.29–30, and see *WN*, I.xi.h.6). This bears a remarkable similarity to aspects of the physiocratic concept of 'fundamental price'. It is clear that Smith considered the natural price of silver a *lowest* price, and consequently that he did *not* consider rises in its price, due to intermittent scarcity, to be increases in its *natural* price. For example, he described how, after the discovery of the American mines, 'its price would sink gradually lower till it fell *to* its natural price' (*WN*, I.xi.g.21, emphasis added).

In addition, of course, he considered that eventually this natural price would itself rise, because all mines 'become gradually more expensive in the working' (*WN*, I.xi.h.8). It is to an aspect of this latter view that Hollander draws attention in defence of his view that 'the "explanation" of price in terms of "supply and demand" or "relative scarcity" was not regarded as an "alternative" to that in terms of costs' (p. 137). For, in explaining the high and rising natural price of silver, Smith on three occasions drew an analogy between the 'scarcity' of the metals and the 'great labour which it requires to collect any considerable quantity of it' (*WN*, I.xi.c.31, see also *WN*, I.xi.h.9 and *WN*, IV.vii.a.19). These instances cannot bear the weight of *theoretical* interpretation that Hollander places on them. Smith did not consider 'scarcity' to have an *analytical* or even a *single* meaning. Apart from the instances cited here, his references to scarcity (including that of precious metals) were to situations where demand was, permanently or temporarily, greater than quantity brought to market, and consequently where *market* price exceeded natural price (see, for example, *WN*, IV.v.b.3–8 and *WN*, I.xi.c.3).

27. Though Smith's explanation of the effects of scarcity probably accorded well with the prevailing notions concerning 'supply and demand' – notions of which Hollander is very critical (pp. 27–51).

28. More generally, Garegnani points out that, given their different theory of distribution, it is not clear that the role assigned by the classical economists to the *content* of the pattern of demand can validly, or even usefully, be conceived as demand relations of the neoclassical kind (Garegnani, 1983, pp. 311–12).

29. In addition, Hollander notes several other important aspects of Smith's treatment of capital and technical change. First, he says that for Smith 'technical change must be "embodied" in the capital structure' (p. 209). Second, machinery was seen as 'complementary' to labour rather than as a substitute to it (p. 239) – a central feature of the classical concept of capital, which came directly from Smith (see Broome, 1983, p. 219).

30. Indeed, Hollander himself says 'what requires particular emphasis is Smith's overwhelming rejection of policies designed to stimulate more rapid expansion by altering the allocation of a given capital stock as distinct from intervention concerned with the stimulus of net capital accumulation' (p. 258).

10   SMITH AS A 'COST OF PRODUCTION' THEORIST

1. See, for example, Schumpeter, 1954, p. 189; Blaug, 1978, p. 40; Cannan, 1929, pp. 169–70; O'Brien, 1975, p. 79; Hunt, 1979,p. 47; and West, 1978, p. 354. It should be noted that several of these writers nevertheless argue that, quite apart from any cost of production explanation of value, Smith should be seen as an important forerunner of neoclassical or at least modern economics. In making this case they draw attention to such things as: Smith's awareness of the interdependence of the economic system (Schumpeter, 1954, pp. 308, 557; Robertson and Taylor, 1957, p. 193; Ekelund and Hebert, 1983, p. 96); the distinction between natural and market price and its similarity to Marshall's long and short run (Schumpeter, 1954, p. 189 and p. 308; Blaug, 1978, p. 42); and his belief that an unco-ordinated market system would lead to a coherent outcome (Arrow and Hahn, 1971, pp. 1–2). Of course these similarities between Smith's work and modern theory are also cited by authors who treat cost of production as a theory of value.

2. Bladen, 1938, p. 41; Blaug, 1978, p. 42; Kaushil, 1973; Stigler, 1952, p. 193; Rankin, 1980, p. 260; Hollander, 1973. This constant cost interpretation can also be found in many textbooks on the history of economic thought.

3. A related view is that Smith explained price by cost of production, not because of specifically constant costs, but because of a general classical failure to take sufficient account of demand (see, for example, West, 1976, p. 201 and Arrow and Starrett, 1973, p. 1).

4. See Marshall, 1890, pp. 420 and p. 627; Bladen, 1938, p. 41; Robertson and Taylor, 1957, p. 193; Kaushil, 1973, p. 67; Blaug, op. cit., Hollander op. cit., Bowley, 1973a, p. 126; O'Brien, 1976a, p. 135; Stigler, 1950, p. 69; Rankin, 1980.

5. To some extent Samuelson can be considered to have put forward a cost of production interpretation. However, his argument is not that Smith be counted as a forerunner of neoclassical theory *because* he equated price to cost of production. Indeed, his stated aim is to 'sustain Smith against the objection of Ricardo and Marx that his eclectic breakdown of prices into wage and rent components is a trivial, surface relation' (Samuelson, 1977, p. 48). However, his defence of Smith consists in showing that such an equation of price to its component parts *can be* derived as an equilibrium condition which equates the price of a good to the factor price multiplied by the partial derivative of the unit-cost function with respect to that factor price. These unit-cost functions are the dual of the production function and hence 'have all the concavity, homogeneity, and differentiability properties' of that function. Such an equation of price to cost of production is certainly not a trivial surface relation – deriving as it does from the simultaneous determination of price and quantities in a general equilibrium of supply and demand (Samuelson, 1977, pp. 47–8). The objection to this argument is that, as an interpretation of Adam Smith's thinking, it is totally hypothetical. We may illustrate one aspect of this as follows. The concavity of the cost functions, in Samuelson's version of Smith, expresses the *substitutability* of factors in response to factor price changes. But Hollander, on the basis of a detailed study of Smith, concluded that 'there is no generalised recognition of factor substitutability', and that Smith 'did not formally introduce the substitution relation into his analysis as a general phenomenon' (Hollander, 1973, pp. 306 and 124 respectively – see also pp. 219–21, and p. 231). This extremely hypothetical nature of Samuelson's argument does not seem to have been noted by West (1978, pp. 353–55) or Recktenwald (1978) – both of whom consider that he has demonstrated his claim that Smith's 'pluralistic supply and demand analysis in terms of all three components of wages, rents, and profits is a valid and valuable anticipation of general equilibrium modelling' (Samuelson, 1977, p. 42).
6. Indeed, Dobb collaborated with Sraffa in editing the collected works of Ricardo.
7. See Schumpeter, 1954, p. 309; Robertson and Taylor, 1957,p. 193; O'Brien, 1975, p. 78; Hutchison, 1978, p. 13, Meek, 1973a, p. 137n; Bowley, 1973, pp. 110 ff; and Vaggi, 1983, pp. 15–17.
8. On the question of the clarification of the true nature of Ricardo's theory Dobb said that for many years this was 'obscured by the fact that the so-called "Jevonian revolution", in its revolt against all "cost" theories in favour of demand-determination by utility, identified the two distinct versions of the former and depicted Ricardo as the main propagator of the rejected doctrine' (1975, p. 330). This seems both theoretically and *historically* implausible. But, on the very next page Dobb gave a different, and much more plausible, explanation: "*Marshall's* interpretation and defence of the so-called Smith–Ricardo–Mill line as a cost of production theory has obscured the real nature of Ricardo's theory for most West European and American economists' (p. 331).

9. Indeed, as Bharadwaj (1978a, p. 168) points out, Dobb's interpretation of *Ricardo's* treatment of natural price contradicts his view that *Smith's* natural prices were determined by supply and demand. He quotes Ricardo's reply to Malthus' statement that 'the great principle of demand and supply is called into action to determine what Adam Smith calls natural prices as well as market prices'. Ricardo's reply – which in Dobb's view places 'it beyond doubt that he was thinking of both wages and profit as being determined *independently* of and prior to market-price or even natural price' (1973, p. 120) – was to say that Malthus *'forgets Adam Smith's definition* of natural price, or he could not say that demand and supply could determine natural price' (Ricardo, *Works*, Vol. II, p. 46, emphasis added).

10. In addition, on the question of the definition of surplus itself, Dobb said that although Smith 'had in mind the Physiocratic notion of *produit net*... the definition that emerges is of something different' (1975, p. 62). Looking only at Chapter ii of Book II of the *Wealth of Nations* (where Smith defined 'net revenue') he concluded, quite correctly, that 'Smithian "net revenue" is a different concept from Physiocratic *produit net* and from Marxian surplus-value' (p. 63). But it has been shown in Chapter 3 of this book that, despite some obscurity (which Dobb correctly identified – p. 62), *when discussing accumulation* Smith clearly defined surplus as that part of produce which was available after replacing fixed and circulating capital (which included worker's subsistence).

11. At several other places in his *History* Schumpeter discussed the relation between Smith and Marshall. He mentioned that they were both British, both liberals, and that they gave approximately equal emphasis to theory and fact (1954, pp. 307n, 835). Thus confirming the point made in the text.

11 CONCLUSION

1. Once a clear definition of a theory is adopted a distinction can easily be drawn between the theory in its ultimate or analytically coherent form and those special propositions and assumptions which it was necessary for the pioneers of the theory to adopt before they could formulate it. Frequently, these special propositions, such as the labour theory of value, are later abandoned – but they remain the essence of the history. A purely theoretical approach to the history of thought could ignore the specific process by which a given theory was developed; a purely historical approach would run the risk of elevating the specific process and equating the theory with the propositions of particular pioneers. These distinctions will be seen to be relevant to the assessment of Smith's role in the development of the classical or surplus theory.

2. The exact same production price equation emerges whether means of production are repeatedly eliminated and replaced by direct and indirect labour, or when prices are eliminated and replaced by wages, profits, and the value of means of production (see Pasinetti, 1977, pp. 90–1).

3. There are several reasons to doubt the argument that the idea of market prices tending to gravitate to natural prices necessarily implies the determination of value by supply and demand. Fisher has stressed that a theory of price adjustment is indispensible to a theory of equilibrium price (Fisher, 1983). However, Arrow has shown that, to date, within neoclassical economics the theory of price adjustment exists on a different and inferior footing to the theory of equilibrium price (Arrow, 1958; see also Hahn, 1970). Indeed, this *distinction* between the 'process by which price is discovered' and 'the ultimate facts which determine it' was made very clear by Wicksteed (1914, p. 785). It is by no means clear that an adequate theory of price adjustment will be cast in the same terms as the existing supply and demand theory of price determination – still less that a theory of price adjustment necessarily implies adoption of the neoclassical theory of price determination.

Quite independent of these problems it has been pointed out by Garegnani that neoclassical theory has changed the notion of equilibrium traditionally used by both classical and neoclassical theorists (Garegnani, 1976). Consequently, neoclassical value theory is no longer concerned with the tendency of prices to gravitate to levels which yield a uniform rate of profit. This would seem to widen the gap between the problems of price adjustment in classical and neoclassical theory (for consideration of this problem within a classical context see Medio, 1978, and Levine, 1980).

Bibliography

ANSPACH, R. (1976) 'Smith's growth paradigm', *History of Political Economy*, vol. 8, pp. 495–514.

ARROW, K.J. (1958) 'Towards a theory of price adjustment', in M. Abramovitz *et al.* (eds), *The Allocation of Economic Resources*. Stanford: Stanford University Press.

ARROW, K.J. and HAHN, F. (1971) *General Competitive Analysis*. Edinburgh: Oliver & Boyd.

ARROW, K.J. and STARRET, D. (1973) 'Cost and demand-theoretic approaches to the theory of price determination' in J. Hicks and W. Weber (eds), *Carl Menger and the Austrian School of Economics*, London: Oxford University Press, pp. 129–47.

BARBER, W.J. (1967) *A History of Economic Thought*. London: Penguin.

BARKAI, H. (1969) 'A formal outline of a Smithian growth model', *Quarterly Journal of Economics*, vol. 83, August, pp. 396–414.

BECKERMAN, W. (1968) *An Introduction to National Income Analysis*. London: Weidenfeld & Nicholson.

BHARADWAJ, K. (1978a) 'Maurice Dobb's critique of theories of value and distribution', *Cambridge Journal of Economics*, vol. 2, June, pp. 153–74.

BHARADWAJ, K. (1978b) *Classical Political Economy and the Rise to Dominance of Supply and Demand Theories*. Calcutta: Orient Longmans.

BHARADWAJ, K. (1978c) 'The subversion of classical analysis: Alfred Marshall's early writing on value', *Cambridge Journal of Economics*, vol. 2, pp. 253–71.

BHARADWAJ, K. (1980) 'On certain theoretical issues in classical political economy: a review article', *Australian Economic Papers*, vol. 19, pp. 349–61.

BLACK, R.D.C. (1971) 'Editor's Introduction' to *Economic Writings of Mountifort Longfield*. New York: A.M. Kelly.

BLACK, R.D.C. (1976) 'Smith's contribution in historical perspective' in T. Wilson and A. Skinner (eds), *The Market and the State: Essays in Honour of Adam Smith*. Oxford: Clarendon Press.

BLADEN, V.W. (1938) 'Adam Smith on value', in H.A. Innis (ed.), *Essays in Political Economy in Honor of E.J. Urwick*. Toronto: University of Toronto Press.

BLADEN, V.W. (1974) *From Adam Smith to Maynard Keynes: The Heritage of Political Economy*. Toronto: University of Toronto Press.

BLADEN V.W. (1975) 'Command over labour: a study in misinterpretation', *Canadian Journal of Economics*, vol. 8, pp. 504–519.

BLAUG, M. (1959) 'Welfare Indices in the Wealth of Nations', *Southern Economic Journal*, vol. 26 (October), pp. 150–3.

BLAUG, M. (1978) *Economic Theory in Retrospect*, 3rd edn. Cambridge University Press (1st edn, 1962).

BLISS, C.J,. (1975) *Capital Theory and the Distribution of Income*. Amsterdam: North-Holland.

260

BLOOMFIELD. A.I. (1975) 'Adam Smith and the theory of international trade', in Skinner and Wilson (1975), pp.*455–81*.

BÖHM-BAWERK, E. (1884) *Capital and Interest*, in three volumes. Illinois: Libertarian Press (1960).

BONAR, J. (1899) 'Adam Smith', in R.I. Palgrave *Dictionary of Political Economy*. London: Macmillan.

BORTKIEWICZ, L. Von. (1906) 'On the correction of Marx's fundamental theoretical construction in the third volume of *Capital*', in P. Sweezy (ed.) *Karl Marx and the Close of His System*. New York: Kelley (1966).

BOULDING, K. (1971) 'After Samuelson, who needs Adam Smith?', *History of Political Economy*, vol. 3, pp. 225–37.

BOWLEY, M. (1937) *Nassau Senior and Classical Economics*. London: George Allen.

BOWLEY, M. (1972) 'The predecessors of Jevons – the revolution that wasn't', *Manchester School*, vol. 40 (1), pp. 9–29.

BOWLEY, M. (1973a) *Studies in the History of Economic Theory Before 1870*. London: Macmillan.

BOWLEY, M. (1973b) 'Review' of Hollander (1973), *Economic Journal*, December.

BOWLEY, M. (1975) 'Some aspects of the treatment of capital in the *Wealth of Nations*', in Skinner and Wilson (1975),pp. 361–76.

BRADLEY, I. and HOWARD, M. (eds) (1982) *Classical and Marxian Political Economy*. London: Macmillan.

BROOME, J. (1983) *The Microeconomics of Capitalism*. London: Academic Press.

BUCHANAN, D. (1814) *The Wealth of Nations*, edited with notes and additions by D. Buchanan. Edinburgh: Oliphant, Waugh & Innes.

BUCHANAN, D. (1817) *Observations on the Subjects Treated in Dr. Smith's Wealth of Nations*. London: Duncan & Cochran.

BUCHANAN, D.H. (1929) 'The historical approach to rent and price theory', *Economica*, vol. 9, June, reprinted in W. Fellner and B.F. Haley (1951) (eds) *Readings in the Theory of Income Distribution*. Philadelphia: Blackiston.

CAMPBELL, R.H. (1982) 'The enlightenment and the economy', in R.H. Campbell and A. Skinner (eds) *The Origins and Nature of the Scottish Enlightenment*. Edinburgh: John Donald.

CAMPBELL, R.H. and SKINNER, A. (1976) 'General Introduction' to the Glasgow Edition of Smith's *Wealth of Nations*. Oxford: Clarendon Press.

CAMPBELL, R.H. and SKINNER, A. (1982), *Adam Smith*. London: Croom Helm.

CANNAN, E. (1896) 'Introduction' to Smith's *Lectures on Justice, Police, Revenue and Arms*. Oxford: Clarendon Press (1964).

CANNAN, E. (1898) *A History of Theories and Production and Distribution in English Political Economy*. London: P.S. Krug & Son.

CANNAN, E. (1929) *A Review of Economic Theory*. London:P.S. Krug & Son.

CANNAN, E. (1937) 'Editor's Introduction' to A. Smith, *The Wealth of Nations*, G.J. Stigler (ed.) (1976). Chicago: Chicago University Press.

CANTILLON, R. (1755) *Essai sur la Nature du Commerce en General*, H. Higgs (ed.) (1959). London: Frank Cass.

CARAVALE, G.A. and TOSATO, D.A. (1980) *Ricardo and the Theory of Value, Distribution and Growth.* London: Routledge.

CASAROSA, C. (1983) 'The new view of the Ricardian theory of distribution and economic growth', in M. Baranzini (ed.) *Advances in Economic Theory.* Oxford: Basil Blackwell.

CASSEL, G. (1932) *The Theory of Social Economy,* S.L. Barron (trans.) (1932). London: Ernest Benn.

CHRISTENSEN, P.P. (1979) 'Sraffian themes in Adam Smith's theory', *Journal of Post-Keynesian Economics,* vol. 5, pp. 94–109.

CLARK, M.J. (1961) *Competition as a Dynamic Process.* Washington: Brookings Institution.

CORRY, B.A. (1962) *Money, Saving and Investment in English Economics 1800–1815.* London: Macmillan.

DAS GUPTA, A.K. (1960) 'Adam Smith on value', *Indian Economic Review,* vol. 5, pp. 105–15.

DAVIES D.G. (1963) 'A note on Marshallian versus Walrasian stability conditions', *Canadian Journal of Economics,* November, pp. 535–39.

DEANE, P. (1978) *The Evolution of Economic Ideas.* Cambridge: Cambridge University Press.

DEBREU, G. (1959) *The Theory of Value.* New Haven: Yale University Press.

DE VIVO, G. (1982) ' Notes on Marx's critique of Ricardo', *Contributions to Political Economy,* vol. 1. pp. 87–99.

DIXIT, A. (1977) 'The accumulation of capital theory', *Oxford Economic Papers,* vol. 29, pp. 1–29.

DMITRIEV, V.K. (1898) 'The theory of value of David Ricardo', in D.M. Nuri, (ed.) *Essays on Value, Competition and Utility.* Cambridge: Cambridge University Press, 1974.

DOBB, M. (1937) *Political Economy and Capitalism.* London: Routledge & Kegan Paul.

DOBB, M. (1973) *Theories of Value and Distribution Since Adam Smith.* Cambridge: Cambridge University Press.

DOBB. M. (1975) 'Ricardo and Adam Smith', in Skinner and Wilson (1975), pp. 324–35.

DOUGLAS, P.H. (1928) 'Adam Smith's theory of value and distribution', in J.M. Clark *et al., Adam Smith, 1776–1926.* Chicago: University of Chicago Press, pp. 75–115.

EAGLY, R.V. (1970) 'Adam Smith and the specie-flow mechanism', *Scottish Journal of Political Economy,* vol. 17, pp. 61–8.

EATWELL, J. (1974) 'Controversies in the theory of surplus value: old and new', *Science and Society,* vol. 38, pp. 281–303.

EATWELL, J. (1975) *Scarce and Produced Commodities.* Unpublished PhD Thesis, Harvard University.

EATWELL, J. (1982) 'Competition', in I. Bradley and M. Howard (eds) *Classical and Marxian Political Economy.* London: Macmillan.

EKELUND, R.B., FRY, C.L., GRAMM, W.P. and HEBERT, R.F. (1972) *The Evolution of Modern Demand Theory.* Boston: Heath.

EKELUND, R.B. and HEBERT, R.F. (1985) *A History of Economic Theory and Method.* New York: McGraw-Hill.

ELTIS, W.A. (1975) 'Adam Smith's theory of economic growth', in Skinner and Wilson (1975), pp.*426–54*.

ELTIS, W.A. (1984) *The Classical Theory of Economic Growth*, London: Macmillan.

FINE, B. (1980) 'The historical approach to rent and price theory reconsidered.' Discussion Paper No. 69. Birkbeck College, University of London.

FINE, B. (1982) *Theories of the Capitalist Economy*. London: Edward Arnold.

FISHER, F.M. (1983) *The Disequilibrium Foundations of Equilibrium Economics*. Cambridge: Cambridge University Press.

GAREGNANI, P. (1958) *A Problem in the Theory of Distribution from Ricardo to Wicksell*. Unpublished PhD, Cambridge.

GAREGNANI, P. (1970) 'Heterogeneous capital, the production function and the theory of distribution', *Review of Economic Studies*, vol. 35, pp. 407–36.

GAREGNANI, P. (1976) 'On a change in the notion of equilibrium', in M. Brown *et al*. *Essays in Modern Capital Theory*. Amsterdam: North-Holland.

GAREGNANI, P. (1983) 'The classical theory of wages and the role of demand schedules in the determination of relative prices', *American Economic Review*, vol. 73, pp. 309–313.

GAREGNANI, P. (1984), 'Value and distribution in the classical economists and Marx', *Oxford Economic Papers*, vol. 73, pp. 291–325.

GEE, J.M.A. (1981) 'The origin of rent in Adam Smith's *Wealth of Nations*: an anti-neoclassical view', *History of Political Economy*, vol. 13, pp. 1–18.

GORDON, D.F. (1959) 'What was the labour theory of value?', *American Economic Review*, vol. 69 (May), pp. 462–72.

GORDON, D.F. (1965) 'The labour theory of value', *International Encyclopedia of the Social Sciences*, pp. 279–82.

GREEN, R. (1982) 'Money, output and inflation in classical economics', *Contributions to Political Economy*, vol. 1. pp. 59–85.

GROENEWEGEN, P. (1969) 'Turgot and Adam Smith', *Scottish Journal of Political Economy*, vol. 16, pp. 271–87.

GROENEWEGEN, P. (1972) 'Three notes on Ricardo's theory of value and distribution', *Australian Economic Papers*, vol. 11.

GROENEWEGEN, P. (1974) 'Review' of M. Dobb, *Theories of Value and Distribution since Adam Smith*, *Economic Journal*, pp. 192–3.

GROENEWEGEN, P. (1975) 'Review' of R.D.C. Black (ed.) *The Marginal Revolution in Economics*, (1973), *Economic Record*, March.

GROENEWEGEN, P. (1980) 'Review' of P. Williams *Competition in Economic Theory*, *Economic Record*.

GROENEWEGEN, P. (1982a) 'History and political economy: Smith, Marx and Marshall', *Australian Economic Papers*, vol. 21, pp. 1–17.

GROENEWEGEN, P. (1982b) 'Turgot: forerunner of neoclassical economics?, *Kenzei Kenkyu*, vol. 33, no. 2, April.

GROENEWEGEN, P. (1983) 'Turgot, Beccaria and Smith', in P. Groenewegen and J. Halevi, (eds) *Altro Polo: Italian Economists Past and Present*. Sydney: Frederick May Foundation for Italian Studies.

HAHN, F.H. (1970) 'Some adjustment problems', *Econometrica*, vol. 38, pp. 1–17.

HAYEK, F. von (1948) *Individualism and Economic Order*. Chicago: Chicago University Press.

HEGELAND, H. (1951) *The Quantity of Money*. Reprinted New York: Kelley (1969).

HEILBRONER, R.L. (1975) 'The paradox of progress: decline and decay in the *Wealth of Nations*', in Skinner and Wilson (1975), pp. 524–39.

HICKS, J. (1965) *Capital and Growth*. Oxford: Clarendon Press.

HICKS, J. (1968) 'Linear theory', in *Surveys of Economic Theory, Vol. III Resource Allocation*. New York: St Martin's.

HICKS, J.R. and HOLLANDER, S. (1977) 'Mr Ricardo and the moderns', *Quarterly Journal of Economics*, vol. 91, pp. 351–70.

HOLLANDER, J. (1928) 'The Founder of a School' in J.M. Clark *et al.* (eds), pp. 1–21. *Adam Smith, 1776–1926*. Chicago: University of Chicago Press.

HOLLANDER, S. (1973) *The Economics of Adam Smith*. London: Heinemann.

HOLLANDER, S. (1977) 'Smith and Ricardo: aspects of the nineteenth-century legacy', *American Economic Review*, vol. 67, pp. 37–41.

HOLLANDER, S. (1979) *The Economics of David Ricardo*. London: Heinemann.

HOLLANDER, S. (1983) 'On the interpretation of Ricardian economics: the assumption regarding wages', *American Economic Review*, vol. 73.

HUNT, E.K. (1979) *History of Economic Thought: A Critical Perspective*. Belmont, Calif.: Wadsworth.

HUTCHISON, T.W. (1978) *On Revolutions and Progress in Economic Knowledge*. Cambridge: Cambridge University Press.

HUTT, W.H. (1954) *The Theory of Collective Bargaining*. Glencoe, Ill.: Free Press.

INTRILLIGATOR, M.D. (1971) *Mathematical Optimisation and Economic Theory*. Englewood Cliffs, NJ: Prentice-Hall.

JAFFE, W. (1977) 'A centenarian on a bicentenarian: Leon Walras', *Elements* on Adam Smith's *Wealth of Nations*', *Canadian Journal of Economics*, vol. 10 (Feb) pp. 19–33.

JEVONS, W.S. (1871) *The Theory of Political Economy*. New York: A.M. Kelley (1965).

JOHNSON, E.A.J. (1937) *Predecessors of Adam Smith – The Growth of British Economic Thought*. New York: Prentice Hall.

KAUDER, E. (1953) 'Genesis of the marginal utility theory from Aristotle to the end of the eighteenth century', *Economic Journal*, vol. LXIII, pp. 638–50.

KAUSHIL, S. (1973) 'The case of Adam Smith's theory of value', *Oxford Economic Papers*, vol. 25, pp. 60–71.

KENDRICK, J.W. (1968) 'National income and product analysis', in *International Encyclopedia of the Social Sciences*, vol. 11.

KEYNES, J.M. (1936) *The General Theory of Employment, Interest, and Money*. London: Macmillan.

KNIGHT, F. (1956) *On the History and Method of Economics*. Chicago: University of Chicago Press.

KOOPMANS, J.C. (1957) *Three Essays on the State of Economic Science*. New York: McGraw-Hill.

KURZ, H.D. (1976) 'Adam Smith's komponententheorie der relativen preise and ihre kritik', *Z.ges. Staatswiss*, vol. 132, pp. 691–709.

KURZ, H.D. (1980) 'Smithian themes in Piero Sraffa's theory', *Journal of Post Keynesian Economics*, vol. 3, pp. 271–80.

LAIDLER, D. (1981) 'Adam Smith as a monetary economist', *Candian Journal of Economics*, vol. 14 (May), pp. 185–200.

LARSEN, R.M. (1977) 'Dmitriev's Smithian Model', *Scottish Journal of Political Economy*, vol. 24, pp. 227–33.

LAUDERDALE, J.M. (1804) *An Inquiry into the Nature and Origin of Public Wealth*. Edinburgh: Constable.

LEONTIEF, W.W. (1951) 'Input-output economics', *Scientific American*, reprinted in W.W. Leontief (1966) *Input-Output Economics*. New York: Oxford University Press.

LEONTIEF, W.W. (1965) 'Input-output analysis', in W.W. Leontief *Input-Output Economics*. New York: Oxford University Press (1966).

LEVINE, D.P. (1980) 'Aspects of the classical theory of markets', *Australian Economic Papers*, vol. 19, pp. 1–15.

LICHTENSTEIN, P.M. (1983) *An Introduction to Post-Keynesian and Marxian Theories of Value and Price*. London: Macmillan.

LOCKE, J. (1690) *Two Treatises Concerning Civil Government*, P. Laslett (ed) Cambridge: Cambridge University Press (1960).

LOWE, A. (1954) 'The classical theory of economic growth', *Social Research*, vol. 21, pp. 127–58.

LOWE, A. (1975) 'Adam Smith's system of equilibrium growth', in Skinner and Wilson (1975), pp. 415–25.

MACDONALD, R.A. (1912). 'Ricardo's criticisms of Adam Smith', *Quarterly Journal of Economics*, vol. 26, pp. 549–92.

MALTHUS, T.R. (1820) *Principles of Political Economy*. 1st edn, as partly reprinted in P. Sraffa (1951) *The Works and Correspondence of David Ricardo*, vol. 2. Cambridge: Cambridge University Press.

MARSHALL, A. (1879a) 'The pure theory of domestic value' reprinted in J.K. Whitaker (ed.) (1975) *The Early Writings of Alfred Marshall, 1867–1890*. New York: Free Press.

MARSHALL, A. and M.P. (1879b) *The Economics of Industry*. London: Macmillan.

MARSHALL, A., (1885) 'The present position of economics' reprinted in A.C. Pigou (ed.) (1925) *Memorials of Alfred Marshall*. London: Macmillan.

MARSHALL, A. (1890) *The Principles of Economics*. 8th edn (1920). London: Macmillan.

MARSHALL, A. (1898) 'Distribution and exchange', *Economic Journal*, as partly reprinted in C.W. Guillebaud, (ed.) *Principles of Economics*, variorum edn, vol. 2. London: Macmillan (1961).

MARSHALL, A. (1926) *Official Papers by Alfred Marshall*, edited by J.M. Keynes. London: Macmillan.

MARX, K. (1844) *Economic and Philosophical Manuscripts*. Reprinted in *Early Writings*. Harmondsworth: Penguin (1975).

MARX, K. (1857–58) *Grundrisse*, Harmondsworth: Penguin.

MARX, K. (1859) *A Contribution to the Critique of Political Economy*. London: Lawrence & Wishart (1971).

MARX, K. (1861–63) *Theories of Surplus Value, Parts I to III*. London: Lawrence & Wishart (1963)

MARX, K.(1867) *Capital*, vol.1. Harmondsworth: Penguin (1976).

MARX, K. (1885) *Capital*, Vol. II. London: Lawrence & Wishart (1974).

MARX, K. (1894) *Capital*, Vol. III. London: Lawrence & Wishart (1959).

McNULTY, P. (1967) 'A note on the history of perfect competition', *Journal of Political Economy*, vol. 75, pp. 395–99.

MEDIO, A. (1978) 'A mathematical note on equilibrium in value and distribution', *Economic Notes*, vol. 7, pp. 97–106.

MEEK, R.L. (1951) 'Physiocracy and classicism in Britain', *Economic Journal*, vol. 61. March, reprinted in Meek (1962).

MEEK, R.L. (1954) 'Adam Smith and the classical concept of profit'. *Scottish Journal of Political Economy*, vol. 1, pp. 138–53.

MEEK, R.L. (1959) 'The Physiocratic concept of profit' *Economica*, as reprinted in Meek (1962).

MEEK, R.L. (1962) *The Economics of Physiocracy: Essays and Translations*. London: George Allen & Unwin.

MEEK, R.L. (1973a) *Studies in the Labour Theory of Value*. 2nd edn. London: Lawrence & Wishart (1st edn. 1956).

MEEK, R.L. (1973b) *Precursors of Adam Smith*. London: Dent.

MEEK, R.L. (1974) 'Value in the history of economic thought', *History of Political Economy*, vol. 6, as reprinted in Meek (1977).

MEEK, R.L. (1977) *Smith, Marx and After: Ten essays in the Development of Economic Thought*. London: Chapman & Hall.

MENGER, C. (1871) *Principles of Economics*, J. Dingwall and B.F. Hoselitz (trans) (1981). New York: New York University Press.

MILGATE, M.J. (1982) *Capital and Employment*, London: Academic Press.

MILL,J.S. (1945) 'Notes on N.W. Senior's *Political Economy*', *Economica*.

MOSS, L. (1974) 'Longfield's supply and demand theory of price', *History of Political Economy*, vol. 6, pp. 405–34.

MOSS, L. (1976) 'The economics of Adam Smith: Professor Hollander's reappraisal', *History of Political Economy*, vol. 8, pp. 564–74.

MYINT, H. (1943) 'The welfare significance of productive labour', *Review of Economic Studies* (Winter), pp. 20–30.

MYINT, H. (1948) *Theories of Welfare Economics*. Cambridge, Mass: Harvard University Press.

MYINT, H. (1977) 'Adam Smith's theory of international trade in the perspective of economic development', *Economica*, vol. 44, pp. 231–48.

NAPOLEONI, C. (1975) *Smith, Ricardo and Marx*. Oxford: Blackwell.

NEWMAN, P. (1965) *The Theory of Exchange*. Englewood Cliffs, N. J.: Prentice-Hall.

O'BRIEN, D.P. (1974) 'The development of economics: a review article', *Scottish Journal of Political Economy*, vol. 20.

O'BRIEN, D.P. (1975) *The Classical Economists*. Oxford: Clarendon Press.

O'BRIEN, D.P. (1976a) 'The longevity of Adam Smith's vision: paradigms, research programs and falsifiability in the history of economic thought', *Scottish Journal of Political Economy*, vol. 23, pp. 133–51.

O'BRIEN, D.P. (1976b) 'Comment' on R.D.C. Black (1976) 'Smith's contribution in historical perspective'.

PASINETTI, L.L. (1973) 'The notion of vertical integration in economic analysis', *Metroeconomica*, vol. XXV, pp. 1–29.
PASINETTI, L.L. (1977) *Lectures on the Theory of Production*. London: Macmillan.
PASINETTI, L.L. (1983) 'Comment' on Casarosa (1983).
PETTY, W. (1662) *A Treatise on Taxes and Contributions*. Reprinted in *The Economic Writings of Sir William Petty*, edited by C.H. Hull. New York: Kelley, 1963 (1st edn, 1899).
PULTENEY, W. (1738) *Some Thoughts on the Interest of Money in General*. Reprints of Economic Classics, edited by P. Groenewegen. Sydney: Department of Economics, University of Sydney (1982).
QUESNAY, F. (1757) 'Grains', translated and reprinted in Meek (1962).
RANKIN, S.C. (1980) 'Supply and demand in Ricardian price theory: a re-interpretation', *Oxford Economic Papers*, vol. 32, pp. 241–62.
RAPHAEL, D.D. (1985) *Adam Smith*. Oxford: Oxford University Press.
RECKTENWALD, H.C. (1978) 'An Adam Smith renaissance anno 1776? the bicentenary output – a reappraisal of his scholarship', *Journal of Economic Literature, vol. 16 (March), pp.*56–83.
REISMAN, D.A. (1976) *Adam Smith's Sociological Economics*. London: Croom Helm.
RICARDO, D. *The Works and Correspondence of David Ricardo*, P. Sraffa (ed.) with M. Dobb, 11 vols. Cambridge: University Press (1951–73).
RICHARDSON G.B. (1975) 'Adam Smith on competition and increasing returns', in Skinner and Wilson (1975), pp. 350–60.
ROBBINS, L. (1930) 'On a certain ambiguity in the conception of stationary equilibrium', *Economic Journal*, vol. 40, pp. 194–214.
ROBBINS, L. (1934) 'Remarks upon certain aspects of the theory of cost', *Economic Journal*, vol. 44, March.
ROBBINS, L. (1935) *An Essay on the Nature and Significance of Economic Science*. London: Macmillan.
ROBBINS, L. (1955) 'Schumpeter on the history of economic analysis', *Quarterly Journal of Economics*, as reprinted in L. Robbins, *The Evolution of Modern Economic Theory*. London: Macmillan.
ROBBINS, L. (1958) *Robert Torrens and the Evolution of Classical Economics*. London: Macmillan.
ROBERTSON, H.M. and TAYLOR, W.L. (1957) 'Adam Smith's approach to the theory of value', *Economic Journal*, vol. 67, pp. 181–98.
ROBINSON, J. (1961) 'Prelude to a critique of economic theory', *Oxford Economic Papers*, vol. 13, February,pp. 53–8.
ROGIN, L. (1956) *The Meaning and Validity of Economic Theory*. New York: Harper.
ROLL, E. (1973) *A History of Economic Thought*. London: Faber (1st edn, 1938).
RONCAGLIA, A. (1978) *Sraffa and the Theory of Prices*. New York: Wiley.
ROSDOLSKY, R. (1977) *The Making of Marx's 'Capital'*, London: Pluto Press.
ROSENBERG, N. (1975) 'Adam Smith on profits – paradox lost and regained' in Skinner and Wilson (1975), pp. 377–89.

ROSENBLUTH, G. (1969) 'A note on labour, wages, and rent in Smith's theory of value', *Canadian Journal of Economics*, vol. 2, pp. 308–14.
SAMUELSON, P. (1977) 'A modern theorist's vindication of Adam Smith', *American Economic Review*, vol. 67, pp. 42–9.
SCHUMPETER, J. (1954) *History of Economic Analysis*. London: George Allen & Unwin.
SCOTT, W.R. (1937) *Adam Smith as Student and Professor*. Glasgow: Jackson.
SEMMLER, W. (1984) *Competition, Monopoly and Differential Profit Rates*. New York: Columbia University Press.
SKINNER, A.S. (1966) 'Editor's Introduction' to Steuart (1767)
SKINNER, A.S. (1974) 'Editor's Introduction' to A. Smith *The Wealth of Nations*. Harmondsworth: Penguin (1st edn, 1970).
SKINNER, A.S. (1976) 'The development of a system', *Scottish Journal of Political Economy*, as reprinted in Skinner (1979).
SKINNER, A.S. (1979) *A System of Social Science: Papers Relating to Adam Smith*. Oxford: Clarendon Press.
SKINNER, A.S. and WILSON, T. (1975) *Essays on Adam Smith*. Oxford: Clarendon Press.
SMITH, A. (1763) *Lectures on Jurisprudence*, edited by R.L. Meek, D.D. Raphael and P.G. Stein. Oxford: Clarendon Press (1978).
SMITH, A. (1776) *An Inquiry into the Nature and Causes of the Wealth of Nations*, edited by R.H. Campbell and A.S. Skinner. Oxford: Clarendon Press (1976).
SMITH, A. (1976) *Correspondence of Adam Smith*, edited by E.C. Mossner and I.S. Ross. Oxford: Clarendon Press.
SOWELL, T. (1974) *Classical Economics Reconsidered*. Princeton: Princeton University Press.
SPENGLER, J.J. (1959a) 'Adam Smith's theory of economic growth', *Southern Economic Journal*, vol. 25, pp. 397–415.
SPENGLER, J.J. (1959b) 'Adam Smith's theory of economic growth' – Part II', *Southern Economic Journal*, vol. 26, pp. 1–14.
SRAFFA, P. (1951) 'Introduction' to *The Works and Correspondence of David Ricardo*. Cambridge: Cambridge University Press.
SRAFFA, P. (1960) *Production of Commodities by Means of Commodities*. Cambridge: Cambridge University Press.
STEEDMAN, I. (1982) 'Marx on Ricardo', in Bradley and Howard (1982).
STEEDMAN, I. (1977) *Marx after Sraffa*. London: New Left Books.
STEUART, J. (1767) *An Inquiry into the Principles of Political Economy*, edited A.S. Skinner. Chicago: University of Chicago Press (1966).
STEWART, D. (1856) 'An account of the life and writings of Adam Smith' in *The Works of Dugald Stewart* edited by W.B. Hamilton. Edinburgh: Constable.
STIGLER, G. (1950) 'The development of utility theory', *Journal of Political Economy*, as reprinted in Stigler (1965).
STIGLER, G. (1952) 'The Ricardian theory of value and distribution', *Journal of Political Economy*, as reprinted in Stigler (1965).
STIGLER, G. (1954) 'Review' of J. Schumpeter, *History of Economic Analysis, Journal of Political Economy*, as reprinted in Stigler (1965).

STIGLER, G. (1957) 'Perfect competion, historically considered', *Journal of Political Economy* as reprinted in Stigler (1965).

STIGLER, G. (1958) 'Ricardo and the 93 per cent labour theory of value', *American Economic Review*, as reprinted in Stigler (1965).

STIGLER, G.J. (1965) *Essays in the History of Economics*. Chicago: University of Chicago Press.

SYLOS-LABINI, P. (1976) 'Competition: the product markets', in Wilson and Skinner (1976), pp. 200–32.

TAKAYAMA, A. (1974) *Mathematical Economics*. Hinsdale, Illinois: Dryden Press.

TAUSSIG, F.W. (1896) *Wages and Capital*. New York: Appleton.

TAYLOR, O.H. (1960) *A History of Economic Thought*. New York: Macmillan

THWEATT, W.O. (1957) 'A diagramatic presentation of Adam Smith's growth model', *Social Research*, vol. 24, pp. 227–30.

TUCKER, G.S.L. (1960) *Progress and Profit in British Economic Thought (1650–1850)*. Cambridge: Cambridge University Press.

VAGGI, G. (1983) 'The physiocratic theory of prices', *Contributions to Political Economy*, vol. 2, pp. 1–23.

VAGGI, G. (1987) *The Economics of Francis Quesnay*, London: Macmillan Press.

VAUGHN, K.I. (1980) *John Locke: Economist and Social Scientist*. Chicago: University of Chicago Press.

VEBLEN, T. (1919) *The Place of Science in Modern Civilisation*. New York: Huebsch; reprinted, New York: Viking press, 1946

VICKERS, D. (1975) 'Adam Smith and the status of the theory of money', in Skinner and Wilson (1975), pp. 482–503.

VINER, J. (1930) 'Review' of E. Cannan, *A Review of Economic Theory*. *Economica*

VINER, J. (1937) *Studies in the Theory of International Trade*. New York: Kelly.

VINER, J. (1954) 'Schumpeter's *History of Economic Analysis*', *American Economic Review*

VINER, J. (1968) 'Adam Smith' in *International Encyclopedia of the Social Sciences*, 14, pp. 322–9

WALRAS, L. (1874) *Elements of Pure Economics*, translated by W. Jaffe. London: George Allen & Unwin (1954).

WALSH, V. and GRAM, H. (1980) *Classical and Neoclassical Theories of General Equilibrium*. Oxford; Oxford University Press.

WEISSKOPF, W.A. (1955) *The Psychology of Economics*. London: Routledge & Kegan Paul.

WERMEL, M.T. (1939) *The Evolution of the Classical Wage Theory*. New York: Columbia University Press.

WEST, E.G. (1974) 'Review' of S. Hollander *The Economics of Adam Smith*, *Canadian Journal of Economics*, vol. 17, pp. 326–30.

WEST, E.G. (1976) *Adam Smith: The Man and His Works*. Indianapolis: Liberty Press.

WEST, E.G. (1978) 'Scotland's resurgent economist: a survey of the new literature on Adam Smith', *Eastern Economic Journal*, vol. 45, pp. 343–69.

WHITAKER, A.C. (1904) *History and Criticism of the Labour Theory of Value in English and Political Economy*. New York: Columbia University Press.

WICKSELL, K. (1893) *Value, Capital and Rent*, S.H. Frowein (trans.) (1954) London: George Allen & Unwin.

WICKSELL, K. (1901) *Lectures on Political Economy*, in L. Robbins (ed.) 2 vols. London: Routledge & Kegan Paul (1935).

WICKSTEED, P.H. (1914) 'The scope and method of political economy in the light of the marginal theory of value and distribution', *Economic Journal*, as reprinted in P.H. Wicksteed (1944) *The Common Sense of Political Economy*. London: Routledge.

WIESER, F. Von (1888) *Natural Value*, C.A. Malloch (trans.), S. Smart (ed.) (1983). London: Macmillan.

WILSON, T. and SKINNER, A. (eds) (1976) *The Market and the State: Essays in Honour of Adam Smith*. Oxford: Clarendon Press.

YOUNG, J.T. (1978) *Classical Theories of Value: From Smith to Sraffa*. Boulder, Colo: Westview Press.

Index

abstinence, 14, 183
accumulation, 1, 5, 9, 11, 12, 27–8,
  33, 34, 38, 39, 40, 43, 48, 58, 59,
  63, 79, 90, 150, 162–3, 173,
  181–2, 183, 195, 207, 212, 213,
  220, 224, 227, 232, 247
  corn model of, 171, 193–6
  and labour command, 72
  effects of monopoly on, 45–7
  price effects, 83–5, 112, 253
  and profits, 28–9, 40–1, 42, 46–7,
    49, 51, 54, 93–9, 100, 101,
    235, 247
  Smith on, 28–9, 38, 39–41, 44,
    45–6, 58–61, 256
  see also capital; wages
adjustment, 181, 252
  v. determination, 252
  gravitation, 23, 53–4, 55, 56–8,
    61, 95–6, 157–8, 160, 181,
    235–6, 259, 277–8
  to natural price, 56–8, 125–6, 181
  Ricardo on, 125–6
  see also competition; price(s)
agriculture, 8–9, 17, 43–4, 45, 46,
  48–9, 76, 80, 98, 104, 105, 107,
  114, 126, 127, 130, 135, 145, 149,
  153, 172, 193, 194, 235, 254
  see also corn; diminishing returns
allocation, 173, 181, 185–6, 193–6,
  227
  see also Hollander, S.
America, 41, 77, 80, 91, 92
Anderson, J., 242
annual produce, 1, 27, 28, 29–34,
  35, 39, 42, 43, 44, 45, 80, 100,
  115, 161, 162–3, 195, 212, 221
  Cannan on, 29–34, 232
  determination of, 39–47, 79–80,
    212, 234
  labour command value of, 72,
    220, 239, 242–3

Marx on, 161–3
  and national income, 30
  equal to revenue, 30–3, 35, 37,
    86–9, 161–3, 221, 233
  not equal to revenue, 33–4,
    86–90
  see also revenue; surplus
Anspach, R., 27, 256
apprenticeship, statutes of, 59
Arrow, K.J., 22, 23, 256, 259
Austrian economics, 204

Barber, W.J., 74, 239
Barkai, H., 27, 95
basic commodity, 238
Beckerman, W., 29
beef, 241
Bharadwaj, K., 72, 88, 113, 141,
  206, 207, 209–10, 216, 258
Black, R.D.C., 1, 27, 232
Bladen, V.W., 2, 71, 72, 77, 113,
  116, 128, 226, 239, 243, 249,
  256
Blaug, M., 2, 3, 23, 30, 31, 35, 56,
  57, 73, 75, 116, 128, 147, 150,
  227, 236, 239, 243, 256
Bliss, C.J., 17, 95, 187
Bloomfield, A.I., 195, 242
Böhm-Bawerk, E., 116, 234
Bortkiewicz, L., 231
Boulding, K., 2, 171
Bowley, M., 2, 3, 40, 41, 61, 94, 179,
  231, 234, 237, 256, 257
Bradley, I., 2, 142, 169, 231
British economics, see classical
  economics
Broome, J., 244, 256
Buchanan, D., 116, 140, 237
Buchanan, D.H., 88, 99

Campbell, R.H., 46, 47, 77, 100,
  177, 234, 239

stone, 251
subsistence, *see* wage(s)
substitution, 184, 196, 257
 in neoclassical theory, 13, 17, 21,
  224, 227
 in Smith, 175, 178, 192, 196, 226,
  227, 256, 257
supply and demand, 2, 6, 14, 56, 57,
  133, 138, 174–9, 183–4, 191, 198,
  199, 203, 206–7, 209, 217, 225,
  258
 and capital theory, 253
 and cost, 21
 development of, 138, 204–7
 Dobb on, 139–41, 197, 199–210
 in neoclassical theory, 13–19, 22,
  24, 133, 138, 174, 224
 Ricardo on, 130, 139–41, 201, 203
 symmetry of, 16, 19, 231
 see also price(s); value
supply function, 16
surplus, 4, 6, 8–9, 12, 32, 33, 39,
  43–4, 46, 83, 100, 195–6
 and accumulation, 33–4
 definitions of, 8–9, 27–9, 49, 83,
  144, 161–2, 167, 195–6, 208,
  212, 215–16, 222, 258
 in different industries, 43–4,
  45–6, 47
 Dobb on, 27–8, 38
 Marx on, 144–6, 150, 154, 161–3
 why misunderstood, 32–3, 35, 38,
  51–2, 161–3, 212
 and parsimony, 8
 and property, 59
 Smith's concept of, 28–9, 32, 35,
  38, 50–2, 167, 215–16, 221
 Spengler on, 27–8, 38, 212
 value, 27, 144–6, 148–9
 see also annual produce; profit(s)
surplus theory, 2, 4, 7–13, 20, 27,
  46, 142, 146, 150, 155, 198, 202,
  203, 208, 211–24
 of accumulation, 27–8, 39–52
 concept of, 2, 3, 7–13
 core of, 12
 history of, 11
 Marx on, 144–6, 165–70

of non-wage share, 39–52, 61,
  101, 212
price-equations approach, 222–3
of profits, 20, 27, 39–52, 91–3,
  96–7, 100–4, 122, 123, 131–2,
  146–7, 154–8, 165–70,
  219–20, 231, 244
Ricardo on, 122–5, 131–3
surplus-equations
  approach, 222–3
of value and distribution, 4, 6,
  7–13, 20, 21–2, 24, 44, 46–7,
  100–4, 113, 122–5, 133–8,
  146–7, 154–65, 211–24, 231
 see also classical theory; price(s);
  value
Sylos-Labini, P., 67, 75, 89, 96, 102,
  128, 237, 238, 243

Takamaya, A., 252
tâtonnement, see adjustment
Taussig, F.W., 117
tax(es), 5, 44–5, 82, 102, 104–6, 138,
  145, 178, 195, 213
 general and particular, 104–6
 on interest, 44–5, 234
 and measure of value, 83, 103–6,
  124–5, 131, 244–5
 on profits, 44–5, 49–50, 98–9,
  104–6, 234, 243–4
 Ricardo *v.* Smith on, 121–2, 131–3
 on wages, 45, 104–6, 107, 127,
  131–3, 134, 201–2, 217,
  244–5
 see also price(s)
Taylor, O.H., 183
Taylor, W.L., 243, 249, 250, 256,
  257
technical change, *see* price(s)
techniques of production, *see* price(s)
technology, 60–1, 90, 127, 149, 195
Thornton, H., 15
Thweatt, W.O., 27
Tosata, D.A., 238
trade, 8, 45, 173, 194–6
 restrictions on, 43
transport, 177, 195

Tucker, G.S.L., 41, 92, 93, 94, 95, 99, 122, 243
Turgot, A.J., 249

undertaker, *see* capitalist
unproductive labour, *see* labour
utility, 13–19, 21, 138, 197, 204–6, 209, 232, 250–2
  and cost, 21
  in definition of social income, 232
  early theories of, 14, 138, 175, 249
  in neoclassical theory, 13–19, 190, 206, 224
  Say on, 138–9
  in Smith, 172, 175–9, 184, 225, 249, 250–2
  see also supply and demand

Vaggi, G., 10, 257
value, 1, 3, 4, 5, 11, 39, 75, 86, 91, 138, 139–40, 164
  added, 29, 30, 31, 32, 35, 38, 45, 48, 83, 115, 144, 147, 162
  change in, 5
  classical theory of, 7–13, 20, 24, 44, 46–7, 57–8, 121, 123
  cost theory of, 197–210
  and distribution, 2, 3, 4, 8, 18–19, 23, 28, 47, 51, 53, 61, 82, 83, 111, 121, 133, 136, 164–5, 169, 172, 184–5, 191, 211–18, 222, 223, 226, 228, 248
  explanation of, 5
  indeterminate theory of, 5, 82–8, 100–4, 110–11, 131–3, 143, 149–52, 154–6, 158–61, 165–70, 174–9, 213, 214, 215–16, 219, 221, 248
  long-period method, 56–8
  Marx's definition of, 148, 156, 164
  methods of production and, 5, 79, 89–90, 248
  neoclassical theory of, 13–9, 21, 23, 24, 57–8, 121
  paradox of, 176
  problem stated, 4, 8, 10, 11, 23, 61, 84, 159, 160, 169, 211, 213, 223
  real, 109
  and riches, 138–9
  Smith's interest in, 62, 67, 68, 70, 126, 213–14
  toil and trouble, 64, 65
  in use, 20, 138, 178, 179, 250–1
  see also classical theory; labour theory of value; price(s); surplus theory
Vaughn K.I., 20, 242
vegetables, 76
Vickers, D., 237
Viner, J., 2, 22, 113, 198–9, 231, 232, 240, 242, 243, 249
vulgar political economy, 143, 155, 156, 164, 170, 247–8

wages, 4, 5, 7, 8, 9, 10, 11, 12, 14, 30, 32, 37, 38, 48, 90, 94, 133–8, 144, 147, 156, 158, 203, 208, 247
  changes in, 67
  corn, 5, 67–9, 70–1, 77, 80, 89–90, 91
  Hollander on, 181–2
  natural rate of, 53–4, 55, 201
  and price changes, 70, 121, 122, 131–8, 201, 207
  Ricardo *v.* Smith on, 122, 207–9
  Smith's theory of, 40–1, 44, 91
  subsistence, 8–9, 40–1, 101, 107, 122, 140, 144, 149, 158, 181, 203, 242
  and surplus, 27, 31, 50–2
  taxes on, 45, 105–6, 131–3, 201–2
  see also distributive variables; price(s); value
Walras, L., 14–9, 55, 56, 171, 181, 185, 231, 236, 252
Walsh, V., 8, 27, 44, 45, 46, 96
wealth, 8, 20, 75, 145
  and accumulation, 9
  Smith's measure of, 35–8
  see also annual produce
Weisskopf, W.A., 117

45.00